THE TURKISH LABYRINTH
ATATÜRK AND THE NEW ISLAM

JAMES PETTIFER

PENGUIN BOOKS

PENGUIN BOOKS

Published by the Penguin Group
Penguin Books Ltd, 27 Wrights Lane, London W8 5TZ, England
Penguin Putnam Inc., 375 Hudson Street, New York, New York 10014, USA
Penguin Books Australia Ltd, Ringwood, Victoria, Australia
Penguin Books Canada Ltd, 10 Alcorn Avenue, Toronto, Ontario, Canada M4V 3B2
Penguin Books (NZ) Ltd, 182–190 Wairau Road, Auckland 10, New Zealand

Penguin Books Ltd, Registered Offices: Harmondsworth, Middlesex, England

First published by Viking 1997
Published in Penguin Books 1998
1 3 5 7 9 10 8 6 4 2

Copyright © James Petttifer, 1997
All rights reserved

The moral right of the author has been asserted

Printed in England by Clays Ltd, St Ives plc

for Sue, Julia and Alexander

The great Sun-God gave a feast and invited the thousand gods; they ate but they were not satisfied, they drank but they quenched not their thirst. Then the Weather-God remembered his son Telepinu, and said: 'Telepinu is not in the land; he was angry and has gone away and taken all the good things with him.'

The Gods great and small set out to search for Telepinu. The Sun-God sent out the swift eagle, saying: 'Go search the high mountains, search the hollow valleys, search the dark-blue waters.'

The eagle went forth; but he found him not, and reported to the Sun-God, saying: 'He is lost. I have not found him, Telepinu, the mighty God.'

The Hittite myth of the Lost God: Anatolia, 2500 B C

Contents

List of Maps

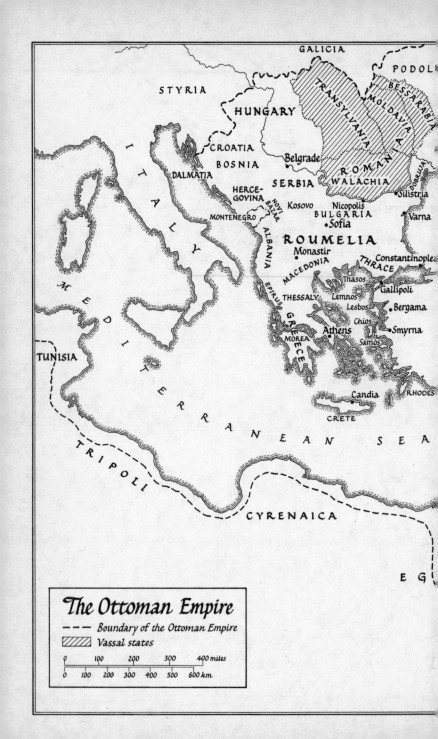

GALICIA

PODOL

STYRIA

HUNGARY

TRANSYLVANIA

BESSARABIA

MOLDAVIA

CROATIA

BOSNIA

Belgrade

SERBIA

ROMANIA

WALACHIA

DOBRUJA

DALMATIA

I T A L Y

HERCE-
GOVINA

NOVI
BAZAR

Kosovo

Nicopolis

Silistria

MONTENEGRO

BULGARIA

Sofia

Varna

ALBANIA

ROUMELIA

Monastir

MACEDONIA

THRACE

Constantinople

M E D I T E R R A N E A N

Thasos

Lemnos

Gallipoli

EPIRUS

THESSALY

Lesbos

Bergama

GREECE

Chios

Athens

Smyrna

MOREA

Samos

TUNISIA

Candia

RHODES

CRETE

S E A

TRIPOLI

CYRENAICA

E G

The Ottoman Empire

- – – – Boundary of the Ottoman Empire
- ▨ Vassal states

| 0 | 100 | 200 | 300 | 400 miles |
| 0 | 100 | 200 | 300 | 400 | 500 | 600 km |

Turkey-in-Europe
in 1834

0   100   200 miles
0   100   200   300km

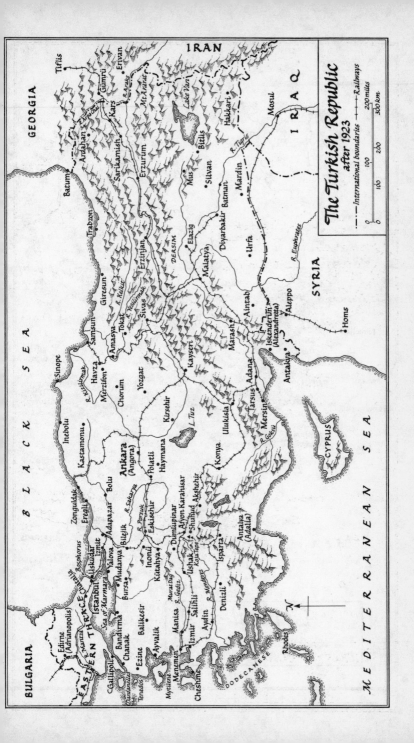

The Turkish Republic after 1923

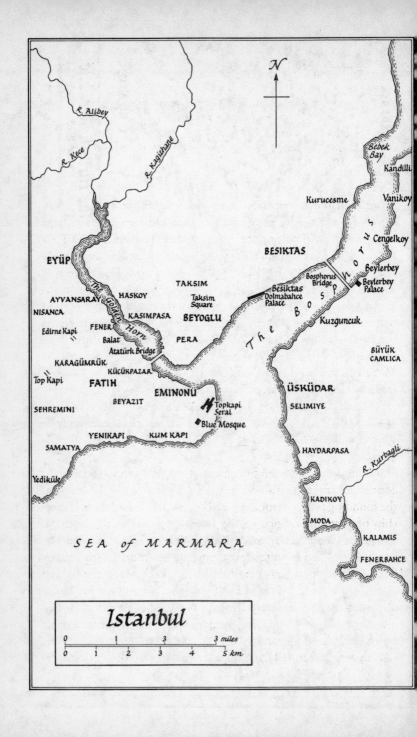

Istanbul

		3 miles
0	1	3
0	1 2 3 4	5 km

Preface

More than most countries of its size and importance, Turkey suffers from a degree of ignorance, even indifference. This was not always so. The popular press in England before the First World War shows regular, if sometimes outlandish and highly prejudiced coverage of the late Ottoman world, and there was serious reporting elsewhere. There is hardly any modern equivalent. Only one or two of the quality newspapers have regular correspondents in post in Ankara or Istanbul. Most travel is confined to a few parts of Turkey. Until 1990 it was difficult to move freely without special government permit in some regions of the country, and there are still large areas where the Kurdish war and associated military activities prevent travel in reasonably secure and relaxed conditions. As a result, debate about Turkish issues is often ideologically charged, based on an exchange of stereotypes and *idées reçues*, in the absence of up-to-date information on many topics.

In this book I have concentrated on a central question of contemporary Turkish society, the survival of the heritage of the founding father of modern Turkey, Atatürk, and the relationship of that inheritance to the Islamic revival in the country. There are many better qualified people to write about Turkey as a Middle Eastern state; I am primarily concerned with Turkey as one of Europe's near neighbours, a participant in the Balkan crisis, and a source of millions of *gastarbeiters* in Europe. I have also attempted to outline at least the main issues affecting Turkey elsewhere, although on many topics readers may need to consult more specialized literature.

I am very grateful to friends and colleagues for their assistance, encouragement and advice with writing this book, particularly Ahmet Ciftci, Ani King Underwood, Anastase Sideris, Dr Celia Kerslake, Ovul Tesisler, Avni Oxcan, Mesut Gunser, Ozker Ozgur, Nevena Georgiev, Christopher Walker, Shaban Murati, Professor Richard Crampton, Professor Sir Dimitri Obolensky, Angela Gillon, Graham Francis, Mahmut Simsek, Elif Osun, Metin Silman, Dr Zoran Pajic, Sir Reginald Hibbert, Michael Christides, Professor Richard Seaford, Martin Fryer, Liz Rawson and George Foster, Bernard McDonagh, Hugh Williams, Martin Stone, Miranda Vickers, Ahmet Sapaz, Hugh Poulton, Bob Campbell, Janet Gunn, Dick and Mary Lincon, Steve Playford and Tina Comely.

I have received wise and patient editorial guidance from Eleo Gordon and Daphne Tagg. The Hotel Hippodrome in Istanbul has been a welcoming home, office and refuge over the years in an often turbulent city. I am also very grateful to the librarians of the Oriental Institute, and St Anthony's College, Oxford, and the School of African and Oriental Studies, London.

I would like to thank the many Turkish and Kurdish people I have met over the years for their help with my travels and research, some of whom, in present political conditions, must remain, regrettably, anonymous.

All errors of fact or interpretation are my own responsibility.

Bath, January 1997

Introduction

> If one takes as a basis the laws, statistics and budgets as printed it is easy to prove that the Ottoman Empire is in a state of unexampled prosperity. Life and property are secure; perfect liberty and toleration are enjoyed by all; taxation is light, balances large, trade flourishing. Those who have not an extensive personal acquaintance with Turkey may regard such accounts with suspicion and think them highly coloured, but they find it difficult to realize that all this official literature is absolute fiction, and for practical purposes unworthy of a moment's attention.
>
> Sir Charles Eliot, *Turkey in Europe*, 1900

In Ottoman times, as today, it was difficult to gain an accurate picture of Turkey from official Turkish publications, although whether this was due to the enormous complexity of the country or to an inherited tradition of official obfuscation is uncertain. The old cliché was that Turkey was a continent, not a country; within living memory it was the centre of a great historic empire that stretched from the Yemen to north Africa, and from the wooded plains south of Skopje to the mountains of the Caucasus. Peoples as far east as the borders of China can see themselves in some senses as Turkish in origin, language or culture, and Turkish identity and political influence are reasserting themselves in many of the new republics emerging from the old Soviet Union. Turkish life and culture have a renewed pattern of complexity and diversity as a result.

When Sir Charles Eliot was writing, the future of Turkey was regarded as part of the 'Eastern Question' – the complex series

of diplomatic conundrums surrounding the fate of the entire
Ottoman Empire. The aftermath of the Congress of Berlin in
1878 saw the emergence and territorial consolidation of the
ex-Ottoman states in the Balkans, such as Serbia, Bulgaria and
Albania, and this was paralleled after the First World War by
the emergence of new Middle Eastern countries carved out from
old Ottoman territories by the imperialist powers. The 'Turkey'
that remained was consolidated by Atatürk into a new republic
in 1923. In the West it tended to be perceived as an ethically and
religiously homogeneous state (which in reality it never was)
and this misconception has often prevented rational analysis and
discussion of some events in the past and in contemporary
Turkey. In that sense, there may be said to be an Eastern Question
now as there was before the final collapse of Ottoman power in
the Balkans.

Until about a hundred years ago Turkish identity in Britain
meant one thing above all others to mainstream liberal opinion:
to be a Muslim, and, therefore, a foe of Western society. The
'Turk' was the 'Other', Muslim, dangerous and untrustworthy.
Resistance to this expansionist and militant religion and the
theocratic Ottoman state that embodied it – at least for the
dominant Sunni believers – was as central to European culture
then as resistance to Soviet Communism and its values has been
this century. Turkey was the deadly enemy of Christendom,
close, powerful, threatening. For generations in Europe, the fight
against the Ottoman Empire was a fight for Christianity against
Islam, as the armies of the Ottoman sultans swept through
the Balkans towards Vienna and northern Europe. In earlier
centuries, the Crusades against the Saracens had the same
impetus: the battle for Christendom, for the free West, against
the tyrannical and doctrinaire East. Turk merged into Arab
according to this way of thinking. Christian society represented
a free society, whereas Turkish society was despotic, the antithesis of the values on which Western civilization was based. In
art, this ideology was embodied in works such as Mozart's opera

The Abduction from the Seraglio, where the Ottoman harem was seen as a symbol of resistance to the values of the Enlightenment and the French Revolution. This ideological prejudice also had a more practical foundation. As an economic entity, the Ottoman Empire meant stagnation and backwardness, compared to the progressive and innovative Christian bourgeois world. In social and family terms, it meant slavery, lack of respect for individual human rights and an absolutist and tyrannical state. This was linked to various notions of unbridled sensuality embodied in the harem and the oppression of women.

In the nineteenth century both England and Germany were strongholds of Hellenism among the ruling élite – a prime minister such as Gladstone could translate Homer from ancient Greek into English in his spare time as a matter of course. The recovery of Hellenism as a political force after the establishment of a Greek state independent of the Ottoman Empire in 1830 was intimately linked to opposition to the Ottoman world as the embodiment of oppression and economic and cultural backwardness. Hellenism was equated with intellectual freedom, the Ottoman world with the absence of intellectual activity or achievement, the world of Milton's 'sensual sty'. Some residual elements of this thinking continue today; the success of a strongly anti-Turkish film like *Midnight Express* in Europe and the USA in the late 1970s was partly dependent on traditional images of Turkish disregard for human rights within a totalitarian state, and the toleration of violence and individual exploitation and the neglect of the rule of law.

In this book I explore how far some of these antitheses have continued to determine our perceptions. In international relations Turkey remains a key country, and all the clichés of Turkey being a bridge between East and West, the meeting point of different cultures, still apply. Despite the end of the Cold War, Turkey continues to occupy a central role as a regional policeman in NATO and Western security thinking. But the Communist period narrowed our vision of Turkey and its role in the world considerably, and little has changed in many minds since.

The preferred Western picture of Turkey and its development portrays the West's multinationals as a central innovating force in the economy and assumes gradual integration with the European Union and a pro-American policy on Middle East issues. It predicts that Atatürk's heritage will be maintained and secularism will be dominant, for the West, faced with the rise of Islamic radicalism in many countries of the world, has equated secularism in Turkey with 'stability'. The complex and incomplete political achievement of Atatürk is reduced to ending the Ottoman theocratic system and demolishing the power of the Islamic religious institutions. According to this way of thinking, Islam largely ceased to matter as a social or political force in Turkey after 1923, yet this view neglects the gradual reassertion of Islam in Turkish life, at least since the 1950s, particularly through the formalities of Islamic education, and the marked growth of Islamic influences in many key institutions since the early 1980s. In most Western countries, think-tanks, the media and political commentators tend to promote this simplistic view of Turkey's recent history; critics, of whatever persuasion, have not enjoyed a comfortable life, any more than serious critics of the Turkish establishment do within the country, even today. The real doubts about these and related issues made writing this book seem worthwhile.

Perceptions of Turkey, prior to Atatürk's revolution, had been dominated by historical images of force, especially that of bloodthirsty, murderous hordes intent on despoiling Europe and placing it under the servitude of a misguided and bigoted religion. Until the late 1980s this view of Turkey as a potential threat to the West was deemed antiquated and out of date; the notion that Turkey embodied any problem to Europe seemed absurd. It was a loyal and vital ally: past threats had been superseded by the collapse of the Ottoman Empire after the First World War, the growth of modern secular culture under Atatürk in the 1930s, and the integration of Turkish nationalism into the security framework of NATO as part of the fight against Communism. Turkey appeared to be turning into a modern European country, at least to the millions of north European tourists who began to visit the Mediterranean coastline – the mosque was merely a picturesque building in the old town, Turkish women were becoming increasingly indistinguishable in dress and manner from European female visitors, and peasants were turning into happy and attentive waiters, as if by a miracle. Turkey's Islamic culture made it different from some other holiday destinations, but that was no longer part of a separate or hostile world, no longer an 'Other'. Turkey was 'democratic', having thrown off its difficult heritage of military intervention in politics; it was reasonable and moderate in its growing links with the European Community; and it was a valued and loyal ally, as the outcome of the Gulf War showed – Turkish co-operation over oil pipeline closures and Operation Desert Storm was vital to Western military success. In the 1980s Turkey under Prime Minister Turgut Ozal was seen as a model of Western economic development, with high growth rates, a liberal and open economic policy based on a good inflow of foreign investment and developing stockmarkets, through which Turks and foreigners could share in the growing prosperity and strength of Turkish industry.

Since the early 1990s, serious doubts have begun to emerge about some aspects of this apparent progress and modernization, partly as a result of the rise of Islam as a political force in Turkish society. The Turkish economy is crippled by high inflation and unemployment and burgeoning public debt. The intractable war with the Kurds, who have been fighting to establish a separate Kurdish state in the south-east for many years, has cost billions of dollars and thousands of deaths since the mid 1980s, and victory seems as far away as ever. The environment is threatened by unplanned industrial development and the ever-expanding cities are running short of water and are suffering gross overcrowding, a rising birthrate, and public health problems. As elsewhere in the world, Turkey has seen a marked revival of radical, if not clearly fundamentalist, Islamic practice: veiled women are now a common sight on Turkish streets; an Islamic political party, the Refah (Welfare) Party, has grown quickly to become a major political force in the country, winning control first of local authorities and then of the government in 1996, and underground Islamic terrorist groups have been established. A new, assertive nationalism has begun to characterize foreign policy after the long stasis of the Cold War, when the United States and NATO shaped Turkish policy largely as they wished. Turkey's co-operation with the United Nations coalition in the Gulf War against Saddam Hussein has left a very uncertain heritage. On every border Turkey has difficulties, and potential and actual security threats. To the south, its relations with Syria, Iraq and Iran are problematic, to the east and north the demise of the Soviet Union has left as many problems as opportunities, and to the west the European Union seems as far away as ever from offering full membership, despite the Customs Union agreement in 1995–6. Turkey avoided military involvement in the Bosnian crisis, but was a closely involved onlooker. It is forming ever closer relations with ex-Yugoslav Macedonia (FYROM), and its troops joined the United Nations force in the Balkan peace-keeping operation, something strongly resented by Serbia.

The Turkish government has seemed indifferent to the concerns of its neighbours, notably the West's liberal democratic values and concern for human rights. The military leaders who ruled Turkey in the early 1980s were responsible, directly and indirectly, for thousands of deaths, often in painful and humiliating circumstances; they have never been charged or put on trial, unlike the Greek colonels from the 1968–74 junta. Many clauses remain in the Turkish constitution and are embodied in individual laws on the statute book that are wholly incompatible with modern notions of human rights. It is far from clear whether they will be removed to facilitate closer Turkish–EU relations, despite the government's incentive to do so. In 1995 Kurdish opponents of the government of Prime Minister Tansu Ciller claimed that hundreds of Kurdish activists had been killed by police death squads. The invasion of Kurdish inhabited areas of Iraq in the early months of 1995 nearly jeopardized the EU Customs Union. Although there may be a superficial and inevitably temporary diplomatic resolution of these issues, the deeper problems remain.

The Turkish population is large and one of the fastest growing in the region, with some 40 per cent aged under thirty. The current population of around 65 million is expected to rise to well over 80 million by the year 2000. If Turkey did become a full member of the EU, in the next century it would have more members of the European Parliament than any other country and could in theory dominate the Community. Opponents of Turkish membership, such as the Roman Catholic right in France, cite these figures as a new manifestation of the old Ottoman cultural threat.

To the visitor, many of these problems may appear marginal and irrelevant. The great continuities of Turkish life are the warmth and decency of the people, the exquisite beauty of tiles and carpets, great empty skies over the central Anatolian plateau, mint tea, dark, sweet coffee, Troy and Ephesus, the ruined towers of Trebizond; it seems better to forget the government and the immoral perplexities of international politics. What is less obvious is how many Turks feel the same way. In Turkey there is less dedication to public life and the interests of the *polis* than there is in Greece. To say this is not to make a value judgement; the Greek passion for politics has not always produced democratic values and institutions, economic progress, or social harmony, in contemporary Greece any more than it did in antiquity. Many individual Turks have made heroic and often lonely sacrifices for democracy and political freedom, suffering intense pain in government torture chambers and prisons.

The scale of the country, which has always created serious

administrative difficulties for governments, has also made it easier for undemocratic forces, in the form of the military, to take and keep power. The army has been the guardian of Atatürk's secular and modernizing heritage, and in the Cold War the West was forced to support it, almost regardless of the political role it played, and whether or not it was involved in difficult and controversial adventures such as the intervention in Cyprus in 1974, or the periodic suspension of democracy, as in the early 1980s. Critics of Turkey often claim that the national identity is essentially military and anti-democratic, ultimately derived from the military caste of the Seljuks who swept westwards against the Byzantine Empire from central Asia and established the Ottoman world. Apologists claim that the facts of Turkish history, geography and politics make a strong, centralized state with an effective military apparatus essential: a country of 70 million people has to defend a land area of over 300,000 square miles, and thousands of miles of coastline.

The United States has been Turkey's strongest supporter in the West, allowing geo-political calculations to overtake issues of human rights or humanitarian considerations, whereas in Europe there has never been the same uncritical support. So, in 1995, the Clinton administration gave support to the invasion of Kurdistan, whereas most of Western Europe condemned it.

But Turkey's future is linked more closely to Europe than to the USA. Kurdish Marxists and Islamic fundamentalist militants have begun to place bombs in the litter bins of Western Europe, just as they have in the bazaars of Turkey, in Istanbul or in Ankara. And Europeans come to Turkey in their millions, compared to the tens of thousands from the USA. If Turkey is ever to become more integrated with the West, European taxpayers will probably have to pay for the modernization of Turkish agriculture; European leaders will have to find a way to help solve the conundrum of Cyprus; European security chiefs will have to integrate Turkey in such a way that NATO does not become defunct in south-east Europe. If relations between Kurds and Turks continue to deteriorate and violence between the different *gastarbeiter* communities in Europe becomes endemic, it will be Germans who are killed by bombs in Turkish owned cafés in their cities or Dutch travel agents who are attacked by Kurds. The Eastern Question, the dreadful pattern of contradictions that beset nineteenth-century statesmen, has re-emerged in some respects within Turkey itself. Before the First World War the problem was what to do about the decaying Ottoman Empire; even then, the empire was the 'sick man of Europe' – not of Asia, or the Middle East, even though it held substantial territories far from Europe. After the First World War, Turkey was much too weak to count very much in international relations; after the Second World War, the Cold War seemed to have produced a 'solution' to the problem. But just as the emerging nationalisms of the Balkans led to the First World War, so the break-up of Yugoslavia may prefigure a future of wider ethnic and religious conflict in south-east Europe. Those laying siege to Sarajevo believed that they were trying to solve some unfinished business from those times – both Serbs and Croats often call the Bosnian Muslims 'Turks'.

The war in ex-Yugoslavia is an important argument for the international importance of Turkey and its heritage – a heritage at the heart of the future of Europe. The modernizing, secular agenda for Turkey has been reshaped as a European problem, however much the Turkish governments may try to attract Japanese or other foreign investment as an economic panacea. The political problem can only be solved in a European context, if it is capable of solution. But Atatürk was one Turk who believed he had found the solution to the Ottoman heritage, and his own inheritance is central to the definition of the new Eastern Question.

To the outside world, it seems as though Atatürk provided modern Turkey with an identity that it did not have before, that he made it a modern nation state. This is certainly how he is

portrayed in the very limited amount of space he is accorded in
English school-books, a kind of Turkish Oliver Cromwell or
George Washington, a 'man of the people who told the Turkish
people who they were to be in the twentieth century', according
to an English school textbook published in 1951. In the view of
most Turks from the secular élite, it is much simpler: it was
Atatürk who gave them their freedom from theocratic government and secured the borders of the modern Turkish state in
the chaos that followed the collapse of the Ottoman Empire.
Atatürk's regime represents, in the 'official' view of modern
Turkey, a complete break with the Ottoman world, in a psychological sense; the beginning of modernism in Turkish life; a
Europeanization of the country, with the abolition of the old
Arabic script and the substitution of the Latin alphabet, mass
literacy campaigns, industrialization and the end of the power
of the mullahs. The military realities were simple: Turkey
appeared to be mortgaged irrevocably to France, Britain and
Greece after the Ottoman military débâcles at the end of the
First World War, and the partition of the country seemed to be
an inevitable result of the deals between the Entente powers and
the last sultan. Atatürk led a renewed Turkish army from the
East, in the manner of the original Seljuks, and drove the *gavurs*,
the foreigners, from Turkish soil. Turkish identity is often therefore seen as racially and ethnically exclusive, and even today the
official definition of Turkishness is partly based on racial and
linguistic criteria.

But as in so much of modern Turkish life, the Ottoman heritage
is present below the surface, powerful and difficult for the forces
of modernity to overcome; what are on the surface national
simplicities conceal complex patterns of difference and multiple
identity. A symbol of this is the life of Atatürk himself. He could
perhaps be seen as the 'ultimate Turk', a warrior hero who swept
from the East to save the country, but his origins were not in
Turkey, let alone eastern Turkey. It has often been suggested
that he had some Albanian or Slav blood among his ancestors.

His family came from the Balkans, from Macedonia, and had their business in Ottoman Greece. His mother Zubeida grew up in southern Albania and spoke Greek well. Many of the other leaders of the Young Turk Revolution in 1908 – a classic modernizing movement mainly led by army officers against the ramshackle imperial system – were also from Macedonia, then one of the most economically advanced and prosperous parts of the empire. (This may seem strange today, when the Balkans are torn by war and bankrupted by United Nations sanctions and associated economic chaos, and when in the old Yugoslavia the Socialist Republic of Macedonia was by far the most backward and poorest republic, with myriad social and economic problems.)

Before the First World War the Macedonian region, including parts of the old territory of *Roumeli* – some of which is now northern Greece, south Serbia, Bulgaria and the Former Yugoslav Republic of Macedonia (FYROM) – was booming: the tobacco industry supplied newly established cigarette factories as smoking became a worldwide habit, mines were opening for manganese and lead in the Sar mountains, and newly built railways running through the region made it a focus of rivalry between the powers in the race for the riches of the Middle East. Construction projects such as the German imperialist centrepiece, the Berlin–Baghdad railway, had the same significance as the Arab oil pipeline routes do today, subjects of national rivalry, intrigue and the struggle for influence over small countries. As Berlin took over one Balkan route, the tsar in Moscow planned a competing line to go through Serbia, a fellow Orthodox Christian country, and meet the Adriatic at Shëngjin on the Albanian coast.

The Balkans and Macedonia offered other resources, some traditional, such as the horses that had been reared in the region since antiquity, giving so many place-names based on the Slav root word for horse, *kono*, as in Kónitsa, in northern Greece, or Konispol, in Albania. And timber. The Thessaly mountains were famed for their timber since the earliest times – Jason cut timber for the *Argo* on Mount Pelion before sailing with his men to the Black Sea in search of the Golden Fleece. Pelion is 10 miles from the modern Greek port of Volos, with its yachts along the harbourside, good fish restaurants and evocative harbourside monument to the Civil War. From there ferries leave for idyllic islands in the Sporades. Above the town the villages are pure rural Greece, with simple stony paths between white houses, small neat churches with bell towers. Mount Olympus, the highest mountain in Greece and home of the ancient gods, is to the north; the Turkish coast, let alone Ankara and the dry stony wastes of the Anatolian plateau, seem a very long way away. Although there are some parts of Greece where echoes of the Ottoman occupation linger on, living links with the past, like the old Turkish cemeteries in Crete where flowers are still laid on gravestones written in the Ottoman script by a scattering of descendants, Pelion seems purely Hellenic, although not Mediterranean. Under the plum trees, wild strawberries grow, not grapes or olives. On the steep slopes above Kala Nera rainfall is high; even in August the heat never singes the chestnuts and beech trees and rare shrubs and bracken. In the autumn the rain starts a thousand streams down the mountain whose head is lost in thick grey clouds. In classical mythology it was the home of Chiron, wisest of the centaurs; during the Second World War the Resistance fighters, the *andartes*, hid from the Germans in the deep tangled undergrowth, guns resting on holly trees above the narrow roads. People hide from the autumn downpours, sitting over dark green bottles of retsina in draughty cafés with *tavli* boards. Below the high limestone cliffs the last tourists read in the sun and swim, the sea a tapestry of blues.

Over the mountains at Makrinitsa, in 1878 Charles Ogle, a special correspondent of *The Times*, was murdered for trying to report on the Turks' battle with local Greek freedom fighters. The Ottoman commander slit his throat himself, in cold blood. In the nearby village of Tsagarada, the chestnuts are laid out to dry on plastic sheets, at night the wooden houses creak in the strengthening wind like old ships. Tsagarada waits for the

betrayals of the winter, the storms sweeping north up the Pagas-
itic Gulf 2,000 feet below. It is home to the largest plane tree in
the country (it needs eighteen outstretched arms to encircle
it) and, in Ottoman times, to the timber industry – the giant
hardwood trees were much in demand for harbour and railway
construction. Tourism then was unknown. Greek *rayahs* (non-
Muslim subjects of the empire) toiled under whiplash to bring
the great trees down from the mountainsides to the coast while
Turkish beys owned the woods and logging rights. It was a
recipe for bitter conflict. Ali Riza, Atatürk's father, was one such
bey, the son of an elementary schoolmaster. As he could read
and write, he obtained a minor post in the imperial system as a
customs clerk, but it was poorly paid. He was stationed with
his wife Zubeida in a lonely mountain village, and, learning of
the money to be made from the timber trade, he found a partner
in Salonika and set up in the logging business. But the mountains
were in turmoil and the bands of Greek irregulars who were
trying to drive the Turks from Greece burnt his timber, persuaded
his labourers to go on strike and disrupted his transport arrangements to the coast. The firm went bankrupt and the Rizas had
to leave the mountains, their hopes of prosperity destroyed. The
empire founded by the great sultans was disintegrating, even in
this out-of-the-way place. With Zubeida, Ali Riza returned to
Salonika, the great rambling, multi-racial and multi-cultural city
on the Axios estuary. There, in 1881, Mustafa Kemal was born.
   Salonika was the Ottoman world in miniature. The streets
were full of Ladino-speaking Jews, Slav speakers from the northern Balkans, Greeks, Bulgarians, Serbs, Romanians, Albanians,
Vlachs, Armenians, the northern European trading community,
and tens of thousands of Gypsies. The Turkish community was
a minority in one of the largest cities of the empire. Here Mustafa
grew up. He became an outstanding military cadet and associated
himself with the Young Turk Revolution in 1908 against the
absolutism of Sultan Abdül Hamit II (1876–1909), known as the
Damned. He suffered discrimination and banishment to the outer

fringes of the crumbling empire as a result of his political views. But he was to save what could be saved of the old territories from the wreckage of the First World War and the foreign invasions of Turkey.

A cynical Islamic friend in Istanbul claims Atatürk is seen by his admirers as the Turkish Elvis, always returning from the dead to haunt the present. Virtually alone among the founding father figures of modern nation states, he is still revered, at least officially; his statues still stand in every town square in Turkey, whereas those of Tito, Stalin and Hoxha have gone. But they stand in a world that has changed. One of the final disasters of the First World War was the anti-Russian war on the eastern front. After the Second World War Turkey became a key NATO barrier against Russian expansionism, but today Istanbul districts like Karikoy are crowded with Russian traders. They arrive in the old port in ships with barely painted-out Communist names, the language of Tolstoy and Turgenev rattles with Slavic consonants around the minarets and domes; Russian shoes are removed by mosque doors, broken, cheap and cracked with wear; atheists for forty years stare at the green baize cloth over the grave of Sultan Mehmet II (1451–81), hammer of the Albanians. He now lies under only 5 feet of grey stone; he was a short man, a fat man, a heavy drinker even by the standards of the early sultans. He unleashed a great blood-bath in the final siege of Scutari in northern Albania. His army was led by 600 drummers and Anatolian *zurna*-players mounted on elephants, and 60,000 corpses littered the battlefield; the eagles and vultures from the Thate mountains must have feasted for weeks. Thate means 'barren' in Albanian; the mountains could not have been better named for the opponents of Turkey that day. Mehmet pushed the frontier of the empire to the mountains of Montenegro, *Mal e Zi*, the Black Mountains – the last few stones left in God's pocket when he made the world, according to Balkan folklore. The Buna river was the sultan's last frontier. It is a windy, wet, lonely estuary, the antithesis of the glamour of Istanbul.

The sultan's grave is trodden on now by a Russian black-market trader, who places a worn-out sock on the baize edge. In the afternoon he will buy leather jackets in the bazaar to take home and sell to the young *mafioski* in Moscow – that will pay for the trip for him. Sultan Mehmet and what he represents is merely a tourist attraction, a monument to pleasure and procreation. A small brass plaque by the tomb notes that he had the three wives prescribed by the Koran and twenty-six children. In the seventeenth century the Turkish population was maybe 8 million people; now many more live in Istanbul alone. Even in these days of one wife, the city planners are assuming there will be 20 million in the greater Istanbul region by the year 2020. In the hot, turbulent streets, it seems as if they are already here.

The great railway stations of Istanbul float like ships on land, great oblong concrete behemoths stranded on solid earth. Haydar Pasha station is on the Asiatic shore of the Bosphorus. A beggar leans against the Ottoman police station nearby, an exquisite little eighteenth-century building decorated with blue tiles. The largest Turkish flag that is made flies from the roof, a billowing crimson banner. (One of the original Ottoman military ranks was that of flag-bearer. It was a job often done by Albanians in the Ottoman army – they were careless of death.) From here the modern servants of the Turkish state catch the night express to Ankara. They take off their smart black shoes and curl their cotton socks under the seat in front of them, relieving some of the tensions created by the perfect external conformity required of Turkish government officials. They are heading east, towards the vast plains of Anatolia, and the capital. Beyond lies the long war with Kurdistan, the problems in the Caucasus, the old enemy Russia, the hated Saddam, the Iranians who claim that most of the interesting elements of Ottoman language and culture came from them. Today they claim the Turks are the most corrupt Muslims of all, hardly deserving the name of Allah's servants. It is very difficult to be Turkish; in the loyal bureaucrats' view great national discipline is necessary to surmount these ever-present threats. And from time to time the army has to be there to enforce order. The arrogant Westerners may dislike it, but they live in less complex and troubled parts of the world and should restrain their criticisms. That is how most of the Turkish ruling élite see things, whether they are bureaucrats in their offices, diplomats with the most perfect manners at their receptions, or soldiers standing in the howling January wind and the deep snow at Mus on the eastern frontier.

On the other side of the Bosphorus, in the safe European quarter of Pera, my friend Ull is musing on the future in his flat. The television shows a huge Islamic demonstration in the Anatolian town of Sivas, with ranks of veiled women enthusiastically tearing up copies of *Penthouse*. Sivas is the fundamentalist capital, if the movement could be said to have one. It is a strange irony that Sivas was where Mustafa Kemal held the Congress in 1919 that laid the foundation of his power in modern Turkey. Like many other nondescript middle-sized towns that few Westerners visit or have even heard of, it is now an Islamic fortress, from where, perhaps, like the original Ottoman Turks, Islamists will have to try to take the Sodom and Gomorrah of Istanbul. It would be the second Turkish takeover of an externally ambiguous and corrupt city that has been colonized by Westerners; the first, in 1453, surged on past Constantinople to conquer the Balkans for Islam and threaten half of Europe. And today, Vienna has no gates. Ull is thinking of history: 'Against the Islamists, we modern Turks must stand and fight. I hate them . . . I hate them. We must defend what Atatürk built. I would die for Atatürk.'

But Atatürk is already dead. On 6 November 1938 his liver finally gave up, enlarged and hardened after years of being washed daily by floods of *raki*, the aniseed spirit that turns as white as milk; according to a Turkish saying, when you drink too much *raki*, you swallow the monster. Atatürk swallowed two monsters – *raki* and the future of Turkey – and tried to shape his life with them.

Part One

CITIES

1. Istanbul I: Origins

> The Greeks have been defeated in a neighbouring land. But
> in a few years they shall themselves gain victory: such being
> the will of Allah before and after ... They care for the
> outward show of life, but of the life to come they are
> heedless ...
>
> Surah 30, the Koran

Atatürk hated foreigners who defined Turkey by its old capital
city. He dedicated his youth to fighting the torpor and corruption
of its government, when it was still called Constantinople. Nowadays, for most visitors encountering Istanbul for the first time,
Constantinople seems to have disappeared as long ago as the
time of the Prophet in the seventh century. The city is a vast,
driving, turbulent metropolis, which often seems to be beyond
individual human control or divine influence. It is wild, often
dissolute, with intersecting centres and localities and suburbs,
much more a labyrinth than any Greek city. It is the only famous
Turkish city, the only place in the country that is not provincial.

In Muhammad's distant Arabian desert fastnesses, the great
city of Constantinople was also the world metropolis, a fabled
centre of wealth and power. Muhammad favoured the Greeks
in their battles with the idolatrous Persians because at least they
were believers, of a kind, if degenerate in their misguided religious
faith and preoccupied with material success. It is an ironic
echo of international politics today, with Muslim Iran as the
arch-enemy of the materialistic and secular West. The words
from the Koran have a contemporary resonance in Istanbul,

although Turkish cynics might say the Greek people have not altered much in some respects, and the Prophet was thinking of them. But Istanbul has changed. The elegant Byzantine metropolis has become a sprawling, chaotic, urban nightmare. In early Western literature the dominant image of the city in Turkey is that of the doomed city of Troy. In 1922 the ruined buildings of Smyrna, modern Izmir, became the new Troy, as the city was razed and the Greek and Armenian populations were massacred by Turkish troops. But Istanbul has been Troy many times: perhaps most importantly in 1453, when the city fell to the Ottoman conquerors, after the final naval assault from Rumeli Hisari; and in 1204 to the Latins, losing most of the hinterland on which it depended for its prosperity. Nowadays the city may fall again, perhaps under its own weight and size rather than at the hand of any outside conqueror.

The old city today is surrounded by suburbs of featureless concrete towers or very tall, barrack-like apartment blocks, set in a wilderness of rubble, old cars and piles of rubbish. They are not the towers of Trebizond but the stronghold of the new Islamic power – in most working-class suburbs of the city the Refah Party has a dominant presence. Tourists are never found in these residential suburbs where the vast majority of the inhabitants of the city live. The progress of the Islamists is hardly surprising, as the only community building of any kind is often the new mosque. Some 4,000 or so are under construction in Turkey at the moment, financed in competition by Saudi Arabia, Kuwait and Iran.

Only a minority of the adults who live in these blocks of flats, structures that resemble the tenement prisons on the outskirts of Moscow, will have been born in Istanbul; they are part of the explosive population growth in the city and surrounding region since the 1960s. The colourful tide of humanity of the centre of the city means little in these sterile blocks, far removed from azure tiles, flashing gold jewellery, girls with black eyes and black curls waiting to cross the street. They were rushed up to try to provide better housing for the mass of people, an honourable aim.

In Istanbul the wealthy are still secular, hedonistic, preoccupied with material life, sensual. However Turkish by birth or culture, they have inherited some of the pleasure-loving habits of the Byzantine Greeks that the Prophet noted so accurately in the Koran. For visitors with some money, pleasure and the senses are central to their experience of Istanbul. In the past, the city was always associated with the crudest sensuality. On the surface, that may still be the case today. East European and German tourists queue outside the doors of the legal brothels in Pera before opening time like shoppers outside Harrods. In one of the annual rituals of Turkish life, the publication of the year's tax returns and the associated competition to be the richest individual Turk, a frequent winner is the Istanbul madam and brothel owner, Matilde Manoughian. She is an Armenian millionairess, who lives in an enormous house with sumptuous internal decorations overlooking the Bosphorus.

The city has always harboured extremes, of wealth and poverty, religion and paganism, hedonism and asceticism. It may seem to be only about the body and its satisfactions, but it is cluttered with temples of the spirit, great churches and mosques at every street corner in the oldest parts of the city. To many visitors, the city seems a long way from the pure and idealized vision of Lord Kinross, the distinguished interpreter of the Turkey of his generation, who could write as recently as 1956 in *Europa Minor*:

Istanbul is a classic example, unusual among cities, of a happy marriage, between nature and man. Land and water are its elements: the land is resolved into architecture, the water forever girdling away from it, the two coalescing to create a city distinct with space and speed and a liquid cleansing light. Its rhythm is in the water, in the Bosphorus, racing like a deep salt river between Europe and Asia, from a cold sea in the north to a warm sea in the south . . . it is a city of windows . . .

their panes glinting gold as the sun dies away from it into the green hills of Europe beyond.

It is almost as if Kinross is writing about a painting of Istanbul rather than the city as it actually exists. The city is seen from a distance, and its beauty is without guilt or responsibility. In this aesthetic tradition – best represented by Kinross, Pierre Loti, the French poet Lamartine and countless other nineteenth-century visitors – Istanbul was somehow beyond morality. It belonged to Flaubert's artificial paradise of *Salammbô*. This vision of Constantinople was a central feature of the Western Orientalist tradition, as represented by the work of a painter like David Roberts (1796–1864). Kinross was a distinguished historian of Turkey, an author of great scholarly works, but some of the admirers of Turkey in our own generation have inherited something of the emptiness of the pictorial tradition of Western Orientalism. As in the Platonic equation, beauty is equated with good. The beautiful buildings of Istanbul become the forms, the content of Turkish society is irrelevant. In political terms power is equated with good: the fact that Turkey is 'stable', allegedly secular, a pillar of the West, exonerates it from criticism of its internal political abuses and human-rights violations. The absence of a moral dimension in perceptions of the city is closely allied to the absence of a moral dimension in the Western establishment view of its politics. The devout political admirers of Turkey in Britain and the United States have frequently been on the right, and sometimes on the extreme right of the political spectrum, just as many Hellenists have, following Byron, been on the political left. Byzantium, in the poems of W. B. Yeats, was a beauty outside time and hence outside society, which excludes the possibility of social change leading to social improvements. For the neo-classicists, the beauty of Greek thought and achievements in the classical world had a strong moral and social content, which raised the question of how the onlookers' society matched up to the ancient model; the

Byzantine and Ottoman tradition in Istanbul was beyond bourgeois political morality, as conceived by implacable Hellenic critics of the Porte such as Gladstone. In Ottoman times this was linked to the nature of the sultan's rule; the admirers of the Ottoman world had to overlook its wholly undemocratic nature.

The old city, in its extraordinarily beautiful and dramatic setting, could seduce by appearance alone, but that is less true nowadays. In contemporary Istanbul dissonance between nature and man is more common than harmony. The Bosphorus has perhaps survived best, in the upper reaches at least. The British diplomat Lord Hardinge wrote in his *Reminiscences* that

locomotion on the Bosphorus was on the most luxurious and picturesque scale. Most people had their own caiques, long graceful boats, rowed by one, two or three caiquejis, according to their position and rank. These rowers were dressed in many-coloured liveries embroidered with gold, and all the cushions and trappings of these caiques were decorated in the same way . . . It would be impossible to describe the wonderful beauty of the moonlit nights, the outlines of the hills on the Asiatic shore, the cries of fishermen signalling passage of fish, the song of the nightingales and the sparkling movements of the dancing fireflies.

Although the magic coalescence of water, air, light and a sense of historical destiny can produce deep emotions in even the most cynical visitor, the complex and difficult reality of life in modern Istanbul and its urban crisis soon intrude. That fierce reality should not be underestimated, and explains why, according to a recent British travel survey, of all major tourist destinations, it has the highest number of people who never return for a second visit. If the view of the nineteenth-century poet Lamartine was that you see the skyline of Constantinople and die, some visitors now find that you encounter the city and then leave as soon as possible.

If Ankara is the Turkish city that is most identified with Atatürk and his revolution, Istanbul is its antithesis. It was a Greek city for far longer than it has been an Ottoman or Turkish city. When the Roman Empire was divided in AD 395, the eastern empire was governed from Constantinople and survived long after Rome had fallen, although after the critical battle of Manzikert in 1071, the empire was on the retreat. In 1453 the followers of the Prophet were to take it from Christian Europe for ever, but it was then the most famous and civilized city in the world, in which Greek was the language of government, the law, and the Church. To understand Greek was to understand civilization. Ankara is identified with ethnically pure Turkishness and the Hittite citadel, Istanbul with ethnic and religious diversity, trade as opposed to government, strong links with progressive Europe as opposed to backward Asia, with the Aegean, a friendly and rich sea, as opposed to the half-lifeless and often sinister Black Sea. And below the surface of Istanbul is old Constantinople, a foreign city for hundreds of years, in terms of nationalist identity, the apex of civilization in its time. Ankara, if it means anything to the average West European, stands for authoritarian government and a terrible climate; visiting businessmen complain about air pollution and smog, the rotting shanty towns at the city edge, and stultifying boredom in the evenings. Istanbul represents the tangible East and the enduring heritage of the Ottoman theocratic state. The 'unspeakable Turk' of so many nineteenth-century anti-Ottoman speeches was unspeakable not just because of his brutal and reactionary actions in government, but because of his allegedly dissipated and hedonistic private life, as important a target for the criticisms of Liberals like Gladstone from the Non-conformist, puritan wing of British politics. Morality overcame considerations of culture or beauty, in the same way that many modern Greeks cannot see any positive value in the exquisite beauties of Turkish material culture.

Atatürk wished Ankara to be free of this dichotomy – the heritage of private pleasure and public degeneration and pain. The new city represented planning, regulation, the military and bureaucracy, centralization and statist ideology, whereas Istanbul has remained the city of freedom, enterprise, economic progress, cultural diversity, openness to Western ideology, sensual pleasure and simple fun. In the post-Communist era, Istanbul has come to the fore again, and the atmosphere of Ankara can seem dated in the same way that many ex-Communist capitals in Eastern Europe seem dated. Within the tangle of the modern Turkish identity, Istanbul has a special place; it expresses the dilemma at the heart of Atatürkist ideology very clearly. This is perhaps linked to the schizophrenic qualities in Atatürk's own dark and divided personality. His revolution was a westernizing movement, but it implied rejection of the most Western city in the country as the centre of government. Yet the rejection was never complete and it is arguable how far it ever took place in practice. As ever in Turkey, past and present, the symbol is important and very different from the reality; by the late 1920s Atatürk himself was spending as much time in what was still called Constantinople as any sultan did, perhaps more than some, and he died in the great palace at Dolmabahce on the Bosphorus in surroundings befitting any late-Ottoman ruler. Ankara may have been his creation, but after about 1928 he chose not to live in it for much of the time.

The Byzantine and Ottoman heritage is embodied in the buildings and archaeological sites of the Golden Horn, the part of Istanbul synonymous with tourism. The tourist industry in Turkey is not simply a matter of money, although it is very important to the national economy. A particular view of the past is constructed for the tourist. Many visitors who come to the city never leave European Turkey, apart, perhaps, from a trip up the Bosphorus, and spend all their time among the Roman, Byzantine and Ottoman monuments. Almost everything on the Golden Horn can be seen and appreciated as if Atatürk had never existed and his revolution and subsequent national history had never taken place. In the Kapali Carsi covered market, the largest souvenir shop in the world, almost everything on sale could have been designed and sold in 1914, if not 1614. It is difficult to find anything connected with Atatürk, let alone one of the busts or portraits that adorn nearly every Turkish shop or office. Even the once banned Ottoman fez is making a come-back, on shop counters at least.

The fact that the visitor's Turkey is essentially the Ottoman and pre-Ottoman world shows how powerful the past is in Turkish culture, and how little modernization of Turkey has taken place in the minds of most Europeans, and, indeed, of many Turks. The modernist images of the secular entrepreneurs have no place here. The world the visitor comes to see was created by the early nineteenth century, and much of it a long time before that. The visitor focuses on institutions that seem quintessentially 'Turkish', such as the palace of the sultans at Seraglio Point, Topkapi Serai, the Turkish baths scattered around the old city, some of great antiquity, and the great mosques and Byzantine buildings. 'Turkey', as the visitor sees it, consists of these great edifices, which retreat into an ever more remote past.

The history, identity and nature of these buildings are very diverse and have little to do with the preferred self-image of the modern Turkish state. It has no central focus such as Windsor Castle and Buckingham Palace in England, the Kremlin in Russia or the White House in the United States. Turkey is very much a republic. The mosque and other Islamic buildings are essentially Arab in origin and inspiration, although the architectural development of the mosques built after the Ottoman conquest owes much to the innovations of the conquerors and great architects like Sinan (1489?–1587). Roman and Byzantine Constantinople left classical monuments, but some of the most prominent were adapted or taken over by the Ottoman conquerors and have become 'Turkish' by default. The ancient Hippodrome next to the Blue Mosque falls into this category. Some of these monuments are not simply buildings, but also social institutions. The much mythologized harem is the most important symbol, along with the Turkish baths. The harem was a symbol of Ottoman 'decadence', and thousands of pages of prose, poetry, pornography and political and sociological discourse have been expended on explaining how it worked, the nature of the oppression of women involved, the architecture of the harem buildings, the violence meted out to unwanted members of the sultan's family, the unnatural life of the eunuchs, and so on. In Victorian England, it was the central symbol of the corrupt dissipation of the Ottoman Empire, the dark heart of mystery, conspiracy, violence and sensuality that exemplified Turkey as the 'Other'. It was where the corrupt body politic and the corrupt physical bodies met in what the anti-Ottomanists saw as a foul and dishonourable marriage. But then and now, anti-Turkish diatribes often take little account of the reality of Turkish history.

The harem was quite unknown to the Seljuk Turks who swept westward from Anatolia in the early Middle Ages and began their long conquest of the Byzantine lands. Their nomadic and austere military leaders may well have treated women very badly, but their way of life was quite incompatible with the sedentary arts and pleasures of the harem, which was a profoundly urban institution. To oversimplify, the sultan could indulge himself in comfort with an endless supply of nubile young females in the city, while the great Ottoman army held the frontiers in discomfort and danger.

The harem was, in many respects, a prison, but of what nature is more difficult to define. It is usually discussed in isolation from the Grand Seraglio, which is misleading, as it was only one part of a much larger palace. According to a crude Freudian interpretation, which has become popular with many Turkish writers, the harem was a symbol of the 'bad' womb, of danger, mystery and solitude, political violence and personal dissipation, as opposed to the 'good' womb of Turkish life embodied in the inner chambers of the mosque, the baths and the church. The harem was corrupting, while the latter were purifying, either spiritually or physically, or both. The sexual politics of the institution seem to support the view that the harem is a symbol of Turkish imperialism in the sexual sphere. Huge castrated men, usually black, represented a triumph over subject peoples,

and women only achieved any power or status by becoming
sultana long after their sexual and reproductive phase of life
had passed. There were exceptions to this rule, of course, like
Roxelana, consort to the great ruler Süleyman I, the Magnificent
(1520–66), but they are very few. Whether many of the sultans
would have behaved differently in their personal lives if the
temptations of the harem had not existed seems doubtful –
Renaissance rulers in the West were hardly chaste, as the lives
of many British and French monarchs indicate. But the practice
of the harem represented a denial of female sexuality as much
as an indulgence of it, a death of freedom and desire.

The origin of the harem lies in the ancient world. The harem
was the women's quarters of a large social, political and administrative unit, the Imperial Palace. According to N. M. Penzer,
author of an authoritative work on the harem, its roots lay in
the Roman Empire, and it was certainly prominent by the time
of Domitian (AD 81–96). Laws were passed under his rule
banning the castration of eunuchs, a key element in all harems,
in all historical periods. It appeared to have already become a
social problem. In Ottoman times, unfortunate boys were captured on the African frontiers, and most of their testicles and
penis were removed in the desert before they arrived in Constantinople. If they survived this terrible ordeal, which many did not,
they were confined in the seraglio for the rest of their lives. Such
savage and barbaric aspects of Ottoman life do not often appear
in the works of writers of the aesthetic Turkophile tradition,
any more than accounts of tortures and human-rights violations
figure in the current writings of Ankara's apologists in Europe
and the United States. Issues of sexuality, in the conventional
meaning of the word, are almost wholly irrelevant here. Most,
if not all, rulers had what are often euphemistically referred to
as 'concubines', and, at one level, the women of the Ottoman
harem were no more or less than that: attractive slave girls who
happened to be in favour with the sultan. The eunuchs were, at
the same simple level, merely symbols of power and conquest.

In appearance, if not reality, it was a house of pleasure, a strange kind of private brothel. This does not seem to have remained the case for very long. The harem developed from being a place of relaxation to being a centre of intrigue, if not of power. For generations of Western visitors, it had the fascination of the unknown; behind its high walls it was secret and closed to male visitors. To break in, or out, as in Mozart's opera, was the height of progressive achievement. It came to represent the impenetrability of Ottoman government and Oriental absolutism.

Constantinople was, and Istanbul still is, the great city of walls. They are the physical manifestation of the cultural and social separations in the old city. In Byzantine times, the Theodosian walls were the symbol of the security of the city, and saved it many times from invasion by the Bulgarians, and the barbarian tribes. They are still a great sight today, the outer walls loping across the Plain of Thrace like a great snake, kilometres outside the modern city. The inner walls are towering landmarks, especially when seen from a car alongside the Sea of Marmara, with deep gates befitting the great triumphal processions of emperors that have passed through them. The Golden Gate, the *Porta Aurea*, is perhaps the best place to appreciate this, and to let the mind dwell on the glorious past. It was built by the Emperor Theodosius I (378–95) to celebrate victory over a rival; his triumphal procession would have been a forest of glittering spearheads, bowed captives and tall men in flashing armour. It was just before the division of the Roman Empire and the Goths were at the door, but Theodosius, aged thirty-three, was master of the Greek-speaking world. Thousands of people would have passed joyfully through this gate in a brief moment of triumph, like Pindar's happy athletes. The gate would witness more triumphs, but never in a united, Christian world, and always with the threat of destruction hanging over the city and the empire. The last imperial triumph was when Emperor Michael VIII Palaeologus (1261–82) passed through with his captives, in a pale imitation of his predecessors, in August 1261. It was only twenty days after the expulsion of the Latin conquerors, the agents of an expansionist, imperialist Vatican, now the enemy of Eastern Christianity.

Walls in the city are not only the tool and setting of the powerful; security for many individuals and institutions is on a Middle Eastern scale. Walls 20, 30, even 40 feet high turn narrow streets into dark alleyways, like the set of a *film noir*. In Kum Kapi, on the Sea of Marmara, down by the seashore, the Armenian cathedral huddles behind vertical cliffs of brickwork, white-painted, austere, a church that would be happy in Calvin's Geneva or Knox's Edinburgh. A dark arch in the walls leads to a brightly lit street of fish restaurants. It is only about a mile from the wholesale fish market. Studded turbot are bent over piles of ice on tables outside, lit by garish bare bulbs. But this is not a tourist trap; most of the customers are Turks who treat the restaurants like home. It is famous for its traditional musicians. Small bands circulate and as the *raki* flows, people break into deep-voiced melancholy love songs. A fat fiddle player runs up and down scales, small brass drums beat, it is the city at its best, warm, human, profoundly Turkish, uncorrupted by Western materialism.

Yet, as always, the Eastern Question is not far away. Like so many other business premises in Turkey, the restaurants have pictures of their founding fathers on the wall, severe, long-departed patriarchs looking down from brown sepia prints to see that the fish are being grilled correctly, alongside the inevitable picture of Atatürk. Unlike Atatürk, the founders of most of these restaurants were Armenian. About a mile away, behind even higher walls than the church, is the home of the Armenian Patriarch. One proprietor gingerly explains, that, yes, his grandparents were Armenians, then, with a sideways glance at his customers, changes the subject and begins to talk loudly about the fine quality of today's mullet, and how stocks of turbot in the Sea of Marmara are being affected by pollution. When I

persist with questions he curtly says that everybody here got on
very well under the Ottoman system until the Great Powers
started manipulating the Christian minorities to help break up
the empire and the Greeks and Armenians began to be seen as
agents of foreign powers. This is what every Turkish schoolbook
says, but the reality is more complex.

The Armenian Patriarch Kazandjian has video cameras above
his door, and security men who look as though they might have
worked for Al Capone. His black Mercedes is armour-plated
and has shaded windows. Yet when he goes to his church, the
atmosphere in the street is relaxed, he stops to talk to some
very Turkish children about their favourite football team –
Galatasaray, inevitably – and how they will get on against the
hated rivals from Edirne. Essential decencies and tolerance are
very strong in Istanbul, where different groups have lived together
for generations. The Armenian Patriarch's congregation is generally rich, some very wealthy indeed, and the whole scene could
be presented as an illustration of the success of Atatürk's policy
of integrating the most difficult and alienated minority into his
new state. (After the massacres of the early twentieth century,
it is perhaps surprising that there are any Armenians in Turkey
at all.) Their standard of living is far removed from the beleaguered life of their compatriots in the stony little fields of the
Armenian homeland to the east – a contrast greater, perhaps,
than that between the rich Jewish suburbs of New York and the
austerity of the kibbutz in Israel.

Their ethnic Greek neighbours are much less happy. The
Armenians are not loved in Turkey, but they have a fairly stable
place, as long as they keep out of certain areas of Turkish life,
and are careful to be loyal Turkish citizens on the key national
issues. The Greek minority in Istanbul has different and much
more serious problems. They are at the heart of a major regional,
ethnic and national conflict that has split NATO and the West
in the eastern Mediterranean. The Greek Patriarch, Bartholo-
meos, is a charming, small, white-bearded man, highly intelligent

and with moderate and conciliatory views, but his flock has diminished in numbers over the years. A generation ago there were about 65,000 Greeks in Istanbul, but many were driven away by violent attacks on their houses and shops during the crises of the 1950s and 1960s in Cyprus. Although Greek culture is alive in the city, there are only about 4,000 Greeks left, and their churches and schools have the atmosphere of being besieged by government bodies, although most Istanbul people accept them as part of the diverse life of the historic city. Many middle-class citizens will admit to some Greek blood, if they know you well, but it is a difficult subject.

It may seem strange to worry about them at all, a few thousand people in a vast city of millions. But the Greeks and the Armenians represent what was once the essential multicultural nature of Istanbul, not just before the Ottoman conquest, but long after it. Greeks quickly rose to leading positions soon after the conquest, and the early sultans opened their doors to oppressed minorities like the persecuted Jews from Catholic Spain. The early Ottoman Empire was far in advance of many Western European states in its tolerance of minorities and religious diversity. Most important of all, the idea of nationalism was entirely absent, and contrary to both Byzantine and Ottoman thinking. Yet our century has been a century of nationalism in Turkey, as elsewhere.

Istanbul dominates Turkey, in one sense. Nobody knows what the population actually is; by the time any census is taken, it is out of date, given the endless influx of people from the east and the relatively high birthrate, but the city and the surrounding region of the Sea of Marmara are thought to run to nearly 12 million people, putting it on a par with greater Cairo. Much of the recent development of the city, as in so many others in Western Europe, has been connected with the car. The answer to the dreadful traffic crisis that has gripped Istanbul for many years has often been to knock down swathes of historic buildings and charming traditional quarters to build new roads. This was a strongly favoured policy during the years of military government in the 1980s – roads and the Turkish military always seem to go together. The city has continued to grow apace, cars have jammed the new roads as well as the old ones, and the whole process has to begin again. In the mid 1980s, under an enlightened mayor, Mr Bedrettin Dalan, the insanity of it all became apparent, although not before great damage to the environment and monuments had been done. Some money was set aside by the city council to preserve some of the last wholly Ottoman streets remaining near the Blue Mosque that were falling into terminal disrepair – charming little wooden houses with latticed balconies that were inhabited by rats and Kurdish refugees in about equal numbers. An inadequate, but welcome, ancient building fund was set up, so that great landmarks like the Byzantine sea walls on the south side of the Golden Horn could be maintained properly.

A modern public transport plan was adopted, with a light railway linking the Sultan Ahmed area with other important inner-city locations. At the same time the British-built Bosphorus bridge was being constructed and the need for ferries to some areas, at least, was reduced. The World Bank financed a new arterial sewer under the Golden Horn, designed to remove the foul waters that had turned the area into a fetid and stagnant bacterial mass. As ever with Istanbul, the city hangs on a knife-edge between survival and collapse. Genuine progress was being made in tackling these problems in the 1980s, when a booming economy helped find the necessary private and public investment to pay for it all, but then new problems appeared. Perhaps the most serious is the water crisis. For hundreds of years Constantinople drew most of its water from the Forest of Belgrade, on the western outskirts of the city, from the little rivers known as the 'sweet waters of Europe'. They are sweet no more, if they exist at all, and water engineers have had to search farther and farther afield for diminishing supplies of even reasonably clean water. Tanker transport of water is the only solution in many areas. The Asian reservoirs are threatened with pollution and present a major public health risk to the city in the future. The water-mains are not capable of conveying the water around the city in many places, and standpipes in the street are all that is available for many poorer inhabitants in the inner districts. In the new suburbs modern supply networks are laid, but there is often little or no water in them, especially to the upper reaches of blocks of flats. Air pollution is another major problem: levels are frequently very high in many inner-city areas.

Istanbul has become akin to many Third World capitals, in terms of population growth and the crisis in basic services – it has much more in common with the problems of Mexico City or Manila than a European city. Yet many friends of Turkey would argue that it is the only European city in the country, in its business and professional culture. Many foreign visitors know little of Turkish history, and find it difficult to relate the apparently modern and commercial culture of Istanbul to the growth of the new Islam. But it cannot be stressed too often that Islam in Turkey has never been an enemy of capitalism, only of foreign capitalism – in the Sultan's eyes or those of Refah. The secular state founded by Atatürk had its roots in a very different Turkey, and in an army that had inherited some of the traditional Ottoman military's aristocratic disdain for any kind of commercial or business activity.

It was in the east, in Anatolia, that resistance broke out, where the Entente powers least expected it. In the chaos following the First World War, the division of the whole Ottoman Empire between France, Britain and Greece was a real possibility, and in the west it became a reality. Foreign capitalist powers seemed to Atatürk to be putting an end to the country. Atatürk raised the flag in old military strongholds like Erzurum, Kars and Mus, names that grate like the peasants' ploughs in the bare fields. Anatolia is a continent away from the streets of Istanbul or the

European frontier with Greece in the Evros delta. In the winter the snow can lie six feet deep, in the summer it is not difficult to die from heat exhaustion if you are working in the fields or in the vast army camps. Atatürk's military revolt was based on a Muslim soldier élite that set out to rescue the country, just as the Osmali Turks had done. In some senses the revolt was part of the anti-imperialist movements that swept the world after the Bolshevik Revolution in 1917, but it was also highly conservative in its mythology: the military marching from the east to rescue the country from foreign domination.

Official Turkey has always felt that there were wider lessons for the world from Atatürk's movement. A government document published in Ankara in 1986 claims that:

the independence struggle carried out against the imperialist states and following the sound reforms of Atatürk constituted an important model for Third World countries winning their independence after the Second World War.

It is doubtful if this was the case, then or since. It is difficult to imagine that Gandhi, Tito or a modern leader like Mandela in South Africa gave much thought to the Turkish experience in developing their own political perspectives. Turkish culture and history has a self-contained quality.

In the landmark election of 1995, when the Islamic Refah Party became the biggest political party in Turkey, Islamic majority areas stretched in a green swathe across the centre of the country from the Sea of Marmara to the eastern border. Constantinople has its own home for a Minotaur, and the city was a byword for random violence and corruption in the ancient world. Western bankers may be wearing the bull's horns now, rather than the Greek mine owners or German railway entrepreneurs of the last century, but they, too, are foreigners entering a labyrinth, with no certainty that there will be any thread of Ariadne to guide them.

2. Istanbul II: Pera and Modernism

And Theseus entered the labyrinth to find the Minotaur,
and he was afraid.

Robert Graves, *Greek Myths*, 1955

If the colour of Islam is green, a green thread in Turkish life,
sometimes dominant, sometimes covered with other colours,
green in Istanbul often means the wooded shores of the Asiatic
side of the Bosphorus. Crossing the fetid and stinking waters of
the Golden Horn seems to most visitors to Istanbul to lead to a
different world, to Asia. In one of his many symbolic journeys
and crossings Lord Byron swam across what was then called
the Hellespont, his physical action, as so often, in unity with
intellectual and cultural exploration. If Europe represents home
and safety, and Asia distance and danger, Pera, lying between
Europe and Asia, is a strange and misleading transition. Or
rather, Turkey has many confusing introductions to Asia. Pera
is removed from the Golden Horn and the continuities of Turkish
history, the interlocking glories and buildings of the Classical,
Byzantine and Ottoman eras. Pera represents commerce, the
emerging bourgeois world, modernity and the institutionalization of Western culture in Turkey. There is a sense in which
capitalism in Turkey has always been a foreign import, run
by foreigners for foreigners, an idea drawn upon by Ottoman
sultans, Atatürk's protectionists and the Turkish left alike.
Within Turkish society, but always above the people and civil
society, there has been a superior state, uncorrupted by the
compromises and distortions of life caused by lowly commerce.

On the far side of Galata Bridge the dark and sinister labyrinth turns into a small, harmless maze, with alleyways to get lost in and meet a family of thin and hungry cats, with middle-brow shops, sensible shoe retailers, a market selling pot plants and tropical fish, and dull restaurants used by junior diplomats discussing the effect of EU regulations on Turkish trade. Pera is the most Westernized part of the city, and to some extent it always has been.

In the Middle Ages the little hill on which Pera stands was more or less empty land that was taken over by Genoese merchants who controlled a good deal of the sea trade of Constantinople. (The Italian Catholic cathedral is still in central Pera.) It later became the home of many foreign communities: Poles, Balts, Latvians, Russians, and other northerners all had their *quartiers* here. But although the area embodied the beginnings of European capitalism, with Italian merchants and Flemish fabric traders in the streets, Pera became a rough and sometimes wild popular district.

Below Galata Tower, the old port is still a vibrant, old-fashioned waterfront, where ships are loaded and unloaded by hand, in a way that has disappeared in the soulless, modern container ports in Europe. In the old days trade in goods here often meant trade in women, and the industry of prostitution remains significant in Pera. The brothels licensed and controlled by the state lead a discreet existence a little way up the hill below Galata Tower. They are, as so often in Turkey, very close to a mosque, bodies and spirits meeting. The area is haunted by pimps, who are having to go through the tiresome process of learning a little Russian. The deal that has not been done within a mile of this dockside has probably never been done anywhere. Little has changed; in 1900 the *Murray's Handbook to Constantinople* described this area as consisting 'of filthy lodging houses in which one of the most depraved populations of Europe finds a home'. A little later a young man called Mustafa Kemal was a frequent customer in the brothels, as one of his early biographers, H. C. Armstrong, describes:

At once he plunged wildly into the nightlife of the great metropolis of Constantinople. Night after night he gambled and drank in the cafés and restaurants. With women he was not fastidious. A figure, a face in profile, a laugh, could set him on fire and reaching out to get the woman, whoever she was. Sometimes it would be with the Greek and Armenian harlots in the bawdy houses by the Galata Bridge, where came the pimps and homosexualists to cater for all the vices; then for a week or two a Levantine lady in her house in Pangaldi; or some Turkish girl who came veiled and by backways in fear of the police to some *maison de rendezvous* in Pera or Stambul.

There were probably far more brothels in nineteenth-century Paris or London than there have ever been in Istanbul, but the institution came to dominate foreign views of Pera, and Pera was the *quartier* the foreigners knew best. Yet the respectable still had their refuges here. Above the dockside, with its grim energy – a place to read writers like Upton Sinclair or Jack London – is the Pera Palace Hotel, a short walk up the steep hill, all late-Ottoman magnificence, with inlaid mother-of-pearl furniture and tiny dishes of exquisite sweet and salted almonds. The hotel was the haunt of exiled monarchs, like Zog of Albania; dictators, like Juan Perón of Argentina; and spies, like Kim Philby. The walls seem to reek of intrigue and conspiracy. Only Mata Hari, the legendary Dutch spy and *femme fatale* of the First World War, is missing from the lounge, although in her heyday here she was very active in the bedrooms. The British flocked to the Pera Palace when the Orient Express brought the danger and mystery of Constantinople within reach of most professional families. Here respectable British and foreign imperialists rubbed shoulders with real intrigue and political danger, or so the myth went. Agatha Christie wrote *Murder on the Orient Express* in Room 304, and Graham Greene is believed to have modelled many features of the Istanbul hotel in his 1930s novel *Stamboul Train* on the Pera Palace. In 1935 Dennis Wheatley published *The Eunuch of Stamboul*, a bestselling popular novel that is full of the traditional racialist stereotypes. Turks are portrayed as corrupt, violent and full of bestial sensuality. These images are significant because modern Turkey has produced very few literary or cultural reflections in England.

If the brothel epitomized disorderly old Constantinople for the traders and visitors, the hotel symbolized a kind of order and accessibility, the great advance in travel to Turkey represented by the railways. From the hotel, Pera could be looked down on in all its teeming and corrupt vitality. It was a haven for imperialists, like the Shepheard's Hotel in Cairo or Raffles in Singapore (all hotels managed by Armenians). Even the name is significant – Pera is the foreign quarter, but the hotel is also a palace, an Ottoman institution, bringing together stranger and despot, where the non-Muslims, the *gavurs* can live like the sultan. The Pera Palace is a little stranded now, above a new inner urban motorway, with a very good view of the local headquarters of the Islamic Refah Party out of the east windows. In the nearby streets, there is nothing more exciting than some cheaper and more dowdy hotels, endless electrical shops and the headquarters of various banks. There are some unnecessarily large Western consulates, like the Swedish building. Most business with the central government has to be done through the Ankara missions and government offices in the capital; many Istanbul buildings, although outwardly magnificent, are semi-inhabited shells that are little more than minor trade and consular offices.

In the British Foreign Office handbook for 1964 it is revealing to note that there were thirty-four accredited officials in post in Ankara, compared to only six in Istanbul. Today there is no real diplomatic corps in Istanbul. Even when the Ottoman world still existed and Angora was a hick provincial town, there was little to do in Constantinople missions, as for so much of the time the future of the Ottoman Empire was being decided elsewhere – in the chancelleries of Europe, the great diplomatic conferences, the turbulent Balkans, or the battlefields of the First World War. The distinguished British diplomat Lord Hardinge, writing in his memoirs on diplomatic life in Pera in 1880, remarks that 'the deadliness of life at the Embassy at that time is inconceivable, and it had the evil effect of driving the young men to spend their evenings in the *cafés chantants* and gambling dens with which Pera abounded'.

Mata Hari was not the only one who contributed to Pera's reputation for espionage. In the mid-nineteenth century the great archaeologist and discoverer of ancient Assyria, Sir Austen Henry Layard, also worked for the British government Intelligence service; one of his memoirs records an unsatisfactory encounter with authority in Pera. He had returned from a dangerous cross-country journey with information he knew the ambassador, Sir Stratford de Redcliffe, was eager to hear, but found himself unable to see him due to an obstructive, 'frilled and scented' second secretary. In the Second World War neutral Turkey was an important espionage centre and academic tradition was respected by SIS, with the distinguished ancient historian Sir Ronald Syme combining a study of the Roman Revolution with a study of German military activities in Ankara.

As in Syme's time, Ankara is where the people that matter in politics usually reside and work, not Istanbul. Today Taksim Square in the centre of Pera reflects the city's attempt to develop Westernized nightlife and consumer culture. Most middle-class Turkish families who can afford to live in the fashionable area have safe and conformist lifestyles, and there is hardly any independent youth culture. The square has the air of a state capital in mid-west America, dominated by traffic and dull shops, burger bars and fast-food establishments, lost in a wilderness of roads and concrete blocks, airline offices and the overarching presence of the Hilton Hotel.

Of course the ascendancy of the foreign is nothing new. In 1900 the official population of Constantinople was just under a million people. It was made up of 384,910 Muslims, 152,714 Greeks, 220,000 Armenians, 44,361 Jews, and 129,243 foreigners, plus a number of smaller ethnic minorities. The Western milieu in and around Taksim Square is essentially a continuation of this cosmopolitan aspect of the Ottoman city.

A major change since Ottoman times has been the development of an independent Turkish middle class, based in the suburbs – pleasant wealthy areas such as Besiktas, with good schools, Paris couturiers, and Italian men's tailors. If all Turkey were like these suburbs, a European destiny would beckon Turkey. Unsurprisingly, they represent all that the new Islamic radicals dislike and it is not uncommon to meet ardent members of the Refah Party there – thin, bearded, intense young men with green scarves or woolly hats. They stand selling pamphlets on the pavement outside Louis Feraud and its satin negligées denouncing Western culture and promoting Islam. And even here the Refah Party polled well in the last election.

With intense security searches at the entrance to the Hilton Hotel, the atmosphere is that of a Hilton in a difficult Middle Eastern state in the mid-1970s. Although the staff are pleasant, and it is a good place to buy expensive carpets, it is awkwardly self-conscious in the Turkishness it promotes, and a little run down, with no water in the fountains and the gardens not very well kept. It is a symbol of the decline in the energy and old certainties of the American relationship with Turkey.

Not far from Dolmabahce Palace, with its opulence and dignity, there is a square of floodlights and concrete walls, near a main road. It is the Galatasaray football ground, home of perhaps the most beautifully named football team in the world. The reality, though, is muscular, male, wild, tribal and frightening, on the field and off it. The stadium is a cauldron of passion and energy; it evokes the primitive fear aroused by the Ottoman army better than any other place in modern Turkey. It has the atmosphere of an ancient amphitheatre, with visiting teams and their hapless supporters being shown all the respect of Christians who have been thrown to the lions. Important matches take place against a background of thundering drumbeats, deafening cheers and wailing *zurnas*. Guns are regularly fired into the air at moments of celebration, and fireworks explode above the supporters on the terraces. 'Galatasaray! Bom, bom, bom,' supporters roar.

Although a football match is only a sports event, it is about war and conquest, or so it seemed to the Manchester United fans who saw their team knocked out of the European Cup there in 1994. Football is one of the few genuinely successful and popular elements in the westernization of Turkish culture. Before the Second World War it was hardly played anywhere in the country, except in the army, but it has become a national obsession and does at least bring some sense of normality to the beleaguered war zones in the east of the country if a major team comes to play. It also provides colour and passion in the poverty-stricken lives of many young Turkish men. And as in the UK, ownership of a football team gives newly rich businessmen an opportunity to acquire a public profile and a populist cultural base.

In a wider cultural sense, this part of Istanbul belongs essentially to the eighteenth and nineteenth centuries, just as much of the Golden Horn belongs to the Middle Ages and the early Ottoman centuries. It was a time of expansion of popular freedom, a move towards a more progressive and modern social system, with attempts at economic and industrial innovation. The sultans had moved from Topkapi Serai to various local palaces, although often not nearer to the people, the most notorious example being Abdül Hamit II at Yildiz Serai, cowering from the masses, an isolated and paranoid neurotic in permanent fear of assassination hiding behind 40-foot-high walls. The Bosphorus was rediscovered as a social space in this period, with giant boating parties of diplomats. Tennis courts were built near the water's edge for foreigners to while away the hot summer afternoons. Love affairs were conducted with gentle decorum. It was a doomed world, a world of beautiful surfaces, exquisite appearances but largely without substance or future, reminiscent of the *ancien régime* in eighteenth-century France depicted by Watteau and Fragonard.

The Refah Party's view of Pera and Galata today is similar, at least as expressed privately by activists over tiny cups of coffee late at night. To them, this part of town is as much the foreigners' enclave as it ever was, only instead of the nineteenth-century foreign merchants and their staff, there are the twentieth-century scourges of video-machine companies, infidels who deal in contraceptives, pornography and jacuzzis, and advise on privatization for large salaries. To the intense young Turks from the provinces, they are the agents of the devil, who would dismember Turkey and sell it to the foreigners.

In the eyes of the foreigners themselves, and of many independent economic commentators, foreign achievements are fragile and less than effective. Ever since Turkish governments began to make serious attempts to liberalize the economy in the late 1970s and early 1980s the same metaphors for Turkey appear in the international press: a broken down train on the way to an important station, a stalled car, and so on. If the foreigners of Pera are the real rulers of modern Turkey since Prime Minister Turgut Ozal began to introduce liberalization and privatization, as some popular newspapers claim, it has hardly been a period of triumphant success. According to the official line, considerable progress was made with privatization in the 1980s and more has been made since. Even this claim does not really stand up to scrutiny. Sales of state-owned industries started in the early 1980s, and have realized about $1.7 billion since then. For an economy the size of Turkey's, it is not much. The programme was slowed down, if not halted, in the Ozal era by the combination of pressure from the left-wing parties and the trade unions, problems with the bureaucracy, and the inertia that makes changing anything in Turkey a very slow and uncertain process. Moreover many of the most valuable Turkish state-owned industrial assets are tied up with holding companies and are difficult to privatize without striking at the vested interests of the Turkish ruling class.

When Mrs Tansu Ciller became prime minister after the death

of Turgut Ozal in 1993, there was considerable pressure on the government to accelerate the privatization programme. She was a true believer in liberal market economics, whereas there were always doubts about how far Mr Ozal had really broken with the old statist system. He presided over a period of high growth and modernization in the economy, so it was easier for him to resist pressure on this subject, which, as the Refah Party realizes only too well, is not simply a matter of economic ideology but goes to the heart of the Turkish identity and sense of independence. Government revenue in the 1980s was also much healthier, whereas an urgent priority for Mrs Ciller is to raise funds. In 1993 about 350 million dollars was raised through privatization issues and flotations on the Istanbul stock exchange, but the thirty-four main state-run industries had lost a staggering total of some £3 billion in the previous year. The endless issues of high-interest government bonds to finance these debts, together with high military expenditure, are prime causes of high inflation. These industries employ more than 600,000 people in 400 associated companies; some economists have estimated that they are so heavily overstaffed that they need to lose at least 60,000 employees to become efficient. Real production is continually squeezed by this crippling burden of debt.

A major obstacle to privatization of important industries, such as the Turkish National Telecommunications Corporation, is the Turkish constitution itself, with its anti-foreign-ownership provisions. Opposition parties and trade unions who disapprove of the principle of privatization, or the methods to be used, have successfully blocked many important government proposals in the courts by appeals to constitutional authority and tradition. The American philosopher W. V. Quine wrote in 1960 that 'the lore of our fathers is a fabric of sentences . . . it is a pale grey lore, black with fact and white with convention'. Convention plays an enormous part in Turkish life. It is a frequent Greek jibe against the Turks that the rule of law is unimportant in Turkey, but in many ways *adet*, custom or convention, has taken its place. In the sphere of the economy, this means that private ownership is often resisted, both at the level of legality, and at an ideological level. Mrs Ciller was always trying to be seen as the defender of Atatürk's tradition and heritage, but at the same time she was continually putting forward proposals to demolish the remaining economic basis of it.

Some progress has been made in the last decade, if privatization of state utilities does represent industrial progress. Private electricity producers have bought out state companies, as have cement manufacturers and parts of the state petrol retailing network, Petrol Ofisi, have been sold. Arrangements are under way for the sale of Petkim, the state petrochemicals company; the Turban hotel chain, which owns hotels, marinas and holiday villages; and the government stake in the Fiat car assembly operation, Tofais. Where privatization has taken place of a part or the whole of an enterprise, the shares sold are mostly held by institutions or foreign investors. United States fund-holders have been very keen investors in Turkey over the last twenty years, and have quickly bought major stakes in the more attractive parts of Turkish business, with optimism based on forecasts of 5–10 per cent growth rates. The problem for investors is that while growth rates have certainly been high, it has often been difficult to repatriate profits in hard currency, despite the openness of the Turkish economy. The foreign companies have resembled mice upon a wheel; generating revenue from the high growth rates which then depreciates in real terms as a result of the endless currency crises of the 1990s.

There is a flourishing stock exchange in Istanbul, but it is a young institution, a creature of the 1980s, and the vast majority of Turks still have little idea how it works or what it does. The ideal of a share-holding democracy has been absent from Turkish privatizations. There are many active investors, but almost exclusively in Istanbul and the western cities. It would be interesting to know how many people in traditional eastern towns like Mus and Kars own any shares at all, or even know what they are. The share-dealing and privatization culture is seen by traditionalist Turks as a sell-out to foreigners, a bonanza for Istanbul wide boys, and has helped the growth in influence of the Refah Party. It runs counter to some deep instincts in Turkish political life in its attempt to make the market the arbiter of all things. A good deal of the old Ottoman belief remains that the humblest man can rise to the heights if his merits are noticed by the powerful. Markets do not notice personal qualities of the individual. This also has a collective social dimension in Turkey.

The trade unions have strongly resisted most privatization proposals and have had a surprisingly strong influence, considering the ineffectiveness of trade union opposition to privatization in most countries, and the long history of hostility of Turkish governments to trade unions and attempts to divide and restrict their leadership. Perhaps this is because of their close links with elements of the Social Democratic Party in parliament. They were able to force concessions of principle out of the Ciller government; for instance, the prime minister had to promise to spend the proceeds of privatization on welfare payments and job-creation schemes. This may help socially, but does little to overcome the problems of chronic debt and inflation in the wider economy. The fact that the government has made major concessions in this area illustrates also that the traditions of state paternalism and corporatist welfarism are still flourishing at a popular level in Turkey; the good and humane side of the statist tradition is that progressive social policies can evolve without the radical disruption caused by market economics.

There are still major problems in Turkey in developing what might be called an enterprise culture, with a real finance capital sector of the economy. The richest Turkish business people, such as the Koc and Sabanci families, attained their position in the times of Atatürk. Vebi Koc could be said to have been little more than a local money-lender who was in the right place – he had the right political connections in Ankara and he was able to undertake a vital task for Atatürk and his advisers: to act as a nucleus for a combination of old state-owned assets that needed to be developed for the common good within a nationalist ideology but with a capitalist ethos. This unusual pattern of development would be impossible to reproduce nowadays, with modern markets and international trading relations. There is no similar route whereby Turkish business can grow in alliance with the benevolent national state today.

The vast majority of Turkish 'capitalism' is very small-scale indeed – people running a restaurant, a tannery or a corner shop. There is little prospect of these people becoming anything other than small businessmen. Business is accepted as part of everyday life, in a very Greek sense, but the idea of business as a new liberating ideology, in the Thatcherite sense, is remote. There is no objection to some state regulation of business by most Turks, given the long statist tradition in the country. There is no large class of slightly constrained and dissatisfied skilled workers, as there was in Britain in 1979, who saw the possibility of a new position in society as a result of privatization and free-market economic reforms. In Turkey the world of the market and the shop is much as it always was, while whole sections of traditional industries, such as coal mining and much of the steel industry, have disappeared. Meanwhile the foreign nostrums espoused by the trendy young men from New York in Pera wine bars are as alien as the free-trade ideas that might have been discussed on the same premises on the same streets a hundred years ago.

If Taksim Square and the inner suburbs of Pera represent the world of the solid and forward-looking middle class, they also represent the world of the intellectuals. Just as most Greek intellectuals congregate in Athens, so most Turkish thinkers and writers gravitate to Istanbul, and always have done. In Ottoman times the radical critics of the sultan and his system found a sympathetic audience here, and most of the time it was possible for secular dissent to flourish. Military dissent was much more difficult, as Atatürk and the Young Turk leaders found in their early days. Sultan Abdül Hamit's secret police were numerous and still quite efficient. The Turkish government maintains that Turkey is a country of free speech, something that has always been central to Turkish claims to 'Europeanness'. It is one of the most tenuous claims of Turkish governments. Uniformed and armed police still patrol the campuses of Istanbul and other universities, and closely monitor student political and social activities. This system has changed little since the end of the military juntas, although it is now operated without the gross human-rights violations that were current then. A large number of laws give the government the right to ban publications and intellectual activity which it considers against the national interest, and repression can always be justified by the constitutional provision which allows the security forces the right to intervene in the life of the country to protect it from internal threats. Although this apparatus of intellectual repression has not been used very often since the mid 1980s, and has sometimes collapsed in ruins in the courts when individual prosecutions have been attempted, its very existence encourages intellectual conformity and timidity in social criticism. Literature is not free from the threat of repression, as many of Turkey's most distinguished and patriotic writers have discovered from time to time. The most famous Turkish poet this century, Nazim Hikmet, spent much of his life in political exile in the Soviet Union. Internal exile and restrictions on the right of publication were the lot of Islamic clerics for many years until the reforms of the 1950s and 1960s improved their rights. Many other lesser figures have suffered imprisonment in Turkey and the banning of their works, including many of the significant authors writing in the Kurdish language.

At an institutional level, the education system tends to encourage conformity and repress individual thought and creativity. University professors have an inordinate amount of power and influence, and many expect their students to reproduce their ideas loyally. Educational standards are reasonable, but innovative work is much rarer than it should be in many subjects. Science and technology are not strong disciplines. In primary schools an extreme and regimented method of rote learning is still common, and the atmosphere, although humane, does not encourage individuality. This didacticism continues in secondary schools, except in the prestigious academies of Istanbul and the big cities, which follow an educational philosophy closer to that of the French Lycées, with a small number of well-connected pupils being educated in a creative and up-to-date environment. Any vocational training for the less educationally gifted only really takes place in the armed forces.

Generalizations can be misleading, but there seems to be an aspect of the Turkish mentality that distrusts abstract conceptual thought, but revels in mysticism, in the 'world of the unseen', as the Koran describes it. It is a refuge from the physical conformity that Turkish society has always demanded. Critical intellectuals do not enjoy high status within mainstream Turkish culture, and professional outlets such as quality journalism and the media do not have the same social status in Turkey as in the West. Most newspapers are not well respected, and Turks do not always believe what they read in them, quite rightly in many cases. The scientific disciplines suffer particularly from a 'brain drain', losing talented people to the better facilities and freer intellectual atmosphere of the United States and Germany. As a result, the Islamic revival has attracted some formerly secular critics of Turkish society, partly because it does provide an institutional focus for social criticism in the mosque and the *madrese*, the Islamic theological school, outside the confines of the university, where the police and the agents of the state have no right to go. Yet the Turkish mosques do not share the traditions of social radicalism of pre-Khomeni Iran or north Africa; there is far less of a tradition of the imams articulating social criticism, particularly in the mainstream Sunni mosques, but none the less they do offer an intellectual refuge that is important to many younger Turkish thinkers who have wholly or partly rejected the Atatürkist secular world with its decline into what they see as mindless materialism and consumerism.

From Pera boats go to every landing stage, large and small, in and around Istanbul. The old diesel engines grind and roar like some component engines of Dante's Hell, while local people use them to get to work or visit the girlfriend's family, just as they might catch the bus in Balham or Clapham. To most business visitors Pera seems to represent life and the hope of modernization in Istanbul, but there is another side to the district. The boat to Üsküdar takes about ten minutes, a remarkable scenic journey with a view of the old sultan's palace at Topkapi Serai that is itself worth the price of the ticket. Üsküdar town was near old Scutari, one of the many *scutaris*, or great forts or strong points in the old empire. It was very important in the Crimean War, and the legend of Florence Nightingale grew from her work in Scutari, in the vast fetid wards of the military hospital that was established in the enormous four-towered Kisla fortress, to try to ease the sufferings of the victims of the Crimean battles. When she arrived, the death rate for soldiers in operations was over 20 per cent; when she left it had fallen to under 2 per cent, and modern military nursing had been born.

In antiquity the area was known as *Chrysopolis*, the City of Gold, and it has always been the obvious place to begin expeditions from Europe into Asia. At the time of the Crimean War – the first serious war of the Victorian era and the first major involvement of British military forces in the lethal politics of the Eastern Question – the costs of these expeditions became apparent. Pera is an incomplete symbol of the foreign world in pre-republican Turkey; to complete the picture visit Üsküdar and walk through its great cemeteries, the British graveyard near the railway station a neat, tidy and very English place near the churning waters of the Bosphorus, while, not so far away, is the vast burial ground of Karaca Ahmed, the largest Muslim cemetery in Istanbul, and possibly the largest cemetery in the old Islamic world. It is a wonderful, endless wilderness of old tombs and cypress trees, best seen in the still of a spring or autumn evening. Many of the Turks buried here were soldiers too, who died in the defence of their empire, just as the hapless victims of the Charge of the Light Brigade and Sebastopol fever died in the service of the British Empire. Nowadays, the efforts of nineteenth-century British Conservatives to keep the Ottoman Empire alive may seem absurd – obviously doomed and informed by misguided political judgement. In this shared suburb of the dead, it is easier to understand that both empires were seen by their proponents as the last outposts of civilization against the threats from Russia and the Asiatic steppes. Trade needed military protection in the region, and so did the inner life of the empire, from the great libraries of the Golden Horn to the meanest market stall by the Blue Mosque. Turkey-in-Europe needed protection on the wild and distant borders of Turkey-in-Asia, as well as in important cities within the heart of the country, like Konya. Then Konya was the city of the dervishes, perhaps the most poetic and mysterious cult of the Ottoman world. Nowadays it is better known as a powerhouse of Necmettin Erbakan's Refah Party.

3. Istanbul III: The Lower Depths

All things created joyfully acclaimed him,
Sorrow was done, new life the world was flooding,
Welcome, the rebel's only place of hiding,
Welcome, the poor man's only sure confiding.

From a dervish poem on the birth of the Prophet, *c*. 1620

Constantinople is the Eternal City – the Rome of the East.

Karl Marx, *The Eastern Question*, 1853

The spinning, whirling dervishes now seen in Konya are mostly a tourist attraction, rather like a folk-dancing display in many Balkan countries. They are only allowed to perform on certain days of the year. In origin they were a movement of popular religious protest, a refuge from the iron military structures and inflexible demands of the high Ottoman system. Dervishes lived as monks in seclusion from the world. Like many other things, the dervishes were banned as part of Atatürk's revolution, and even their passive spiritual accomplices, the dissident Bektashis, had to leave Ankara in 1926 and set up the international head-quarters of the Supreme Bektash in Tirana, in Albania. The Bektashis do not believe in many orthodox Muslim tenets, such as praying to Mecca. They revere nature and find God in quiet rural spots and beautiful mountain shrines, rather as the ancient Greeks did. Bektashis have a kind of communion service. Like the much larger Alevi sect, and many other dissident Islamic groups in Turkey, they attracted the poor and the outsiders within the old system, such as the numerous Albanians who held imperial posts. The modern Refah Party draws on aspects of this largely forgotten tradition. Few people in Konya would agree with the prevailing Western view that Turkey is a successful, 'secular', Sunni society.

In Ottoman times and since, Turkish Christian and Jewish minorities tend to be wealthy. Despite the energetic efforts of Protestant missionaries in the nineteenth century, Christianity has never made headway in Turkey. Despite the poverty of the workers, Karl Marx preferred to concentrate on analysing the Crimean War and the international relations crises of the late Ottoman Empire. Like most nineteenth-century liberals and socialists, Marx felt that the internal condition of Ottoman Turkey was largely beyond hope or reform, but, sensing little revolutionary tradition amongst the Turkish masses, had little to say about them. Saint Helena's Anglican church in Mesrutiyet street in 1996 is a quiet, lonely Victorian building. A Ghanaian is sweeping and watching a cat in the porch. At first glance he could be a devoted black supporter of some struggling inner-city church in the north of England. But this was a church of rich exiles, traders and diplomats. On the walls inside there are lengthy brass memorials to all manner of British worthies, most of whom were members of the large nineteenth-century British community in the city. The diplomats, vicars and businessmen of the Levant Company had a secure place in the Ottoman world; the Ghanaian does not have anything but a tenuous right to exist in contemporary Turkey. His ship was stranded in the port and there was no way to get home; he is an economic refugee, who has managed to make himself indispensable to the church and as a result can eat and has somewhere to sleep, a wrecked African Odysseus, washed up here, with no Circe to help him.

Most of the native Turks living in the nearby rat-infested tenements are as poor as he is, and some of them do not even have the shelter that the church provides. What was a fashionable district of the city in the nineteenth century has fallen on hard times. The tall houses of eight or nine storeys have become ramshackle tenements, the lower floors crowded with tiny dark workshops, the upper storeys a rabbit-warren full of refugees and economic migrants from the east and from the countryside. Modern Istanbul is in many ways a city of the poor: millions of people live at basic subsistence level, just as they did on the small farms in the east from which many of them have escaped. Nobody knows exactly how many: estimates vary from one to four million people technically living below the defined basic living standard, only saved from utter destitution by cheap, good quality, plentiful Turkish food and low housing costs in the slums.

Some political analysts and historians have argued that the food policies of successive Turkish governments, going back to early Ottoman times, have been the determining factor which has made the Turkish working class instinctively conservative. There has rarely, if ever, been the real hunger in Turkey that many surrounding countries have experienced and often had to live with, like the Arab nations to the south-east, with their deserts, or the Balkan provinces of the empire, with their mountains. The productive fields of the western littoral have fed the cities, even if the peasants working on the farms have received a miserable return for their efforts. The Ottoman state gave considerable attention to food production, building on the Byzantine social tradition. Self-sufficiency in food was an important weapon against the long sieges that dominated barbarian and foreign attempts to capture Constantinople. In Muslim thinking it has always been part of the duty of the ruler to ensure as far as possible the means of subsistence of his subjects. In Turkey this has not generally been difficult. The country is very large and much of it is productive agricultural land; even today the population is small in relation to the land mass.

Constantinople was well placed on the coast of the Sea of Marmara, which used to be one of the richest fishing grounds in the Mediterranean, and within easy reach of fishing ports on the Bosphorus and the Black Sea. Fishing by rod and line from Galata Bridge for tiny sprats was a traditional activity in the city. The cereal-growing land of the interior is enormous in its extent, if often arid and less productive than it should be, and good grazing land for herded animals is found virtually everywhere throughout the country. If it succeeds in its objectives, the GAP irrigation scheme in the south-east (officially known as the South-East Anatolian Project) will boost national agricultural production dramatically.

Turkey remains a very rich agricultural country. This fact was fascinating to eighteenth-century mercantilist students of Ottoman Turkey, who felt that the country should be far richer and more powerful than it was, given its great natural advantages of land and population density. Many of the cynical and even abusive views of Turkey expressed by the French philosopher Voltaire have their origin in this contradiction. The 'sage of Ferney' could only conclude, like many others before and since, that the real reason for the country's problems must reside in the corrupt character of the Turkish people themselves and the failings of their social system, since there was such a huge gap between Turkish potential and achievement. If this was seen in terms of agricultural production by the eighteenth-century thinkers, nineteenth-century opponents of the sultan saw the problem in terms of Turkey's failure to exploit its mineral resources and thereby create an industrial revolution. Turks have never been short of Western critics with theories that readily explain the weaknesses of their society, and make ill-informed and misleading comments on the moral and practical character of the Turkish people.

'The poor' is, of course, a highly unscientific term, despised by many modern sociologists, and it would be wrong to see the whole population of the poor Istanbul suburbs, the inner city and shanty towns, as a vast, inchoate, undifferentiated mass, ruled by a corrupt and rich élite, as some Greek commentators tend to do. There are fine differentiations among the Turkish poor, just as there were among the London masses studied by Henry Mayhew in the nineteenth century. In some ways the two cities are quite similar. As in London in the 1880s, in modern Istanbul there is a large artisan class, many of them employed in traditional occupations that members of their families have followed for hundreds of years. Their jobs and status are often threatened by technological development. An attendant at the Cumiyet Baths once told me that he could trace uninterrupted employment of his ancestors in the establishment for over four hundred years. Although these people are often not well paid, and may depend heavily on tips to make ends meet, they have an absolutely secure and respected place in society, and have organizations with roots deep in the Ottoman past that resemble medieval guilds. Membership is often hereditary, the association offers some basic social benefits, such as assistance with funerals for impoverished widows, and employment rights for sons and grandsons. There are similar organizations for many craftsmen, like coppersmiths and leather-workers, and the late development of mass production in Turkey has prevented them from being displaced by modern trade unions. They often exist in what are thought of as 'honourable' trades, with long craft traditions. A member of one of these guilds has a high status in artisan and working-class society, and daughters from one of these families can expect a good marriage, for, if the family is short on direct male heirs, a bridegroom may sometimes be accepted as a tradesman by the guild.

A little farther down the social scale are the skilled workers in modern industries. There are relatively few in Istanbul, with its strange mixture of old industries and modern finance capitalism, but are more numerous in cities like Bursa and Izmir. They do belong to trade unions, and are often better paid than the older craftsmen, but are also taxed by the state at source, and have little or no job security. Although the trade unions command considerable loyalty among Turkish workers, they have always been divided by ideology and personalities, and have rarely become as influential as their northern European counterparts.

Below the skilled workers, there are the unskilled workers, often employed by the state, who also belong to trade unions but whose social status is low. They are ethnically Turkish in every sense, and operate a closed shop that excludes important minorities and marginal groups such as the *roma* (gypsies). Istanbul has a disproportionately large number of these workers, mostly occupied in trying to keep the city running properly, as dustmen, labourers doing road repair work, and so on. They are not well paid but can usually manage to bring up a family by dint of long hours of hard work and often a long journey home to a small flat in a grim tower block in the outer suburbs.

Below this group lie the 'lower depths' of city society. Hundreds of thousands of people exist on the economic margins in the private sector. Sweat-shops employ huge numbers of unskilled workers in the textile and shoe manufacturing trades. Some are long-term employees, but many are employed on a casual basis, depending on supply and demand. Wages are very low, and working conditions often abysmal. Large numbers of workers are also similarly employed in the tourist and restaurant trades. Women are often employed as casual workers, and there is substantial home-working, making items such as lampshades, for pitifully small wages. In the sweat-shops conditions are often very unhealthy and, although factory inspectors do exist, they are badly paid themselves, and can all too easily be bribed by employers to turn a blind eye to offensive working practices. Young women are sometimes expected to provide regular sexual favours in return for a job, and young men are worked mercilessly and are sacked at the slightest complaint, because employers are secure in the knowledge that replacements can be easily found among the hundreds of thousands of migrants who reach the shanty towns each year from the countryside. The employers are themselves subject to ruthless competition; as subcontractors for large combines, they feel they have to extract every ounce of labour value from their workers in order to remain competitive.

Some of the traditional trades which have been very successful in recent years, such as the leather and tanning trades, discharge large amounts of unpleasant and dangerous chemicals into the environment. The tanneries are particularly bad in this respect, with their extensive use of chromium chemicals, and the city lacks a proper disposal system for industrial effluent. Their waste finds its way directly into the Sea of Marmara, and then into the marine food chain.

At the very bottom of the social scale are the scavengers – people who arrive from the countryside with nothing and search the rubbish tips and industrial waste sites for saleable items. Recycling of cans in Istanbul is largely in the hands of these people, who walk round the city sifting through litter bins for empty drinks cans to collect in their black plastic sacks. In the great markets, people collect odd scraps of material to stuff cushions, which can be made at home by old women, or even items as small as nails and screws. Just a little better off are the thousands of street sellers who do not have a position in one of the official markets but set up a stall selling tourist goods, or clothes, or cigarettes, or whatever.

However much this cheap flexible labour supply may be said to contribute to economic growth and to the sense of dynamic commercial activity that pervades modern Istanbul, it is typical of the economic development of a Third World society. In the better areas of Turkish agriculture and in traditional manufacturing industries such as carpet-making, Turkish products can compete favourably with any in the world, and the development of some new industries such as car manufacturing and electronics is positive. Ultimately, however, the dynamism of Istanbul is based on ruthless exploitation of labour and the ethics and employment practices of the ant heap. It is not surprising that these exploited sectors of society have become the supporters of the Islamic and anti-Western political parties, and that there is a profound yearning for the stability of Islamic rural societies. The inhumanity and anonymity of Istanbul life has produced a strong critical reaction among the very poor, with unpredictable long-term social and political consequences.

Turning to Islam is not, however, the immediate problem facing the Turkish authorities among the very poor; it is the crisis caused by mass migration to the city and the associated pressure on the environment. Water is a key issue. Turkey has good aquifers, but they are not in the right part of the country to be useful for Istanbul. So the Istanbul local authority is more concerned about cholera than the introduction of Sharia law. Shanty towns have grown up on the outskirts of the city, particularly on the Asiatic side, where conditions are appalling. Whole families live in tin shacks with two tiny rooms between them, and the only water supply is a stand-pipe, if that. Open sewers run through the muddy lanes, in an atmosphere more reminiscent of Calcutta than a country seeking European Union membership. Some 60,000 squatters live in the vicinity of the main water reservoir for the city, with no proper sewage disposal facilities. It must only be a matter of time before there is an epidemic of one of the diseases that plagued Mayhew's London. As it is, at least a quarter of the population are hepatitis carriers; diseases of childhood like rickets are very common; tuberculosis is endemic in the shanty towns and is a common cause of death among older people, as is pneumonia in the winter. The most feared scourge of all is cholera. There have been some cases every year in Turkey recently, and some experts consider that the Ankara health authorities have suppressed the true figures for outbreaks in remote districts. The small Albanian epidemic in September 1994 was blamed on visitors from Turkey. Apart from the human costs, the economic effects of a significant epidemic would be devastating and would decimate the important tourist industry.

Occasionally dead bodies can be seen in the street: victims of traffic accidents who seem too poor to have a home, half-starved and destitute women with sick children, Kurdish refugees living on fresh air and hope. Sometimes they float down the Bosphorus, attended by sea-birds. But more often the vast lower depths of the city are hidden from visitors, who never visit the shanty towns or fetid sweat-shops.

To survive in this grim world, some sort of social order is at a premium, and it has always been a difficulty for the Turkish left that some of the strongest supporters of military intervention in civilian life have come from the poorest strata. The Istanbul police are not widely respected, and are seen as inefficient and corrupt by many people. They often take little notice of complaints from the poor, and it is easy for the local bosses who dominate so many areas of the city, particularly the factory owners, to do what they like. Small-scale protection rackets are widespread, and mass immigration into the city has given rise to all kinds of local *mafioski* based on kinship, ethnic groups and religious adherence. When serious rioting broke out in a suburb of the city in 1995, between Sunni and Alevi Muslims, the local people turned out in the streets to cheer when the army was sent in to intervene. In *Journey to Kars*, his fascinating memoir of travel in Turkey a few weeks after military rule started in the 1980s, Philip Glazebrook notes the relief even peasants in remote areas felt at the end of the near civil war between different guerrilla groups, even though they had no illusions about what a period of military rule would mean for the poor in general.

The 'lower depths' is also the world of most poor women. Westernization has produced greater 'progress', in terms of job opportunities, good education and medical care, in Istanbul than elsewhere, but not for all women, some of whom suffer systematic oppression and exploitation, whether in the family, the factory, or the school. Supporters of Turkey frequently claim that in the sphere of women's rights great progress has been made, but it is indicative of the plight of many women that more women than men voted for the Refah Party in the 1995 election.

Of course some progress has been made from the near-medieval conditions that Atatürk inherited – the famous state dictum that a woman should walk several paces behind her man in public still applied. According to the first census taken in the republic, in 1927, only about 4.5 per cent of the female population were literate, a figure that may be an exaggeration, in any event. Although considerable efforts were made to improve the situation, progress has been very limited in some respects. For instance, in the 1980 census only 17 per cent of men over the age of six were illiterate, yet 46.6 per cent of women could not read. In higher education the same disparity was evident, with men taking 77 per cent of the places, women only 23 per cent. In rural areas the situation was worse: only 4.5 per cent of rural women could read and write, and 61 per cent were totally illiterate.

The public perception of these inequalities has been a major problem for Turkish governments for many years. According to the propaganda of the 1930s, the literacy problem was well on the way to being solved, and in the absence of much research in rural areas, many foreign writers, academics and journalists cheerfully and naïvely reflected the government view, just as they tended to do in Soviet Russia. With the political liberalization that took place after 1951, when a more genuine multi-party system was introduced, the publication of books about the reality of rural Turkey was possible. An outstanding work was *A Turkish Village* by Mahmut Makal, in which a gifted, naïve peasant writer gave a moving and accurate picture of the primitive and backward world of the Anatolian villagers. The drudgery and brutality of the women's lives was portrayed with particular accuracy. The book caused immediate uproar in Turkey and was banned and the author arrested. But the government was unable to disguise the fact that very little had in fact changed in these societies since Ottoman times. The vast majority of women still worked as housewives or as unpaid labour on the family's subsistence plots.

In the industrial sector, only the tobacco and weaving industries employ significant numbers of less educated women, although the well-educated girls leaving school and university in Istanbul and other towns have a good foothold in the banking and finance sectors. There are also real opportunities for élite girls educated at one of the foreign institutions, such as the American schools and colleges in Istanbul. Women become teachers and doctors and enter the caring professions much as they do in most of Europe, but in women's employment opportunities there is perhaps a clearer class differentiation than in any other field in Turkey.

The same ideological currents that conflict in society as a whole are evident in the family. The rural birthrate is still high, although not as high as it was, and women who wish to have many children are encouraged to do so. The imams generally approve of large families, and control of fertility is difficult. When the rural poor move to the cities, and frequently find themselves in desperate conditions, on the margins of society, a large family can be an asset in the absence of any social security network or community facilities. If the slum has a strongly Islamic population, very large families may be encouraged on ideological grounds. Abortion is legal under certain circumstances, but is very expensive, and illegal abortion is widely practised. Contraceptives are on sale but are very much a male preserve. Class and economic position are the determinants of a woman's fate. If she is born into a wealthy family, none of these constraints is likely to affect her, and if she is intelligent and moderately determined, she can lead a life identical to that of a woman in London or Athens. If she is some way down the income scale, it is possible to lead a reasonably free life but without much economic independence; after marriage the extended family and her children will be her main concerns in life. For the respectable poor, a life of procreation and hard, poorly paid work is all that is on offer; for the very poor, only appalling drudgery and degradation. It is not surprising, therefore, that the old Gladstonian metaphor for Istanbul life – sexual corruption and exploitation – still applies in the 'lower depths'. Straightforward prostitution and the myriad mansions of the Istanbul sex industry offer a way out, of a kind, and hundreds if not thousands of girls take it every year. It may have none of its old glamour, but for some women it is a great deal better than the sweat-shop or early marriage and a child every year.

This situation is perhaps indicative of the terrible impoverishment of some aspects of Turkish popular culture under the governments of the last thirty years. The images of sensuality, from the harem to the street, were not fictitious. The belly-dance may have been exploited by the Western visitor – and there are few more unpleasant ways of spending an evening than watching a poor dancer messing about in Istanbul in front of jeering tourists – but a good dancer is a figure of female celebration, of strength, cultural assertion and freedom. Her dance is wild, pagan, Asiatic, in the best sense; clicking handbells, shaking long black hair, pounding bare feet, endlessly stretched and moving arms, she seems like a strange and beautiful sea creature who finds herself on land. But it is a difficult skill to find nowadays in the city without knowing where to go. For the Islamists, belly-dancing is a symbol of Western imperialism, with the young Turkish female body reduced to quivering semi-nakedness before unknown men. It is effectively banned during Ramadan, and on the retreat for the rest of the year. As in Iran, the genuinely sensual and deeply human side of traditional Islamic society is being throttled between the cheapest forms of Western materialism and the understandable Islamic puritan reaction to it. Like traditional rural Greek culture in the 1960s, which Patrick Leigh Fermor described in *Roumeli* as being crushed between the hammer and sickle and Coca Cola, the wonderful diversity and richness in personal identity and daily life in Turkey are being lost: the Islam of mystery, imagination and *The Thousand and One Nights* is being reduced to a grim Koranic legalism, as a response to the emptiness of the technocratic West and its secular juggernaut. It is perhaps a tribute to the Refah Party that its social policies have so far avoided the worst excesses of the more austere zealots in its ranks.

The richness of Turkish life and imagination is obvious from a glance at any tile, carpet or porcelain dish, even though much has been lost beneath the statist uniformity of the modernists, and capitulation to the world of McDonald's hamburgers and the Internet. It is not surprising that many intellectuals, who might in other countries support leftist and secular causes, now support the Refah Party, because Islam seems to be the only way to recapture elements of the heritage of Turkish life, identity and experience. Turks are practical people, Refah are too intelligent to wish to take on the army with an Islamic revolution in the streets, where they would surely lose; the revolution can be made in small ways, without a major confrontation with the state and the army. Islamic activists have been infiltrating the Ministry of the Interior for ten years. They are making a long march through the institutions, unnoticed, until recently, by foreigners. No soldier, however dedicated to the ideals of Atatürk, can possibly object to the new Refah restaurants offering the variety and sophistication of traditional Turkish food, even if *raki* is not served – it is a good deal better than burgers and Turkish 'chips'.

Atatürk believed in his time that national self-sufficiency could save Turkey and establish a new national life that would be just and fair, would transcend old class divisions and preserve what was good and valuable from the Ottoman world; but he was living before the time of the satellite dish. The technocratic future seems to offer many Turks little compared to the Islamic and Ottoman past. The singular power of Refah is embodied in its understanding of this reality.

In Ottoman times, until the Tanzimat reforms of the 1830s, the status and position of women were very straightforward. Production was centred on the self-sufficient family, and women had no political rights at all. A woman was not considered a man's equal as a human being. If she lived in rural society, as the vast majority of women did, life would consist of grinding hard work in the fields and the great demands of reproduction. If she lived in a wealthy family in the city, she would be exempt from the former, but not the latter. In many ways, little has changed. The ancestors of the girls who work computers for the banks probably worked abacuses for the sultan. The ancestors of the women who pick broad beans for a refrigeration plant in Adana picked broad beans for the pasha.

Above them all are the very rich, the few families who control great swathes of Turkish wealth and industry, whose names are well known, even outside Turkey. The merchant princes are the Koc and Sabanci families, equivalent in wealth and status to the Niarchos or Onassis families in Greece. Their personal wealth runs into billions, which is perhaps not surprising as there has never been an efficient system of taxing capital in Turkey. Below them are some 100–200 families who are multi-millionaires, people who are mostly unknown outside Turkey but who have made fortunes from the booming tourist industry, from agri-business trading with the Middle East, construction and, above all, property speculation. The thirty years from the mid-1960s have turned Istanbul and some of the more prosperous cities such as Izmir into speculators' paradises; with government emphasis on better housing and roads, and on lack of planning and environmental controls, it has been easy for the astute to make money. The radical right economics of Milton Friedman which have been followed in the last twenty years have given the rich more and more opportunities to make profits out of the public sector. All this has had a social cost. The financial corruption of the élite has become a public scandal, and the interaction between the state and the private sector recalls elements of the old Ottoman tax system, where public assets are squeezed ruthlessly for the private profit of officials. The state itself has become corrupt, even 'debauched', in the view of a leading British writer on Turkey, Andrew Mango. The process has continuously given ammunition to its Islamic and left-wing critics.

Although the very rich have enjoyed an economic paradise, the same cannot be said of their social lives. The ostentation and corruption has seemed so entrenched and unchangeable by democratic means that some desperate radicals have turned to terrorism. Many rich Turks have been shot down over the years, one of the most recent, in 1996, being Ozdemir Sabanci, one of the heirs to the family industrial combine. Life for the ultra-rich in Turkey is often life under siege, and a good deal of time is spent under armed guard. Bolt-holes abroad are a psychological necessity, as are yachts. The sea is a good deal more secure than land.

The rich also suffer the same problems of identity as everyone else. The previous generation were, emphatically, very rich, and old industrial patriarchs like the recently deceased Vebi Koc – who was worth 7 billion dollars and smoked just five cigarettes a day – were national institutions. Their offspring, however, are not self-made men with careers based in the early days of the republic and the idealism of the Atatürk years. They have usually been educated abroad, probably in America, they are fabulously rich and move in the international jet set. In the eyes of many Turks, they have been born with undeserved silver spoons in their mouths. The family firms suffer from the usual problems of management succession, with a fair ration of playboys and playgirls and a shortage of hardworking management talent. This is not universally the case, but the paternalist ethic that led a man like Koc to wander round his factories checking the lights were turned off in the evenings has largely disappeared. It made a valuable contribution to social stability, and it is not clear what will replace it. The radicals see Turkish assets being stripped by the multinational companies that partner the Turkish industrial combines and holding companies, which benefits the individual billionaire and millionaire families but impoverishes the country. It is a process that seems to be sanctified by the remote and increasingly corrupt élite in Ankara.

4. Ankara: The Kemalist Monument

> After three days of Taxim we were told that it had been
> decided to send us to Angora, where we would enjoy perfect
> liberty. None of us had a clear idea where Angora was, but
> we knew it must be a pleasant change from Taxim. We left
> Taxim early in the morning of the 25th August and were
> ferried across the Bosphorus to Haida Pasha station. Tech-
> nically speaking, we stood now for the first time in Asia,
> though, morally speaking, where the Turk rules there is
> Asia.
>
> Captain John Still, *A Prisoner in Turkey*, 1920

The train from Haydar Pasha leaves in darkness, escaping from
the station on the edge of the streaming Bosphorus current late
at night and disappearing into the Asiatic shore like a ghost or
a Koranic *jinn*. Haydar Pasha is at its loneliest and most dramatic,
the pigeons are asleep on beams under the cavernous roof, the
inscription near the door recording the activities of Lawrence of
Arabia in old Scutari is encrusted with salt from the winter
waves. The tiny Ottoman pavilion on the waterside is closed, a
couple of gypsies play cards on a bench. The tall board in strange
English says nothing about how Lawrence loved the Arab cause
and despised the Ottoman Turk as a degenerate; echoes of
Nietzsche, he thought the vital Arab like a superman would
sweep away the decadent and spent Turk. Only a few years
afterwards the author of *The Seven Pillars of Wisdom* left Scutari,
Atatürk swept all before him and proved Lawrence wrong.
Turkey had produced its own superman. On the hill above
Üsküdar stands the vast sprawling barracks of Scutari, hospital

for British troops in the nineteenth century and torture house for Turkish radicals in the twentieth. The late diners in the restaurant doze over *raki* and aubergines and *borek* and wonderful fragrant cigarette smoke. Iznik tiles surround the doorways, delicate rippling blues in traceries of flowers and leaves; they have been there since the station was rebuilt, at the time of great statist idealism between the wars. In Russia nothing was too good for the workers and Stalin built the Moscow metro; in Turkey it was the same, the best of the Ottoman crafts were to be restored and made available to everybody. Atatürk, according to Turkish mythology, was thinking of the rail traveller as well as everyone else in Turkey. The humble rail traveller could enjoy the tiles from the old sultan's factories. Atatürk would make him the sultan, or the pasha, at least. The more egocentric could promote themselves to be sultan if they wished.

The army is never far away. An elderly Australian, a historian of the Anzacs who fought at Gallipoli in the First World War, boards the train at the last minute, scattering a packet of photographs over the seats. They show long-dead young men in swagman's hats sitting around campfires, high buttoned boots under their trousers. They were volunteers, pulled from the creeks of Victoria and New South Wales into a Balkan hell; like the men who went to the Somme or Passchendaele and never came back, they were sacrificed to a new invention, the machine-gun. It was one of Vickers' classic deals: Sir Hiram Maxim's murderous invention was sold to both sides by Sir Basil Zaharoff, who, like a Homeric god, cast a deadly spell over the Dardanelles, where so many young Turks and Australians were never seen again. The professor of history is going to talk to an academic conference in Ankara, telling the tragic story to a new generation of Turkish university students.

At the end of the platform the Turkish soldiers carry short-stocked Heckler and Koch machine pistols, in case Kurdish terrorists come to visit the station, although bombs in tourist resorts are more fashionable at the moment. There has never been any shortage of weapons in this country nor of people capable of using them. The Turkish defence budget in 1994 totalled 777,700 billion Turkish lira, or 4.9 billion dollars. The soldiers are part of one of the largest effective infantry forces in the world, consisting of millions of personnel. The force is so large that it is divided by the Ministry of Defence in Ankara into three separate armies, plus the paramilitary forces and Ministry of the Interior special units. The army never sleeps, the conscripts are neat and well trained and wear neat uniforms; they are Turkey in their own eyes just as much as the omniscient Atatürk, whose vast bronze death mask statue is a hundred yards away, shining, colossal, like a late Roman emperor peering out into Istanbul. The great bronze eyes stare out through the station booking hall into the turbulent street. Atatürk made the army, he made it so that it would educate them, civilize them, turn hick boys into trained mechanics and carpenters. Many people still believe that the army is the only real centre of power in Turkey; the National Security Council can move prime ministers like puppets.

In their villages these station guards were nobodies, semi-literate, poor, sitting idly over pin-tables and backgammon boards and wondering if a visa and a job in Germany might come along. Carrying their Hecklers on this station platform, they carry Turkey forward, keep secure the great nation in which for centuries so many have been born, lived and died; they are armed masculinity at its most direct and unambiguous. They defend the Turkish state that in theory protects its loyal citizens all their lives if they conform and keep to the rules. Sometimes that is difficult, for Americanization and consumerism have destroyed many of the unspoken conventions, the rich are so corrupt nowadays, and have destroyed the good old state way of doing things for their own profit. The poor and the little people are cast adrift, but are trying to find bearings. It is not uncommon to see fellow soldiers reading the Koran in the barracks; they are looking for the often banned rules again.

Out of the right-hand windows of the carriage there is a rush of lights, then more darkness before we see the ships and industrial towns of the Sea of Marmara. Marmara means marble in Greek. Other feet have trodden the land and sailed the sea here before the word Turk meant anything in the world. Only half an hour from Istanbul the train seems to be entering the great unknown, and Ankara, old Angora, seems a very long way away. Then, after the derricks and bright lights of Gebze – in ancient times a small Greek port called Dakybiza – nothing. It is as if Turkey has been hit by a neutron bomb: the streets are deserted, depressing, with glowing street lamps shining over damp pavements. Outside Istanbul, this is a country without much Western nightlife. Athenian business visitors who come expecting to die from nationalist hostility in the street discover they are more likely to die of boredom first.

The train is warm, it is easy to sleep as the lights disappear and only the occasional tiny neat station building breaks the opaque monotony. Each station has its name in identical-sized letters in the same place on the building façade – this is Turkey, where there is order and the state has thought of many things for the welfare of its citizens. Small matters such as the legibility of the names of railway stations from passing trains caught its attention, there was a meeting in Ankara, or several, perhaps, a regulation was made, it was transmitted to the relevant offices across the country, on documents that were correctly stamped, on time, by the officials with that responsibility, of the correct grade to make these regulations and enforce them. In time, the regulation was acted upon, and the state made progress. But at least 20 per cent of Turkish citizens are still illiterate, and cannot read any sign, of whatever size.

Dawn breaks very slowly, there is a sense of a great empty landscape unfolding, a pale pink and white sky above a vast, open land, ramshackle wooden houses with disintegrating balconies stranded in the middle of huge, featureless fields of dry brown grass. An old woman brings a goat out from a shed and throws an armful of foliage down in front of it. She represents the rural decline and despair of Turkey, with her sons perhaps working in German factories or in Istanbul, perhaps making trainer shoes. In Germany she probably fears they will forget they are Muslims and become dreaded Communists; the young one in Istanbul may get scrotal cancer from the rubber and die long before his time, like her friends' boy. His job is to lower the press that welds the rubber and kangaroo skin together to make the trainers hundreds of times a day; each time the hot rubber vapour will escape and he will breathe it in. Perhaps he will become concerned about his breathing after a year or two, but people will make jokes – Turks are expected to trust their own sturdy bodies and powers of endurance to overcome health problems. Nobody tells him how the rubber will affect him.

This is Asia; individuals are diminished by their surroundings and their fate, whether in the factory or on the farm. The goat seems more important to Allah than the woman. Browsing on scrub, it looks permanent, typical, part of an eternal order, whereas she seems small and transient. Wider, lonely, well-maintained roads wind across the dry, ochre-coloured tableland. An occasional distant Mercedes or Audi kicks up a cloud of dust – this is a poor landscape, but not a poor country. Rich men with more money to make are nearing the capital. An attendant passes along the train with rose-water to shake over stale hands, and a beautifully pressed linen towel is available to dry them, as if the Ottoman world is not dead, yet the train toilets have no paper and it is easy to believe they have not been cleaned since the pasha might have visited them. In the carriage the service is exquisite, democratic; the attendant is performing a small task to remind his passengers that they are Turkish, and therefore special. They are in contact with the Turkish state, and the Turkish state can always perform a small service for them. And they must serve the state in return.

Turkey finds accommodating its citizens in reasonable housing more difficult than shaking rose-water on their hands. Nearer Ankara, the train rushes through dereliction and ugliness – a shanty town built of old railway sleepers, plastic sheets and corrugated iron posts from the farms that were once there. 'Gypsies', an arrogant German civil servant murmurs to his companion. He is reading classified papers about EU and NATO relations; he is careless and unprofessional as well as grossly overweight. There is not a single gypsy in sight – these people are just refugees from rural unemployment and poverty. The *gecekondu*, or shanty town, is where the peasants live when they first move to the big city. It might be Bombay or Calcutta. The bureaucrats are rushing past on their train and are offended by what they see. The water of a small stream is pale grey and stinks of raw sewage, but there is probably no other water supply to the settlement. A child with skin disease stares up at our train; there are not many vitamins to be had here. There is no school or doctor or local government officer for miles. This deprivation does not appear in government statistics, or the tourist brochures. Then there are the bare flats, with their peculiarly narrow proletarian style. It is no wonder Islam is reviving when the mosque is the only social centre, the street market below its steps the only shop, providing the only colour, the only possibility of intellectual exchange or cultural dignity, the only club. The shadow of the army is evident here – when Turks build flats they build barracks. For Atatürk's generation and that of the Second World War, industrialism, secularism and modernity became an adequate substitute for religion; now the factory and the small modern flat are taken for granted. The void is there and Islam is beginning to fill it.

When Captain Still of the Sixth Battalion of the East Yorkshire Regiment was taken prisoner after the disasters of the Dardanelles campaigns in the First World War, Ankara, in the modern sense, hardly existed. Still known by the Byzantine name of

Angora, from the Slav *gora*, meaning hill, it was a one-horse town on the way to the east, on the main road across Anatolia. A few thousand poor and backward people lived around what amounted to an oasis in an otherwise bone-dry plateau, surrounded by malarial swamps. Old Angora had a flourishing market, a derelict Byzantine fortress on top of the citadel rock in the middle of the town, a railway station, and little else. It was only known in England by cat lovers for its famous breed of Turkish cats. The new railway line, opened in 1893, was the first sign of economic progress in the region for centuries.

A few events of note had once taken place, mostly a very long time ago, such as the visit of Alexander the Great in 333 BC on his way to world conquest after he cut the Gordian knot. Julius Caesar called briefly in 74 BC, and did political deals with the local Celtic tribes who by then had overrun the area. It became part of a Roman province, prospered under the Byzantines and was taken permanently by Mehmet I for the Ottomans in 1414 after a period when it was held by Tamerlane and the Golden Horde. Even then, Angora was not safe like Constantinople on the Bosphorus; it was an isolated, threatened fortress open to the barbarism and turmoil of Asia. When Atatürk made it his capital in 1923, after his great military victory against the Greeks in 1921, it had a population of only some 30,000 people and the atmosphere of an Ottoman country town. Almost fifty years earlier, in 1876, the English traveller Frederick Burnaby had captured its sleepy, backwoods atmosphere and the torpor surrounding a local businessman-cum-diplomat:

In a few minutes the English Vice Consul arrived. He was dressed in his official uniform, and was accompanied by a young Bulgarian, who was a merchant in the same business as himself.

Mr — was very surprised to see an Englishman in Angora, no one of our nation having visited that town for some years past; and he informed me that a telegram had just been received from Constantinople with reference to the proclamation of a Constitution. In consequence of this the town was to be illuminated the following evening: cannon would be fired, and the Pasha would read the telegram to the populace in the Courtyard to the Palace.

It had been a miserable, backward place for a long time, symbolic of the old Turkey Atatürk was determined to destroy, and ripe for transformation. Angora was everything that Constantinople was not, and could be shaped by the *Ghazi* to his will. Most importantly, there was no existing élite for Atatürk to displace. The last sultans' promises of parliaments and liberal reforms did them little good in the end and their power in Angora had disappeared, as in most other parts of the country. The despised foreigners in Constantinople had exploited Ottoman economic assets, but they had also brought a sense of the possibility of other economic systems and political rights for the growing commercial middle class. None of this mattered here. The town had no particular importance in the Ottoman world; it did not have the Greek associations and identity of places like Smyrna and Bodrum on the Aegean coast, nor the problems of minority domination by Kurds or other non-Turkish groups of towns further south and east. From the military point of view, it was secure against air attack, something that always preoccupied Atatürk, given the large size of the Turkish army but the technical backwardness and paucity of his air force. It is exactly in the centre of the country, with excellent rail communications, a symbolic benefit for what was to be a highly centralist and *dirigiste* period of reform. It was an easy city to change, which appealed to a man who loved the grand simplicities of life – perhaps because they concealed his own inner complexities and conflicts. Changing anything in Istanbul is very difficult, as rulers have always found, even the nineteenth-century sultans who moved their residences farther and farther from the city – a symbol of their failure to change it. No doubt the Islamists will find the great seething metropolis of the west equally intractable even if they are in government for a long time.

In a decision full of old cultural resonances, German and Austrian architects from the new Fascist states in Europe were employed to design the great boulevards and roadways of Ankara. In its architecture and ambience it is profoundly Atatürk's town; Tito never succeeded in defining Belgrade to the same degree, nor Stalin, Moscow, nor Hitler, Berlin, however hard all tried to do so. By the mid-1930s, the population had risen to 135,000 and the swamps had disappeared. Perhaps the nearest modern equivalent, although an ultimate failure, was St Petersburg, where the will and energy of Peter the Great was central to the construction of an urban identity.

On arrival, that identity is forcibly brought home to the modern visitor. A huge, garish neon head of Atatürk, 20 feet high, dominates the park over the road from the railway station. A few coins are dropped into the entrance turnstiles underneath it. Turkish families demurely walk beneath it, with small, well-dressed children ready to feed the ducks on the pond. To Turkey's detractors, this is the dull, conformist, suburban aspect of Turkish life, so unlike the fizz and energy of a Greek town in the evening; to its admirers, it is a sign of the essential, solid basis of Turkish family life and of a stable, ordered society. (Turks see themselves as sensible, cooperative, rational, the Greeks as personally of loose morals and international troublemakers in world affairs.) But whichever is true, Atatürk is watching, just as he watches in spirit over the whole city from his vast, grandiose mausoleum, Anit Kabir, although it is perhaps strange to think in terms of the afterlife for such a secular, materialistic man. Under his gaze Ankara has prospered and grown. In the 1930s the town was the playground for the new rich, who did well out of the construction of the new capital city. In 1938 Howard Robertson of *The Times* noted that 'the fashionable women of Ankara have taken to civilization wholeheartedly. They smoke, they tango, and they look slim and elegant.' Twenty years later the British authority on Turkey, Geoffrey Lewis Lewis, observed that Turkish women in an international beauty contest were becoming more the size and shape of the other contestants, but had clearly not achieved parity. The process of modernization and westernization is often an incomplete one in Turkey.

In the revolutionary period of the 1920s and early 1930s, Ankara was a symbol of the dynamism and achievement of the new Turkey, which was knocking away the props of absolutism and the clerical state, and building a new society with an industrial and secular ethos. It was a town with very few mosques – there were few before the First World War and even fewer were built under Atatürk – but many health centres, schools and sports fields, and even a scattering of cinemas. The few imams who operated in the town were unrecognizable in their mainstream clothes, and were kept under some surveillance by the new civil information service, which later grew into the modern Turkish Internal Intelligence Service, with its large budgets, vast networks of informers and high-technology surveillance systems. If Turkey ever becomes a fully democratic country, its archives will no doubt reveal as much as the old Stasi files did about Communist East Germany.

When Atatürk died in 1938, numerous volumes were published celebrating his achievements and it is interesting today to see how much of the material is actually about Ankara. For example the commemoration volume that *The Times* published on 9 August 1938 is completely dominated by pictures of the city, not just of the new buildings like sports arenas and clinics, but of the inhabitants. Many show women taking part in public events, being educated or at work, apparently on a par with men and enjoying fruitful lives in a modern industrial society. There is evidence of considerable regimentation, but the images are not those of orthodox militarism or Fascism. They show a people building a new capital city in an atmosphere of strict social conformity. Ankara was not merely a symbol of the new Turkey; it *was* the country. Atatürk did not need a monument, for Ankara was his monument (although thousands of museums and statues throughout the country were built after his death, as if the God might return if enough statues of him were constructed). In political terms, the late 1930s were the high point of Atatürk's achievement, and he died at a fortunate time, before the difficulties of the Second World War and the subsequent takeover of whole areas of Turkish security policy by the United States and NATO. In 1938 *The Times*'s correspondent was able to write confidently that 'today we find the Ottoman past quite picturesque, which shows how quickly it has receded' – a statement that was perhaps more convincing at the time of Atatürk's death than at any time before or since.

The Ottoman world was built on the Ottoman army. The terrifying military machine that besieged Renaissance Europe, led by hundreds of drummers and the howling wail of massed *zurnas*, was central to the Turkish identity in Europe. The end of the empire came with the catastrophic military defeat of the First World War. It is something that is still engrained in the national consciousness. The armed forces are still much the largest organized body in Turkey, just as they were in Ottoman times. The size of the army varied at different periods of Ottoman rule, but it is possible to argue that the Turkish forces are now larger than they were in the Ottoman centuries, relative to the population as a whole, despite the absence of an ostensible empire to defend – 'ostensible' in that Turkish radicals and critics of the military often argue that the Kurdish question has been conducted by the military on an imperial basis, that the 1974 Cyprus occupation was essentially an expansionist, if not neo-imperialist, adventure, and that a good deal of Turkish military commitment was taken up in defending Western interests throughout the Cold War period.

The Turkish constitution remains an important factor in national political life, and the role of the armed forces in the constitution is central. If the document is read in one way, it can be seen as providing a framework for the army to dominate the country. In a key passage, its job is defined not merely in terms of defending Turkey against external aggression, as any military does; its function is also to make

the timely and correct identification of threats against the unity of the country and the nation . . . and to protect the territory against internal threats which may necessitate the use of the Turkish armed force within the framework of the Constitution and the law against any overt or covert attempt to destroy the democratic parliamentary system . . . and the indivisible integrity of the Turkish nation, regardless of the source of the threat.

This in essence gives the armed forces the authority to intervene in politics and to play a specifically political role in the internal life of the country when it feels it wishes to do so, or is ordered to by the National Security Council. In practice it provides the government with draconian powers against dissenters of all kinds. The Turkish constitution is a document that has no parallel in any European country, nor in many countries in the developing world. Its defenders claim that all armies have this power, but most constitutions do not spell it out as clearly. A simple answer is that if Turkey were as democratic a state as is claimed, the clauses would not be needed and should be deleted from the constitution. However, reforming or changing anything that appears to have been laid down as law by Atatürk is extremely difficult.

It is strange that opponents of Turkish membership of the EU have not paid more attention to the constitution, rather than concentrating on the resulting human-rights abuses. The fact that they take place is a result not simply of malpractice by individuals but of the continuous intrusion of the military and security forces into areas of life where it is inconceivable they would be allowed to intervene in a democratic country. This could not take place without constitutional sanction. Equally important, the influence of the constitution protects wrongdoers within the army and security forces from effective investigation or punishment. Excesses by the political police will take place from time to time in every country, but a democracy provides means of redress and a clear commitment to the principle that the security forces are subject to the rule of law, just like the private individual. Turkey's political leaders pay lip-service to this principle, and interminably reiterate commitments to reform, usually when a cut-off of international aid is threatened, but there are very few examples in recent Turkish history of the official perpetrators of torture and other less serious crimes being investigated, arrested, or brought to justice, let alone convicted. Literally thousands of policemen, security personnel and local officials involved in the most ruthless and systematic repression under past military governments are still living normal lives, untroubled by any prospect of prosecution. Today, secret-police death squads operate with impunity in cities like Diyarbakir, Kars and Batman. If similar killings had taken place during the Cold War in a Communist country with a comparable level of development, like, say, Hungary, there would have been an international outcry. As it is, the grim records of organizations like Amnesty International make bitter reading, but have little effect on Western political calculations, and the 'international community' failed to take any action against the leaders of the military intervention of the 1980s, unlike their Greek equivalents, who were put on trial promptly.

The size and scope of Turkey's internal security and policing operations are extremely expensive. There are, for example, no fewer than 513 offices of the Directorate of Security throughout the country. Each of the sixty-seven provinces also has a director of security, answerable to Ankara. The security personnel are well paid, by Turkish standards, and are part of a large bureaucracy that is difficult for Ankara to control from the financial point of view. There has also been a considerable investment in high-technology surveillance equipment over the years.

Another contentious issue is the efficacy of the army as a force to defend the country from external threat. There is little evidence on which to make a judgement. Even in the Second World War,

Turkey played no military part, only declaring war on Germany in February 1945, when, cynics might claim, it was clear who was going to win, and there was little risk to Turkish lives in taking part at that stage. Small numbers of Turkish troops have been involved in various operations going back to the Korean War, and appear to have discharged themselves honourably, but never in very testing circumstances where the defence of their own country was at stake. Turkish forces take part in NATO operations, and appear to be well trained by international standards. Operation Attila, the invasion of Cyprus in 1974, was conducted on the basis of overwhelming force against a largely defenceless population, and provided no guide to what would happen in a major conflict against serious opposition. In the various Middle East wars over the years, Turkey has avoided commitment. In the political conflicts with Greece land war has been avoided, although there have been minor air and naval actions. Unlike most participants in the Cold War, who downsized their armies after 1989, Turkey has continued to spend heavily on the military, and has been assisted by American, German and British policy to build the country into a regional superpower. Ex-NATO central theatre equipment has also been virtually given away free to Turkey and Greece to rebuild their arsenals under the 'Cascade' programmes.

It seems likely that a much smaller professional or partly professional army could defend the territory as well or better than the current overweight behemoth, but the obstacles to change are many and entrenched, and are ultimately linked to the internal security and constitutional role of the military forces. The obsession with equipment modernization that pervades the navy and air force may stem in part from the notorious neglect of the navy in late Ottoman times. Writing in 1903, W. E. Curtis noted that

the annual allotment of money for the supplies of the navy is about $3,200,000, but according to popular impression, a very small part of it is ever applied to the purpose for which it is intended. The navy yard at the Golden Horn is the most extraordinary marine morgue in existence. Long rows of vessels of the most antiquated pattern lie side by side, stripped of their machinery and equipments and fit only to be knocked to pieces for junk. Students of marine architecture will find there types of vessels that have not been used for a century, and the Sultan still appropriates money to maintain them.

Technology and equipment continue to hold an obsessive fascination that has disappeared in many other defence forces. The army equivalent of the naval mausoleum was perhaps the death of typhus and starvation of tens of thousands of troops on the Eastern Front in the First World War. Critics of Turkish militarism need to bear in mind these terrible national memories, and the overwhelming support throughout society for strong and modern military forces. After all, nobody in Britain would object to the influence of memories of the chaos of the Western Front.

The Turkish military are at pains to tell its critics that it is neither an army of occupation of its own country, nor a bloated and old-fashioned defence force of doubtful real competence, but a modern armed force with real technological skills and an involvement in many useful social welfare and educational functions. This aspect of the Turkish system should perhaps be better understood in the West. Ever since Napoleon became emperor of France, and perhaps long before, armies have offered a route to the very top for the gifted man without means or connections. As the rise of a black man in the US military like General Colin Powell shows, a humane and democratic army can provide a good career for the poorest and least favoured youth. Turkey is an extremely conservative society where money and family links are still very important and it is often difficult for a talented provincial boy to make his way without connections. The army is very democratic in its formal operations and at least some of the officer corps are drawn from non-privileged families, although as a graduate education is becoming more important in controlling modern forces and weapon systems, even this route to the top is becoming a little constricted. The Turkish military does provide basic education, trade skills and training for many jobs, and gives many callow youths the chance to become men.

Yet within this enlightened and forward-looking framework, there is a marked emphasis on barrack-room conformity and the implantation of a dogmatic nationalist ideology. Basic training is often brutal and spirit-breaking. Individual personality is assaulted in the name of 'Turkish' identity, although the crude version of Atatürkist ideology put forward is conformist, thuggish and virtually racist and Fascist. In the tougher training camps suicide by conscripts is fairly common. Rape by non-commissioned officers is sometimes reported to families or human rights organizations, along with unpleasant initiation rituals involving physical humiliation and degrading physical practices, linked to the unrestricted use of severe punishments for the most minor disciplinary offences.

Ankara is ultimately a garrison town as well as a town of government and industry, although both of these have flourished in the two-million-strong capital. The great cast-iron stag horns that tower above a central traffic roundabout in the city provide an image of an ancient past. The citadel was used by ancient peoples such as the Hurrians and the Hittites, long before other occupiers came and went. The Hittites invented cast-iron technology, in part to celebrate their gods. Their majestic sacred deer and cows are now to be found in the citadel museum, a short walk up a hill through a spice market and a good place to shop for fine linen bearing Hittite motifs in black and white. The museum, too, is black and white, with exquisite models of ancient metalwork in jet black displayed against the white walls. Much of the history is artificial, the words 'Greek' and 'Armenian' never appear on the display boards, and I am told that the account of ancient civilization in eastern Anatolia resembles science fiction. It is the only museum in Ankara without a noticeable presence of Atatürk. It seems to be little visited, except by school parties. The present of Turkish modernism, exemplified by Atatürk, seems to find it difficult to connect with the reality of the ancient world, so beautifully set out in the citadel museum. This is so different from what most visitors to Athens see as the seamless web of Greek history and culture from the ancient world through Byzantium to the present. There are in fact many fractures and dissonances in the Greek tradition, but they never impinge on foreign visitors unless they begin to take a more scholarly interest in some aspect of Greek history. In Turkey the lack of connection with the past is exacerbated by the politicization of many museums, and the deliberate distortion of basic historical realities. However, in recent years, more enlightened governments have sought to unlock the tourist potential of classical antiquity. A lead was given by Prime Minister Turgut Ozal in the late 1980s, with the acknowledgement of the ancient Greek heritage of the Aegean coastal cities and the use of the term 'Greek' in official tourist literature. Elsewhere, there is little change. Atatürk's absence from the citadel illustrates the great difficulty official Turkey has with integrating important aspects of its past into the projection of the contemporary national identity.

Ankara can be a harsh city. Even the weather plays its part, with burning heat in the summer, and snow that even in late March can be so deep that chains are needed for the cars. Ankara is a little like Madrid in its climate and situation, as in its instinctively authoritarian politics, the capital of a centralized country that is difficult to govern democratically and where many of the people on the periphery do not want to be subject to its power at all. Perhaps part of the solemnity and conformity of many of its inhabitants, especially the all-pervasive civil servants, stems from this knowledge and their inner sense of insecurity, even inferiority. It is a dignified, pleasant capital, but it is an island, and it is not the best place in the world to have fun.

North from Ankara towards the Black Sea coast, the roads

are wide, but relatively unfrequented – much wider and more impressive than the level of traffic would demand. This is not one of the great east–west routes, linking Istanbul to the rest of the country and Europe to Asia. Yet it is one of the most important roads in the country, as it links Ankara with the old industrial centres of the Black Sea coast, such as Eregli, and the coal fields. In Atatürk's time the north was intended to be the centre of the long-awaited Turkish industrial revolution. In the 1920s the *Ghazi* was a frequent visitor to the coast, and made it a priority area for his literacy campaigns. There are many photographs of him standing bolt upright by a blackboard under a tree in some small village, pointing out the new letters of the Roman alphabet that was to replace the old Ottoman script. He swept along the carriageway towards the people waiting for enlightenment, the Turkish proletariat who would capture the future and the modern world for him.

Part Two

COUNTRYSIDE

5. *Zonguldak and the Black Sea*

No one who has not lived in the Near East can understand
how utterly incapable of progress the Turk is. No one who
has not travelled through the Turkish villages or through
the back region of the Turkish Empire can understand how
totally unprogressive a people is who, holding for five
hundred years the fairest and richest part of the earth's
surface, has never made a sewing machine or a plough, nor
a steam engine, nor a battleship, nor a pin, nor a match.
Anyone who hopes for the progress of Turkey inhabited
only by Turks is hoping for the leopard to change its spots.

Dispatch from the American consul general,
Constantinople, 26 September 1922

Ankara is only a few hours by car from the damp and deciduous
woods of the Black Sea coast, but in electoral terms, it is a long
way from the conservative and increasingly Islamic heartlands
around the capital to the radical and progressive Black Sea coast,
where the moderate left has nearly always been pre-eminent and
the extreme left has always had some presence. The industrial
Turkey of the Black Sea steel and mining regions is perhaps the
least known part of the country. On the world stage, even in
Atatürk's time Turkish heavy industries were not seen as having
an important role to play, although in the late Ottoman period
they had considerable status and importance for the region.

Industrialism and economic progress were not new to Turkey
in the nineteenth century. They began in ancient times. The
New Testament reports that copper exports and artefacts of the
Assyrian Empire were sent from the Anatolian plateau to the

Black Sea coast, and silver from the huge mine at Bolkar Maden in the Cilician Taurus was used for coinage by ancient Greek colonists and their forebears. In Biblical times the climate was probably less severe than it is now and a sophisticated civilization was built with the labour of the slaves who grew vines and olives, often at considerable altitudes, which modern weather has reduced to empty and barren grasslands. The technology required to mine the copper was simple and well understood: a big fire lit at ground level was often enough to melt the ore from surface deposits. Working iron was much more demanding, and it was the great achievement of the Hittites to have begun to develop technologies to use it. The temperature required to make even low level pig-iron is far higher than that needed for copper and can only be achieved by burning charcoal or coal. For hundreds of years in the later ancient and Byzantine worlds Turkey was an important supplier of raw materials to the sur-rounding region, as the copper of Anatolia was made into manu-factured goods in the bazaars of Syria or Beirut, or chrome from Cenkoy was mixed with pig-iron to make steel in local furnaces. Romanian cities burnt Turkish brown coal for hundreds of years. But there was no development of large-scale factory production until very late in the imperial era, and then only of a very limited kind.

The Ottoman torpor resulted in a lack of economic develop-ment, according to historical orthodoxy, and one of Atatürk's resounding themes, which has continued to be expounded by all political parties up to the present, was the need for Turkey to secure control of its own resources and to prevent the 'plunder' of the nation by foreign exploiters. It is as resonant now in the Islamic movement as it was among the Nationalists seventy years ago. It is implied that the 'plunder' is the reason for the relative lack of Turkish development, although this has often been belied by the last twenty or thirty years, when considerable progress has been made in Turkish business through partnerships with foreign firms. A good example is a British multinational like

Unilever, which from small beginnings has become a major force in soap and detergents in Turkey.

This heritage and ideology should be examined a little more carefully. Just as the Communist rulers of the early Soviet Union claimed credit for a foundation of industrialization that had actually been laid in Tsarist times, so the Kemalists built Turkish industry on an Ottoman foundation. The achievements of the industrialists under the late sultans have been downplayed by most historians, perhaps because the traditional iron and steel industry was not only Ottoman, but owned, built and developed almost entirely by Greeks. Many commercial areas of the Ottoman Empire were dominated by ethnic Greeks, descendants of phanariot Greek families who had their roots in Byzantine Constantinople. (The phanariots were Greek officials who, in later Ottoman times became vassal rulers of whole Ottoman realms, such as Romania.)

In the 1930s, and to a lesser extent more recently, the suggestion that there was any real industrial progress in Turkey in the nineteenth and early twentieth centuries was viewed as heretical. Although its mineral resources were not of a scale to allow Turkey to play a major role in the world economy in Ottoman times, they were not used in an irrational way; modern government policies to create a Black Sea Economic Cooperation area correspond closely to late Ottoman industrial trade patterns. Some worthwhile development did take place under the aegis of the nineteenth-century 'foreign' owners, but it was remote from Western eyes, and successive Turkish governments have been able to make what they wish of the economic truth. The fact that in the last stages of the Ottoman Empire the government was controlled by the imperialist powers was equated not only with economic exploitation, but also with economic backwardness. The Kemalist denunciations of foreign capitalists who prevented the country from attaining its real economic strength as a world power now seem as illusory as some of the Ottoman visions of Turkey and its imperial potential, or the current

Islamist doctrine of a world Muslim economic commonwealth based on Turkish leadership. In between there have been variations on this theme, exemplified by the 'anti-bureaucratic' economic initiatives taken after 1950 that were supposed to reduce direct state control of economic life.

As with so much in Turkish life, a real evaluation of the past is difficult: history, even in the field of technical and economic development, becomes a religious myth, as much as in any Balkan country. The image of the nation as victim, manipulated and ruined by selfish neighbours and outside powers, is common to much Serbian, Croatian, Greek, Albanian and Turkish thinking, despite opposing political and religious outlooks. The response of most of these ex-Ottoman economic 'victims' was to try to achieve self-sufficiency. In Turkey the means used were almost identical to those of Stalin's Soviet Union: widespread nationalization, the development of state-owned firms and holding companies, and restrictions on foreign involvement in the economy. Until quite recently it was illegal to keep any savings in a foreign currency in Turkey, a more extreme nationalist measure than that attempted by most Communist or Fascist states. It helps account for the palpable absence of any understanding of the workings of modern finance capital in whole sections of modern Turkish society. 'Business' and 'value' are equated in most Turkish minds, particularly those of the older generation, with material production, rather than with secondary values in stocks and shares or other financial instruments.

Since the Second World War, programmes to increase industrial production similar to that of Atatürkist Turkey have been adopted by socialist, revolutionary and anti-imperialist movements throughout the world. Although Turkey tends to be seen as a right-wing country by Western liberals and socialists, the means used to control the economy until the 1970s owed much to the traditional left, if left means state planning and a directed economy. Modernist Turks will not generally agree with this view, pointing to the development of privately owned industrial combines such as the car industry since the 1960s, and claim there has been a reduction in state economic planning. But the reality deserves close examination. In the 1980s Turkey was a byword among the international financial institutions for economic 'progress': financial markets were set up – much to the surprise of many Turks – and industry was opened up to what was seen as fundamental transformation by partnership with foreign capital. Now much of that achievement seems to have been built on sand. In the motor industry, for instance, the cars produced are often retooled versions of obsolete models written off by European and Japanese companies and are unlikely to be competitive in the world markets. In the 1970s and 1980s that did not matter, as a central tariff system protected Turkish vehicles from international competition by making European imports extremely expensive. This will not continue under the 1995–6 EU Customs Union arrangements, if they ever come into full operation. The Turkish vehicle companies do not have the state-of-the-art technology of the Japanese and Korean manufacturers, and low wages are a diminishing asset in a business dominated by capital-intensive high-tech machinery. Since the end of Communism, equally low wages are available in countries much nearer the European industrial heartlands, such as the Czech Republic. The pattern of state capitalism in Turkey that has developed through the great industrial families such as the Koc and Sabanci dynasties relies heavily on protection from the old planned economy for its success, however much the modernization of the 1980s may have obscured the fact. The failure of the new is less important than the failure of the old. As always in Turkey, the past overshadows the present, but often it is a much more distant past than is at first apparent.

One of my Turkish companions was philosophical on this theme: 'The Americans have been alive for two hundred years. How long have we been alive?' In terms of industrialization and some factory production, if not a fully fledged industrial revolution, the answer is probably longer than most people think.

In terms of international investment, the weak link remains the limited development of finance capital; all too often, as in Ottoman times, it only seems to be a vehicle for foreigners to buy Turkish assets cheaply, rather than a means of accelerating the economic development of the country.

An interesting illustration of this thesis is provided by the crisis that overtook Asil Nadir's Polly Peck company in the late 1980s. Asil Nadir, a Turkish-Cypriot businessman, made what appeared to be a fortune by buying up and integrating textile companies in London and then using the financial markets to build a 'Turkish' multinational turning over hundreds of millions of pounds a year, which extended its interests into mass-market citrus production, cardboard boxes, hotels in Cyprus, and electronics on the Turkish mainland. Despite its industrial success, Polly Peck remained a creature of the London and international financial markets, built up by massive bank borrowings against what appeared to be an ever rising share price. As a Cypriot, Nadir was an outsider to the Turkish industrial establishment, if not something of an upstart. This did not matter when the business was going well, but when market conditions changed, there was little Nadir could do to prevent the crash of his empire and bankruptcy. Although he was a close friend of the then Turkish prime minister, Turgut Ozal, who tried to raise support for him in Turkey, little was forthcoming. The old industrial and commercial dynasties were indifferent to his fate, even though to Ozal, and to fellow leader Margaret Thatcher, Nadir was a shining beacon of what Turkish capitalism might become if it was fully liberalized – if it was opened up to world economic competition, what they saw as the outstanding industrial potential and natural resources of Turkey could be set free by the beneficial action of the international financial markets. These ideological considerations, so typical of the 1980s, meant little to Turkish industrial leaders, whose lives had been lived in a web of support from the Turkish state that sustained them.

The whole sorry affair is perhaps a better commentary on

the real relationship of much Turkish business with radical free-market capitalism and more illuminating than the endless, intractable arguments among experts about the exact degree of financial liberalization that has taken place since the 1970s. When business is going well, the big Turkish combines are happy to appear open to the outside world; when their position in Turkey is threatened in any way, they are ruthless in defence of their own interests and quick to seek the protective canopy of the Turkish state.

Zonguldak is a black town, hanging precariously on the cliffs of the Black Sea coast, above the dark swirling waters once navigated by Jason and the Argonauts. The coal basin dives deep below the Black Sea to emerge thousands of miles to the north in the great Donetz coal fields in the Ukraine and southern Russia. Coal is something else the two old enemies share. Zonguldak is not only far from the tourist routes, it is also a place of bad news and darkness. People do not go there unless they have to, almost everybody who can leave tries to do so. The capital of Turkish heavy industry is in the ancient terrain of the Paphlagonians, drenched with rain for much of the spring and autumn with an uncertain and short summer. Huge waves swept up by the northern gales in the winter soak cars with salt spray along the quayside, thick fogs blind the coast in autumn, making this northern fringe of Turkey seem more like Dickensian London or Manchester. Workers trudge to the steelworks in the early morning gloom like the classic Marxist proletarians, huddled in thick scarves and cheap anoraks, people bowed in spirit by filth and impassive heavy machinery. Foreign visitors to the coal mines are not particularly welcomed. The security guards took a very active interest in who I was, asking to see my passport, expressing disapproval at the word 'writer'. The air still breathes conflict, although the last of the great Zonguldak strikes took place in 1987.

The ancient Greek name for Zonguldak, *Acherousias*, is

derived from Acheron, the Homeric River of the Dead. It seems very appropriate. In mythology, Zonguldak is associated with difficulties and defeats. On the way to Colchis, at the other end of the Black Sea, Hercules lost his page and lover here, the beautiful Hylas. The unfortunate Hylas was left behind and had to follow the heroes on foot. The final labour Hercules had to perform involved visiting the underworld to subdue the savage dog, Cerberus; he brought back white poplar bark from the Stygian depths, the only wood permitted in sacrifices to the Olympian Zeus. The ancient Greek colony that became modern Zonguldak, and Eregli, the home of the largest steelworks in the Middle East, are both named after him.

The ancient Greeks, attempting to spread civilization along the Black Sea coast, originally called it *Ineuxine Pontus*, the inhospitable sea. It is so different from the Mediterranean. Even where the water is not polluted by untreated sewage or spoil from the mine workings and the natural coal strata, it is dark, uninviting and only supports marine life on a narrow top strip. The fathomless water underneath is effectively dead. Modern pollution, mainly from the River Danube, is building up in the sterile depths. The holy dolphins that were the symbol of ancient Trebizond have long gone, Black Sea trawlermen struggle to make a living from diminishing catches of fish, and the songs to celebrate the great anchovy harvests are a thing of the past. The dark poetry of the land and the dark mythology of the sea meet on the deserted beaches. It is a lonely, difficult place to live in and to struggle with the elements.

The mineral wealth of Zonguldak has always seemed worth the price, though: in Ottoman times half-starved miners hacked at the coal with wooden picks in appalling conditions thousands of feet below ground. The Zonguldak basin contains the most substantial coal reserves in Turkey, estimated to be over 1,000 million tons in December 1989, divided between poor quality lignite brown coal and high quality coking fuel, the latter essential for steel making. Until 1994, production ran at about 5 million metric tons a year. Here, in the heart of Turkish industry, the valleys resemble those of the Rhondda in South Wales. There is the same rain-swept vegetation, with little birch and beech trees clinging to sodden hillsides, deep valleys gashing the dark green mountainsides that drop sheer into the sea, the same pervasive sense of everything covered in coal dust. Outside the kitchen windows of the miners' little houses clean washing turns grey in a few hours, white cats are turned black by life in the backyards. It is the industrial landscape of the nineteenth century, a smoke-stack industry, suffering from poor geological and mining conditions, with an ever-present danger of flash floods. In 1977 a major disaster destroyed whole shafts and winding gear as well as the lives of hundreds of miners. Such disasters receive international publicity, but they only add to an already very high death toll. Until recently, all mining was done by pick and shovel, as in Ottoman times, explosions were common, safety training or rescue training minimal or non-existent. To work in the dark realms was a terrible fate; men signed on for a few weeks, worked without training or technology until they had earned some money, then tramped home to villages in the hilly areas behind the coast for the agricultural work season.

This coast has always been severe and difficult, even compared to the other parts of the 'inhospitable sea'. Towering waves in winter gales have drowned thousands of mariners in all sea-going generations. The winter rain nowadays destroys the roads with underground streams and landslides. Like Hercules completing his grim assignation with death in Hades, every day the miners descended to the depths, their only weapons being basic tools that many people in England use on allotments. The most plausible site for the entrance to the ancient underworld was Cape Herakleia, where the mountains drop most steeply into the sea and deep caverns are common. The glow from the huge steelworks along the coast at Eregli dominates the evening sky, and the sense of being near the infernal regions cannot escape even the most phlegmatic and practical traveller. Smoke belches from the tall chimneys, showers of sparks blow up from the blast furnaces like a firework display, and an acid smell of sulphur dioxide spreads for miles along the coast. It could all be taken from a painting of the early Industrial Revolution by Wright of Derby. But there are more modern, more disturbing things alien to countries that have always been democratic: oblong concrete blockhouses with old military insignia near the entrance gates to the spoil tips, 30-foot-high military guard posts at the mine entrances – during the last period of military government, guards were posted at the entrance to the mineshafts. This is the world of the old authoritarian states of Eastern Europe and elsewhere. Here slave labour was enforced at the point of an M-16 carbine, just as in antiquity the slave miners near Athens would have been coerced by sword or whiplash. When labour unrest occurred in the early 1980s, as it was bound to, and the workers protested against their miserable conditions, strategic industries were effectively militarized, strikes banned and the armed forces used to terrorize hungry miners back to work. Some Western diplomats quietly murmured approval over their sherries at Ankara cocktail parties. However, because many Zonguldak miners are employed as casual labour, rather like the migrant labourers of the South African mines, many were able to avoid the worst of the military excesses of the 1980s by returning to the family farm or finding some sort of job in Istanbul. It was possible to escape, if only back to a life of poverty helping an elderly mother survive on the little family plot.

The damage done to this coast by Turkish governments has not been confined to human society. In 1977 new coal-washing plants were built by Romanian 'experts' that completely ruined the remains of the local fishing industry within two years. Black Sea cooperation across political boundaries has sometimes meant just that: cosy arrangements between corrupt rulers for their own short-term profit, financed by World Bank loans.

But political imperatives remain. Without the brown coal from the basin, Turkish lights would have gone out in the 1970s, and the potential industrial power of the miners was never far from the minds of Ankara politicians. As part of the turn to the economics of the radical right under the military governments of the 1980s, collision with the miners was inevitable, as in Mrs Thatcher's Britain. Turgut Ozal and the British prime minister had a close personal and political relationship and no doubt discussed their mutual struggles with their mineworkers. To the government in Ankara the miners represented residual – although never much used – class power and a stronghold of support for the political left. Cheap imported coal from South Africa and Australia was available to replace their hard-won local product and in the 1980s, the share of Zonguldak coal used in Turkish power generation fell from over 90 per cent to less than 40 per cent. It is arguable how far the motives were wholly political, for the Turkish miners had never brought down a government, as Arthur Scargill and his men did in Britain in 1974. However far the banned Turkish Communist Party had spread its tentacles in the post-war years along the damp and gloomy Zonguldak valleys, where it acquired its first, and only, mass support in the country, until the early 1990s the government was always able to use force to break strikes, as the ivy-coloured military watch-towers testify.

In 1991 the miners revolted against their primitive and danger-ous conditions (in 1989 an explosion at Yeni Celtek pit killed sixty-eight miners in a methane explosion). They went on strike and the valleys running down to the narrow beaches were sud-denly and strangely silent. The government was shocked, as it had not expected the strike, nor the massive public support for the strikers. The military option was impossible in the new world order for a government in Ankara pledged to social reform. The miners sensed their strength and marched on Ankara. The government ordered the police to set up road-blocks to protect the capital. The march was a very orderly affair, very Turkish in its way. Little communities along the way, where everybody had believed that Ankara knew best, suddenly found themselves mobilizing to feed hundreds of thousands of poor people they had never met before. Ultimately the strike was futile. The government made vague promises of improvements that split the miners' leadership, and the strikers drifted back to work. As soon as it was practical, and a decent interval had elapsed, Ankara began to close down the mines. Zonguldak was dying, and with it the older part of the Atatürkist national economic development programme, based exclusively on heavy industry.

If the old world of Zonguldak was simple and essentially brutal, the new world of Turkish industry has many complexities and contradictions. According to radical economic thinking, and countless reports on the economy written since the 1960s, what the country needs to develop a modern industrial economy is widespread privatization, a new business culture, a reduction in the size of the bloated state sector, and an end to the nationalized state monopolies. This would, it has been claimed by the World Bank and other international institutions, bring a rebirth of enterprise, more foreign investment, and an end to the traditional Turkish cyclical problems of inflation, under-investment and the accumulation of vast debts. As the problems of the contemporary Turkish economy show, there is much to be done in many directions before any of these virtuous objectives are achieved. The prescription of the international banks and the radical right appeared to work in the 1980s to some extent, but have not done so since. Although the comparison would be a little crude and misleading, many economic years in the time of the last sultans could show better figures for investment and production, related to the technology of the times, than the 1990s.

A glance at the streets of any Turkish town or village will show why some of the laws of radical free-market economics do not apply very well to Turkey. The street market outside the mosque in Zonguldak is, in a sense, the whole economy in microcosm. The first thing a visitor from Mars would notice is the multitude of stalls and street traders, selling goods of every description. Turkey has had a flourishing bazaar culture since ancient times. There is no shortage of entrepreneurs or small businessmen that has to be filled by breaking up publicly owned assets and selling them off. Almost everybody in urban Turkey has deeply entrepreneurial instincts, irrespective of their economic position or their political views. This may account, in part, for the relative lack of envy of the Turkish rich. The market has been the arbiter of economic life for most people for a very long time, and in a society with poor social security provisions, if you fail in the marketplace, the consequences for you and your family can be very serious. So there is no need for a Thatcherite revolution in that sense in Turkey, where the work ethic is as entrenched as in Victorian England, and there is no expensive welfare state to discourage vigorous enterprise and self-sufficiency.

The second thing that an intelligent Martian might notice is the relative homogeneity in the standard of life of the vast majority of the population in front of him. Although there are some very rich people in Turkey, and an increasing number of the very poor, there is a vast and fairly homogenous mass of working-class and lower-middle-class people who are the foundation of Turkish political populism. They are conscientious, reasonably hard-working, usually Sunni or Alevi Muslim, and feel they are the backbone of the country. These people find it difficult to accumulate assets, although many own their own home, and there is often a family farm or smallholding left somewhere in the country, although it is often not worth much in a market sense. Money is earned and spent, and in the Atatürkist era there did not seem to be particular merit in encouraging individual capital accumulation. The accumulators might have become a nuisance if they wished to exert control of their assets outside the state framework and the dictates of the five-year plans. As the sultans knew so well, despite the wealth and riches of Turkey, there is always a strange shortage of capital, if not of capitalists.

*

The north and the Black Sea have a place in the Turkish psyche that is difficult for outsiders to understand. In the distant past the Black Sea meant trade and migration, the very opposite of the settled, authoritarian nation state. Perhaps there is a grain of this mentality left in the secular and often radical inhabitants nowadays. The dominant myth is Jason's search for the fabled wealth of the far Black Sea shores, where the wild Scythian tribes with their fierce shamanistic religion ruled the steppes unchallenged. There is a particular kind of loneliness about these shores, even in the domesticated, modest seaside resorts scattered along the thousands of miles of the coastline. In the past sea trade here was important; in the early Ottoman period, it was often contracted out to Genoese traders, who built chains of forts on top of the Byzantine fortifications or the remaining defensive walls of the early Greek cities. Now these places are only visited by Turkish holiday-makers in midsummer – places like lonely Amasra, ancient *Sesamus*, which was established by Greek colonists from Miletus in the sixth century BC. It has a beautiful harbour, a sea wall and little else.

Every Amasra Turk has one or more relatives working in Germany; the height of economic achievement and social prestige is to be able to retire from a menial job there, drive an old Mercedes home, restore it lovingly and sit and play cards on the seafront waiting for passengers who never come. But Amasra illustrates another dimension to the crisis in the Turkish economy that is rarely seen: the continuing vitality of the craft sector and traditional industries such as carpet-making. In Amasra pottery is made which is charming and finds admirers as far away as Scandinavia. It is a cottage industry, with little potters' wheels and kilns humming away in sheds and outhouses. Production is never going to be large enough to affect Turkey's dreadful economic statistics, but it is nevertheless a stable and effective local industry. Most of its output probably never appears in government figures anyway, as nobody comes to Amasra to collect them.

There are literally thousands of local industries of this kind scattered throughout the country, from the traditional metal-work of the south-east to the glorious tiles of Iznik and the equally renowned carpet-makers near Istanbul. As they are labour-intensive and often dependent on skills handed down through the generations, it is not surprising if many of the laws of economics do not appear to affect them very much. These businesses are already wholly privately owned, so the concept of privatization is quite meaningless. Carpet-making skills can be taught, but the only sensible way to do it is within a family framework, given the time and discipline needed. It is not some-thing where production could ever be increased significantly by governments setting up training courses for the unemployed. The Turkish genius in business and manufacturing is practical, with an organic relationship between materials and design, con-sumer and producer. Turkish business friendships, once formed, are immensely loyal and rewarding relationships, indifferent to time and place, unlike the relationships with state officials, many of whom display such pride and arrogance that they deserve to be brought low. These responses depend on often highly conservative, inherited identities as workers and skilled crafts-men and women; the Turkish state can set up a framework, as Atatürk and his reformers tried to do, to enable production to flourish, but that is about all. The little industries of towns like Amasra, which are well away from the planners and bureaucrats in Ankara, simply go on regardless. It is almost inconceivable to imagine a Turkish craftsman carefully writing down how many painted tiles he has produced in a day. Hence it is a very underestimated section of the economy, but in the rush to try to develop finance capitalism since the 1960s, many Turkish craftsmen feel forgotten and neglected. It is not surprising that some of them have begun to turn towards the Islamic movements and the Refah Party. In many small towns the Refah secretary often seems to have a small dark shop and to be making something that has been made there for generations. In his heart he may be worried about whether the tradition can continue and Refah seems to offer some reassuring answers to his political questions.

Mehmet spent twenty years cleaning out Hamburg power station and, as a religious man, sat on the committee that raised funds for the first Turkish mosque in the city. Now there are over thirty in north Germany alone. He is fifty, but looks nearer seventy, a sad, bowed figure in a brown anorak sitting dangling a fishing line off the great concrete blocks that protect Amasra from the violent winter storms. It is the one tangible contribution of Ankara to the life of the town since the war, to stop it being assaulted by the sea. The fishing fleet in the harbour that the wall was supposed to protect has mostly gone, the 20-foot-high concrete wall an absurdity that has found a new role: it is the background for inspired popular art, wall paintings of huge fish and graffiti – messages of love, accounts of conquests, an address from someone who was offered a job in Munich unexpectedly and had to leave at short notice. Perhaps he will never see again the woman he wanted to marry. She was always busy in her shop; with her tiny feet she had to stand on steps to reach the top shelves where the sugar was stacked; she was always neat in her dark blue skirt and patterned *chador*. She would have been an ideal partner. Elderly petulant little men with wandering eyes and squeaky voices tried to stop them meeting. Freedom in Amasra was a scarce commodity for them, just as it was in ancient Paphlagonia, a country of slave-traders, colonists, refugees from Greece who would betray their Hellenic education and heritage to hide in Turkey from the justice of the gods. It is hard to hide in Amasra now. There are not many hotels or other places for a visitor to stay, and the cockroaches are large and hungry and eat shit and run fast in the bathrooms and kitchens. And along the beach the pollution is washed up; the Greek tragedian Euripides wrote that the sea washes away the ills of man, but every wave of the Black Sea washes them back towards him.

6. *The Armenians and the Kurdish Crisis I*

From the earliest period to the present hour, Armenia has been the theatre of perpetual war.

Edward Gibbon, *The Decline and Fall of the Roman Empire*, 1776

Whole districts were abandoned to Kurds when the Russian armies retreated in 1829, 1855 and 1878 from Turkish soil, because violence was bound to follow. We found on all hands villages now Kurd which were till lately Armenian.

Noel Buxton MP, *Travels and Reflections*, 1929

Late Ottoman Turkey was the locus of the Eastern Question – for northern Europe an intractable, endlessly complex international-relations dilemma. In the eyes of many Turks modern Turkey has an eastern question of its own. To secularist and modernist Turks, the west has represented order and progress – the civilizing Greeks on the Mediterranean coast, and wealthy, dissolute Constantinople, for so long the greatest city in the world, facing Western Europe. The east has often brought disorder, it has always had a long and often barely defensible land frontier, a brutal climate and landscape with long hot summers and arctic winters, and alien political and social forces. The social structure, economic development and mental attitudes of the east have always been generations behind that of the west. Here lies a problem: in the mythology, and to a degree the reality, of Turkish origins, the heart of the modern Turkish people has been central Asia, the 'original home of all Turks', as a 1988 Ankara government booklet puts it.

The east has been purely Turkish, and so implicitly 'good', while the west, notably Istanbul, has been of mixed race and religion and was the home of the difficult minorities, such as the Greeks. In reality the east has always been a frontier – in recent history with the Arabs and the Russians. Before the Ottoman conquest the Byzantine occupiers had considerable difficulties with their Arab neighbours, as did the Romans with the Parthians. In the east during the First World War Russia's defeat of Enver Pasha's army was a terrible blow to the Ottoman sultans, and the east was the scene of the Armenian crisis during the same period. The Kurdish war is the modern-day nightmare of this frontier, it is the contemporary manifestation of a long-standing disorderly political situation. Kingdoms and regimes have come and gone in the East but few of them in the past have been friends of Turkey. Few of the neighbouring states are today either.

The Asiatic steppes of the Turkish ancestral home have for generations been controlled by Russia, Turkey's most serious and long-standing enemy. There is a geographical correspondence between the two countries, each having a westernized west, but an alien and wild east, in the case of Russia the frozen forests and tundra of Siberia. For both the east embodies promise – of wealth and, in the past, of territorial expansion – and a threat to national security. Just as in Greece disorder has usually come from the north, whether in the Dark Ages or in the Second World War, in Turkey it has often come from the east. The traditional enemy to the north, Russia, has threatened or attacked from the east, not usually from across the Black Sea. Although in Europe the decline of the Ottoman Empire represented the progress and democracy of the Greek, Serbian and Bulgarian independence movements, for Turks it meant loss of territory and national prestige and influence, and the eastern parts of the empire being menaced by increasing threats from Russia. These culminated in the Armenian uprising during and after the First World War, when, in alliance with Russia, a serious attempt was made to create a new state on Turkey's eastern borders which included part of what is contemporary Turkish national territory.

During the seventy years of Communism, the traditional Russian threat that had existed since the eighteenth century was magnified to become the central determinant of Turkish foreign and security policy. This was reinforced by the policies of the friends of Turkey abroad. For example, British foreign policy, particularly under Tory governments, has been based on supporting Turkey as an anti-Russian or anti-Soviet force in the region. A whole genre of British popular literature has been based on growing concern about the political future of this region, from John Buchan's *Greenmantle* to the world of anti-Russian espionage explored in Peter Hopkirk's book *On Secret Service East of Constantinople*. But the political intrigue and melodrama rested on a real foundation. Many ordinary Turks have a serious (their critics would say paranoid) fear of disorder from the east, just as many otherwise rational and politically moderate Greeks adopt extreme positions over the Slav-speakers' problem, which occupies a very similar place in their political psyche as Kurdistan does in the Turkish mind, and for the same reasons. In each case, an ethnic minority, Slav-speakers or Kurds, threatens the illusion of national religious and cultural homogeneity the government is anxious to maintain. It is the same mentality that allows the Turkish government to maintain a pattern of serious human rights violations and constitutional backwardness over the Kurdish issue that would be unacceptable elsewhere.

Until 1914 hundreds of thousands of Armenians constituted the majority population in many parts of eastern Turkey, and had strong nationalist ambitions. There are very few Armenians left in Turkey today, and the recovery of the ancestral lands lost during the First World War massacres is no longer a political

possibility. Although the Armenians in Istanbul have their problems, they appear to have reached a *modus vivendi* with the
government, many of them are prosperous and some of them
are rich. The Armenian diaspora is powerful and well organized
and has an influential lobby in the United States that can protect
their human rights. A homeland exists, its capital at Yerevan,
based on the old Armenian Soviet Socialist Republic, and has
many new problems and opportunities of its own. It is largely
surrounded by ex-Soviet republics which have populations of
partly or wholly Turkish culture and Islamic religion, and has
fought a long and bitter war with Azerbaijan for the enclave of
Nagorno-Karabakh. The extent to which the Armenians and
their cultural heritage disappeared from contemporary historical
consciousness in the Cold War is shown by the fact that in 1959
the gifted and open-minded English travel writer Freya Stark
could describe the far eastern Van and Diyarbakir regions of
Turkey without ever using the word 'Armenian' in her book
Riding to the Tigris. It is also worth bearing in mind that even
the well connected found travel permits hard to come by in these
regions until quite recently, and that within Turkey independent
or investigative reporting about what takes place there now is
often difficult.

The Armenians, as Christians occupying parts of the old
Ottoman east, have held a peculiarly sensitive and delicate position in the Turkish psychology. But the official version of events
about the massacres under the Ottoman Empire and the culminat-
ing bloodbath in 1915 is a myth, promulgated with much the
same aim as Stalinist justifications of the massacres of rich
peasants in the Soviet Union in the 1930s. Although Armenian
propagandists may have exaggerated the ethnic cleansing, there
are too many independent witnesses from Europe and the USA
for the official version of events to have much credibility outside
Turkophile circles. The forced marches of Armenians across the
deserts into Syria and the Lebanon, where tens of thousands of
innocent people died of hunger and thirst, must count as some

of the most terrible offences against humanity in the twentieth century, and the precursor to later genocides.

But as always, order in the Turkish state seems to outweigh the loss of individual rights. Most members of the Turkish élite will admit privately that the history of Armenia taught in Turkish schools is little more than nationalist propaganda, just as the account of ancient and medieval Armenia in the official handbook for the Ankara museum approaches fiction. But as in the Balkans, history merges into contemporary political debate in Turkey. The struggle against Kurdish nationalism today is presented in an equally distorted light, although many members of the élite do not believe the propaganda and understand a change of attitude is needed if Turkey is to overcome the Kurdish crisis.

At the heart of the Kurdish struggle is the great but forbidding city of Diyarbakir, Byzantine *Amida*, built on the Tigris where it first becomes navigable. In a way it holds the key to modern Turkey and the renewed eastern question. It is a city of two forts, the ancient citadel built around the cone of an extinct volcano, and the modern NATO and CIA installations that are central to Western defence policy in the Middle East.

The modern fort belongs to the world of CNN, Peter Arnett in his dug-out, and the war against Saddam Hussein. But the city was a great fortress long before man learned how to fly or listen to telephone conversations made hundreds of miles away. Travellers usually find it the most Arab of any Turkish city. The great black basalt walls that wind around the cone of the extinct volcano like a sinister python are one of the longest continuous fortifications after the Great Wall of China. Flying into Diyarbakir evokes the Gulf War and many other Middle Eastern conflicts. The vast, empty landscape unfolds below the aircraft, semi-desert to the south, the same strange mixture of high-technology aerospace equipment – the silver darts of the Lockheed fighters stand in lonely multi-million pound isolation in bomb-proof pens by the side of the runway. Heavily armed paramilitary troops guard it all, and there is a nervous, itchy air among the military officials. Foreigners are not popular in south-east Turkey, especially if they look like journalists. The defences of the West are exposed here as if the Cold War had never ended.

Diyarbakir is better reached by air. The Kurdish Workers Party, the PKK, has many guns but it does not have anti-aircraft artillery, so the Turkish military have complete control of the skies. They do not effectively control large areas of the land. Travel on buses and in cars in the south-east is dangerous in many places, the roads in the mountains especially so, for a serious, old-fashioned guerrilla war is being fought here. The PKK swoop unexpectedly from their hide-outs to attack buses and take tourists hostage.

The eastern landscape is elemental: the horizon stretches down towards the Syrian desert and the grim basalt walls of Diyarbakir, the endless severity of the mountains unfolding towards the far distant border with Iran. The wild, lonely plateau seems as uninhabited as the surface of the moon, an impression enhanced by the scale of the landmarks: the 17,000-feet-high peak of Mount Ararat, where Noah's Ark was beached; the Tigris and Euphrates rising in the area and rushing southwards towards Iraq, waters that saw the birth of civilization. Both the Kurdish people and the Turkish soldiers who have been bogged down in a bloody counter-insurgency war since the mid-1980s feel their struggle has gone to the heart of the Turkish state, to its identity and its sense of the future. But it is being fought in a landscape dominated by primeval images from the ancient past, the kind of place where the mythical slouched beast in W. B. Yeats's poem 'The Second Coming' might emerge to destroy the world.

In all Mediterranean and Balkan countries, there have been endemic patterns of conflict between mountain peoples and plain-dwellers throughout recorded history. The mountain peoples have sought to spread down to the better pastures and easier life on the plains, while the vulnerable towns there have felt threatened by these movements. Mountain dwellers usually prove to be the tougher fighters and have often lived by raiding traffic through the passes or on the plains themselves. The Kurds are a classic example of this type and for centuries their predatory ways seemed to have changed little since they were first mentioned by the ancient Greek military historian Xenophon. In the case of the Balkans, the Montenegrans lived similar lives and preyed off Adriatic shipping and Turkish caravans. The mountains preserve older and more primitive forms of social organization, while on the plains there is development towards urban life. Most important of all, the mountains are difficult for regular armies to control, as the Romans, the Byzantines and the Ottomans found here and in the Balkans – keeping order was a very unrewarding pursuit.

These factors would exist in eastern Turkey even if the Kurdish people did not. The country is a bridge between East and West in a very literal sense: the narrow coastal strip and its roads lead towards the Caucasus and Russia, the central plateau dominates the route to Iran, while the south-east, with the Kurdish inhabited areas, straddles the borders of Syria and Iraq. In ancient times Western civilization was first brought to these lands by the conquests of Alexander the Great, and after his death came the Selucids, the Parthians and the Romans. But Roman rule was never secure in the mountains, and the imperial peace was only maintained by the construction of huge fortresses to control the strategically vital roads. *Amida*, modern Diyarbakir, was one of these strong points and became an Assyrian trading post on the road to Edessa and Malatya. Emperor Constantine I (324–37) enclosed part of the city and began the building of the great walls that continued on and off for a thousand years afterwards. But they did not prevent the city from being captured by the Persians in 359. After a terrible siege, it was taken and the conquerors found the narrow streets crowded with starving villagers from the nearby mountains, the ancestors of today's

Kurds. They must have looked very similar to the hundreds of thousands of refugees who fill the city today, fleeing the cluster bombs and anti-personnel weapons of the Turkish air force. The Roman historian Ammianus recorded that the Persians slaughtered 80,000 men by starvation in the amphitheatre while keeping the women to 'bake for them and satisfy their lust'.

Internecine wars continued for hundreds of years, as *Amida* remained a strategic frontier town. In 503 the Persians again recaptured the city. After 636, it was taken by the Arabs, and given to the Beni Bakr tribe, so acquiring its modern name, Diyarbakir, the home of the Bakr tribe. They held it until 1085, when it fell into the hands of the Seljuk Turks. Under the Ottoman sultans, it became a key administrative centre for the empire, and all caravans for the Iranian provinces were forced to pass through the town. The tax farmers of Diyarbakir were very powerful and controlled enormous revenues. In an interesting irony, given Turkey's problematic relations with fundamentalist Iran today, one of the duties imposed on the local administrators was to enforce the list of prohibited goods that could not be exported to Iran. These were iron, copper, horses and silver.

Diyarbakir's role in the world has remained largely the same. The city is of central importance to the economy and defences of eastern Turkey, and it is the heart of the Kurdish rebellion. Some 25 miles away are the great white globes of the American CIA listening post – domes like huge ping-pong balls lying in the arid grassland that leads to Mardin, the crusaders' town on the way to Syria that looks like a set for a film of the *Arabian Nights*. Diyarbakir is a frontier in the West's struggle for the Middle East as well as a Turkish border. Beyond lies fundamentalism, disorder, fanaticism, and the undemocratic regimes that threaten the West. Behind is Turkey, part of the new world order, secular, reasonable, a pillar of the West, or so the propaganda goes.

*

In the bar of the Caravanserai hotel the Americans gather to drink furtively during Ramadan. Hizbollah is attacking any liquor shop that opens in the city, so none do. Devout shopkeepers cover their windows with brown paper to make sure they escape the fury of the mullahs. But the hotel is a foreigners' refuge built on the ruins of an old Ottoman *han*, or wayside inn, and is a glorious, atmospheric building with dreamy interior courts with tinkling fountains and white marker stones set in the basalt block walls in severe geometric patterns. They resemble the Greek key patterns from the ancient world. In Ottoman days hundreds of camels would have been kept in the stables here, while the merchants haggled in the *han* courtyard and deals were struck that enabled a caravan to be assembled. The restaurant is a strange place, sunk into the ground, the only customers visiting intelligence and national security officials from Ankara, who smoke heavily, staring into the distance, wishing there were more customers to mingle with them and hide their activities. On the television there is a continual diet of rock videos, the worst of Western consumerism, but all around the *han* there is Ramadan and piety; so a Victorian traveller stranded there might have read a sensual love story in the rooms so like monastic cells.

At the bar the talk is of a great snake that was found wrapped around a radar disk inside one of the domes. Security against human intruders is awesome but ineffective against the creatures of the desert. Harry, a black computer expert from Louisiana, takes his pet wolf spider out of its box and gives it a walk along the bar top. It is called Assad, after the Syrian president (Harry spends all day listening to him and to his military communications). Unlike President Assad, who is clean-shaven, the wolf spider is huge and hairy, the size of a small tarantula, and very over-sexed. Harry extends his ballpoint pen carefully towards the spider, who mounts it and begins to copulate with it rhythmically, the fur on its rear end standing out and up. 'You could make a rug out of this guy's arse, man,' Harry muses philosophically. Perhaps the Byzantine garrison commander allowed his men to keep wolf spiders as pets too, in the eleventh century. It would have made a good story for the functionaries back in Constantinople. They told lies for the empire, the garrison commander would have had to die for it. A mouse would frighten them, but they depended on his intelligence reports on the Seljuk threat over the eastern walls on the volcano cone. And a wolf spider would travel well, to produce at the right moment in some *polis* social gathering. This Assad's future is to the west, over the ocean. Harry is planning to take him home to Louisiana, to the Mississippi delta, the home of the Blues. There will be billions of mosquitoes for him to devour. Harry is optimistic about his future. 'He'll make a good home with us. No doubt. Away from this goddam war, man.'

But it is outside that you find the war, with children living like rats, orphans scavenging in the rubbish tips below the loops in the basalt walls. They fight over oranges and peaches that drop off passing carts coming into the town. By the great Gate of Mardin, facing south over the surging Tigris, there used to be a water cistern. Diyarbakir was one of the cleanest cities in the Middle East, it was said. Not only visitors from the surrounding countryside but also their horses and camels had to be washed here. In Ankara, few officials would be happy to hear any part of Turkey described as the Middle East, but the reality is inescapable here. A camel sits chewing the cud by a new Mercedes, a chic, sinister C-class with dark smoked windows. There is money to be made here, but legal means are not common or usual. The camel feeds from a tiny plot of grass under the outer bailey. Diyarbakir is at the centre of a huge hinterland, hundreds of miles ravaged by war, ethnic cleansing, attacks by the army on villages, attacks by the PKK on richer Kurdish peasants and right-wing villages that do not support them, attacks by Islamic groups on the godless PKK, murders of decent non-political businessmen who refuse to pay protection money. Murders of all kinds can be studied in Diyarbakir: there is no shortage of bodies. Most sinister of all are the corpses of idealistic young men lying in alleyways at night, killed by faceless gunmen from the Turkish government death squads. About five hundred people were liquidated hereabouts in this way in 1995. But there is still money to be made from selling salt and sugar and cheese and washing-up liquid.

It is not a clean city today, as its population has risen from about 300,000 in 1980 to over one and a quarter million. The government military campaign against the PKK is emptying villages of their inhabitants and it is being fought on classic Cold War counter-insurgency lines: the rural areas are being depopulated to deprive the guerrillas of support, isolating them from their supplies and safe houses and herding them to towns where they can be more easily controlled by the security forces. Very handsome Kurdish women with deep black eyes walk the streets to the market in complex, elegant, traditional costumes – swathes of brilliant white cotton, deep blue beads, gold jewellery. The Turkish state campaign of terror has taken their homes but not their pride, nor their open and relaxed sexuality. Within Diyarbakir, armoured cars patrol the streets with all the nonchalance of English police Land Rovers at a pop festival. But there are also open-sided old pick-up trucks loaded with conscripts, armed to the teeth. They ride shotgun through the town two or three times a day, brandishing machine-pistols in the air. They could be the US cavalry terrifying a Red Indian camp a hundred years ago. I am prevented from photographing an innocent scene in a crowded market, but am able to rescue my camera when the Turkish plain-clothes official hears I come from Oxford. In the courtyard of the old mosque, old men sit and read the Koran, the book resting on little carved wooden stands. This is one of the oldest mosques in the region, famous for culture and learning and social welfare, with a great hospital as well as a library. Ancient Greek medical knowledge passed to the West through places like it, like vital blood through an artery. Now it is a refuge from genocide.

*

In this city of Kurdish blood and pain it is not easy to find the Armenian church. My friend Abdullah thinks it a strange request anyway, and although a long-time resident of the city, with an encyclopaedic knowledge of the narrow streets, he finds the route difficult and we get lost.

The Emperor Justinian made the area around the city a Byzantine province in 536 and called it the Fourth Armenia. Despite its centrality to the Kurdish struggle, it was an Armenian town long before the Kurds moved in. And it was hundreds of years before the word Turk had any meaning in Europe at all. We turn down a narrow alleyway that looks like the setting for a shadowy episode in Kipling's *Great Game*, and pass a crumbling, rambling mosque on the left, with cats playing games on the ancient red-tiled roof. The minaret is separate, and stands on cut-off Byzantine stone columns in the alleyway. According to tradition, infertility can be cured by passing around the minaret with your wife several times. It points phallic and grimy into the Turkish spring sky. Down an even smaller alleyway, there is a boarded-up Catholic church to the right. This was the old Christian quarter but it is not shown on any official Turkish map.

Deeper into the rabbit warren of alleys, there is a blue iron door with number four painted on it. Through it there is a little house, then, amazingly, a vast open courtyard surrounded by high walls, in the middle of which is an echoing, ruined roofless church, an enormous building that could hold hundreds of worshippers. It is like Tintern Abbey, stranded and hidden in far eastern Turkey. A hapless refugee family are living in a tin shack built in the roofless crypt. A rat hurries across a rubbish tip towards the family chickens. The organ loft door swings at a crazy angle in the wind, above the few pathetic children's toys scattered on the stone floor. It is the world of John Buchan's *Greenmantle*, the souks and sewers of Baghdad that can tell a tale. Today Diyarbakir is the Kurdish city *par excellence*, but before the First World War it had a very large Armenian population, who dominated trade throughout the whole region and administered whole parts of the empire. The Armenians were murdered and the Kurds moved into their empty buildings, just as Vlachs moved into so many northern Greek villages emptied of Slav-speakers after the Greek Civil War. When Diyarbakir was first made a vilayet in 1867, it had a population of 471,462 Turks and 133,818 non-Muslims, of whom 79,129 were Armenians. They had been in the city for hundreds of years. The traveller Simeon of Lwow, who visited Diyarbakir in 1612, described the residents has having

1,000 Armenian houses and all of them are wealthy, luxurious and glorious. And whatever business and riches exist, they possess; the mint, the customs, the caravanserais and the rest . . . and when it is a Sunday and the Armenians do not open their shops and do not work, you think the town is empty and desolated.

Armenian officials dominated certain professions (one nine-teenth-century traveller found that every architect and doctor in the place was an Armenian), they had numerous members on the local councils, they were great teachers of crafts such as metal work and carpet-making. Many worked as administrators in the departments of education and public health, in the judiciary, the postal and telegraphic service, and on the agricultural boards. Only the police force was dominated by Turks, and even in wholly Armenian districts only one or two Armenians would be allowed in each police station. Greeks seemed to be more trusted in the army than the Armenians, and army doctors in the south-east were almost invariably Greek.

Diyarbakir is yet another Troy, the besieged city in Turkey that always falls, drenched in blood. The Armenian Troy was a hundred years ago, the Kurdish Troy is happening today. This is the worst side of Turkey, where war is won through vigour and strength, then the peace is lost because of the political vacuum. Ankara's only answer to certain political problems has always been to slit throats, or to use torture: the pincers on the toe-nails or the truncheon up the vagina in the basement of the police station. My friend's uncle will not live long after a week in custody in Diyarbakir police station. He was kicked on his back for hours and he passes blood with his urine. He cannot close his carpet shop to seek medical treatment because there are so few customers that his family would not eat if he did. It was not a political problem – he is not a PKK supporter. But to protect himself from the extortions of the PKK and the four separate underground Islamic fundamentalist groups operating in the city, he is allowed to have a pistol by the police. But he has to bribe them continuously to keep the licence. When he could not pay, he was assumed to have handed the money to the revolutionaries, and so became a guest of the Turkish state for a week. He will die very soon from kidney failure, in all probability. His world is far removed from the world of the suave apologies for the Turkish human-rights record at some diplomatic receptions in Ankara, the calm assurances that while there are problems, the situation is improving all the time and journalists who write too much about it can be 'unhelpful'.

A small woman in a beautiful red tribal dress explains why she is living in the ruined church on her own with her two children. Her husband disappeared one day, three years ago. Death is not uncommon among Kurdish activists – the Turkish army do not mess about. The greystone Christian passions of Armenia died here, too, the dour priests, the beautiful, sensual but gloomy and dogmatic women; their tumbling black curls were cut off to humiliate them before they were raped and murdered, perhaps near these organ pipes that lie among the piles of rotting timbers and lumps of old plaster. Christian music will never be heard here again.

The Turks are once more making a waste land of eastern Anatolia and calling it peace. To them, reality is more mundane, conventional. The Kurds and Armenians shared much territory in Ottoman times. Their ideal homelands overlapped in many places – lands they wished to detach from the Ottoman then the Turkish state. But the sultan 'solved' the Armenian problem first. And the great genocide of the First World War is passed over in silence.

On 1 November 1895 the sultan took his revenge on Diyarbakir's Armenians, as earlier that year he had in Erzurum, Urfa and many other towns and cities in the east. Most of the massacres followed a common pattern. In Urfa an Armenian killed a Turk in a quarrel, then the family of the Turk killed the Armenian's family, and in a day or two an orgy of inter-communal violence began that left over several hundred dead. Another common cause was a provocation by the terrorist wing of the Hunchak, the Armenian national movement, as in Erzurum, where one of its members tried to shoot the chief of police. In Diyarbakir three days of blood and mayhem gripped the town, but this was only the prelude, the Armenian equivalent of *Krystalnacht*, when the Jews received their first warning from Hitler. The 'final solution' came during the First World War, in the terrible years of 1915 and 1916. In the aftermath of the Young Turk revolution in 1908, what in the West was seen as legitimate nationalism and renewal became fierce racism in the East. The Armenians had been issued with weapons in 1905, as a barrier against the Kurds, but they soon turned them against their Ottoman oppressors. The government ordered the army to move against the Armenians in early 1915, in the wider context of the Russian threat and the chaotic conditions in the east of the country as the First World War unfolded. It became clear to the Turkish government that some sort of Armenian state was emerging, likely to be based on territory to the east of the modern border. A programme of massive ethnic cleansing was undertaken to exterminate the Armenian population and its cultural and religious traditions in the traditional eastern strongholds. By so doing, the capacity of the Armenian people to form a state would be severely restricted or possibly removed altogether. The methods used were systematic and brutal. Long columns of Armenians were formed and forcibly marched out of eastern Turkey in the direction of Syria or Cilicia. Most died from thirst, hunger or exposure in the burning heat of the semi-desert. The vultures picked their bones. Attractive women were raped then beheaded in front of local bystanders, men were castrated and tied to trees to bleed to death with their genitals stuffed into their mouths. If the columns stopped along the way offenders were mercilessly whipped by Turkish irregulars until they died. Christopher Walker, a historian of the Armenians, notes that 'far from being the "clean fighters" who figured among the legends of British Turkophiles, they were worthy heirs of Attila the Hun and Genghis Khan in their remorseless brutality'.

However horrendous, the policy worked: there was never an Armenian political movement of any substance in Turkey again, and the little Armenian state that eventually emerged as a constituent republic of the Soviet Union, with its capital in Yerevan, was a poverty-stricken and ineffective homeland. The only other land left to the Armenian people was these stony and bare uplands. The Nationalists had a deliberately racialist policy that involved cleansing the areas within Turkey of non-Turkish elements in preparation for the foundation of a racially and ethnically pure state; multi-racialism and multi-culturalism were seen as vices of the old empire.

Unsurprisingly, in view of the nature of what was involved, Turkish governments since have attempted to deny or obscure what happened. In doing so they have been aided by the silence of the international community over the issue, in a manner that has become deeply familiar to human-rights activists and critics of Ankara's policies. It could be said that, more than any other single factor, the failure to confront the reality of the Armenian issue has made it difficult to improve Turkish human rights over the years. The genocide has been used by Armenian propagandists for their own purposes, of course, but there are too many independent accounts of what happened from foreign observers for official Turkish denials to carry much weight. Even these accounts have not prevented apologists for the various Turkish governments from claiming that massacres never took place, or that, if they did, they were part of the undeniable chaos of the First World War and should be forgotten. This tendency was particularly strong among American historians and Turkish 'experts' during the Cold War period, when notions of academic objectivity were abandoned in the interests of propaganda and disinformation. Americans have been notable among the Western apologists for Ankara throughout the last seventy years on many topics. As early as 1922, Admiral Mark Bristol, the United States high commissioner in Constantinople, was claiming that the Armenians were being moved 'to the most delightful and fertile parts of Syria where the climate is as benign as in Florida . . . all this was done at a great expense of money and effort'.

The most telling comment on the whole process and its real status in international politics was made in the early 1930s by Hitler in an internal debate within the Nazi Party on the feasibility of the Final Solution for the Jewish people, when he said, 'Who remembers the Armenians?' The episode set a precedent for legitimizing genocide and ethnic cleansing throughout the twentieth century. The Turkish nationalists had crushed the nascent Armenian republic and brought on the Sovietization of what remained. But they had also begun a tradition of international political obfuscation of the true nature and *modus operandi* of some aspects of Turkish history and the Turkish state machine that has continued to the present day. This flourished in the Reaganite era in the United States when, under Secretary of State George Shultz, the administration fought attempts by the Armenian community worldwide to have the genocide recognized. This was countered in 1987 by the European Parliament's vote to recognize what had happened. In response to veiled threats from Ankara to pull out of NATO, the US administration bitterly resisted attempts to put a similar resolution through Congress. The few remaining Armenians in the country are conformist pillars of the community, yet the United States kowtowed to the Turkish government, just as Britain had in the nineteenth century when Sultan Mahmut II (1808–39) threatened to move closer to Russia.

A central problem for many neighbours and internal critics of Turkey is to evolve a policy to deal with the ever-present threat of military blackmail. Greece, as the neighbouring country most immediately involved with the problem, usually relies on international law. The training of Greek diplomats places a heavy emphasis on law, and it is necessary to pass an examination in it before entering Athens government service. It is a response the English prime minister Gladstone would have appreciated; he often contrasted the Greek concept of the rule of law with the Ottoman technique of rule by force. Other countries can follow suit if they wish. But it does little to help the people of Diyarbakir and other eastern cities, where lawyers are few and are subject to as much intimidation as anyone else. The atmosphere of a coercive army of occupation is overwhelming. The answer, for even the best-intentioned, is often to counter force with the guerrilla struggle. This leads to a city where carrying arms is as normal as wearing a shirt, and bullets are a new currency, more reliable than the inflationary lira, and of more practical use.

It is easy to forget all about Istanbul and the West and see the city as part of the great Middle Eastern arms bazaar. But although the government would like to confine the crisis here, it is difficult to do so. The long years of NATO equivocation with Ankara and the false definition of national and social issues such as 'terrorism' and 'internal security' have left a bitter heritage, which allows the West to play politics with the Kurdish people over borders and the inner machinations of regimes.

7. The Kurdish Crisis II

Kani kanla yumazlar, kani su ile yurlar (Blood will not be washed away with blood but with water).

Kurdish proverb

Only a few minutes walk from the Blue Mosque in Istanbul a line of people waiting to go home from a day in the office or travel agency are standing demurely at the tram stop. A beautiful but grubby grey-and-white cat sorts through rubbish by a burger bar. If this is not Europe, it feels very close to it. But in a side street running south towards the Sea of Marmara, below the white-painted concrete balcony of a jeans factory, an arrest is in progress. It does not take long. A young man with the unmistakable hawkish features of a Kurd is rushed across the crowded pavement and bundled into the back of a police van. It seems a very routine process, he clearly knows what is happening to him, the policemen are muscular and domineering and bored. One of them takes an aimless kick at a pile of cardboard boxes on the pavement before they drive away. Perhaps a hundred young Kurds will be questioned today in Istanbul. Some will be treated well, questioned superficially, photographed and let out into the street. Others will be subject to more serious interrogation; the police will want to know who their friends are and what they are doing in Istanbul. A few will be beaten and humiliated and frightened. Every so often, someone is tortured, rather than simply maltreated. His toe-nails will be pulled out with pliers, or his foreskin stapled together, or he will be forced to drink a gallon of water, then hung upside down and beaten.

Or maybe just beaten on the soles of the feet. Women have their own separate and specific pain and humiliations to endure, not orthodox rape, as a rule, but physical humiliation, cruel, direct and insulting, legs tied apart and pubic hairs pulled out one by one with tweezers. Or immersion in a bath of cold water while the police urinate into the bath.

It is a great engine, the Turkish security apparatus, and sometimes even the politicians who most wish to stop and dismantle it cannot do so. Over the whole country, at any one time, thousands of people are in detention for what are basically political reasons, even if the authorities justify them as arrests for minor civil misdemeanours. Successive Turkish governments when faced with press allegations about what has been happening have adopted a policy of denial. It relies on the inertia of much Turkish public opinion, and the quiet understandings that have been built up informally with Western partners. Now the Kurdish crisis has become a crisis for Istanbul. Although the war has been confined to the south-east in a military sense, in another it dominates the country. Istanbul is the biggest Kurdish city in the world. Hundreds of thousands of displaced people have moved here during the long years of the Kurdish *intifada*. Public order in Istanbul is a key element in the government's strategy to confine the Kurdish movement. One of the successes of the strategy has been to keep the big city largely free of terrorism, at least from Kurds, and security planners in Ankara would probably be prepared to risk almost any degree of international opprobrium as a result of repressive action if that achievement were ever threatened. A regional war is acceptable, in Western terms, and does not call into question the security of an otherwise stable state. In the same way, nobody would suggest that the British state is fundamentally threatened by the long-running crisis in Northern Ireland, however expensive it may be and however intermittently disruptive to British cities.

Some of the Kurds who have moved to Istanbul are well integrated and virtually unrecognizable except by informed insiders. In other places there are Kurdish cafés and restaurants where even the best-intentioned and trusted visitor finds it difficult to relax. In Ankara and many other large towns it is possible to forget the Kurdish problem, but this is much more difficult in Istanbul. The city has experienced an immigrant invasion in the last twenty years, but it cannot admit it, as to do so would expose the official myth of social homogeneity. Near the Blue Mosque, on a sunny March day, a young red-bearded German tourist is explaining to a carpet trader where he is going for the next stage of his holiday. He says he is taking the long-distance bus to Konya, then Kurdistan. '*Kurdistan?* Where is this Kurdistan? I have never heard of it.' The hitherto relaxed and charming rug salesman turns almost immediately into an angry nationalist. 'There is no Kurdistan. Please do not talk to me of Kurdistan.'

A couple of weeks later is the feast of Nevruz, an ancient Kurdish festival celebrating the spring equinox, now suddenly taken over as a public holiday by the Turkish state after many years of being a traditional day of protest against the government. In an odd irony, it is still banned in Germany, where it has given rise to violent demonstrations in favour of the Kurdish Workers Party, the PKK. But in Istanbul it is now encouraged, in an effort to demonstrate the endlessly assimilative qualities of Turkish ideology and to show that the Kurds have a respected place in Turkish society. Although bizarre, it is perhaps something of a tribute to the strength and resilience of the Turkish state.

But the far east is not only about the Kurdish problem. The social and economic effects of the war have spread far beyond the fairly narrow area of conflict; in the ten years since the Kurdish *intifada* started, these ripples have severely damaged the Turkish economy and gone to the heart of Turkish self-confidence. The war shares some of the characteristics of the war in the Balkans. It is not fought by very many people, using low technology armaments – at least on the Kurdish side – and not that many people are killed in relation to the population of the area affected by the fighting, but the economic and social effects are devastating and spread hundreds of miles away. A war fought by 20,000 or 30,000 people has destroyed the old Yugoslavia. Not many more are involved in the Kurdish conflict at any one time, yet it is possible that it will destroy the social order in Turkey. To the chagrin of the Foreign Ministry in Ankara, even comparatively small outbreaks of fighting, such as the conflict in the mountains in Diyarbakir province in April 1996, are extensively reported in the international media. In economic terms, in the south-east, the ordinary middle class is being destroyed or emigrates, and new bosses take over, gangster groups or worse.

In other ways it is a very old-fashioned war, with a large army whose officers are still fighting a classic counter-insurgency campaign against a guerrilla force with a Marxist ideology. Or it may be older than that in the tactical sense. Ottoman power in these backward and outlying areas was based on control of the roads, a strategy inherited from the Byzantine and Roman imperial systems. Local chieftains who were thought to be politic-ally reliable were paid from central funds to maintain their own private police forces and prevent disorder, just as today Ankara pays anti-PKK peasants in the Kurdish areas to resist the Kurdish leftists. Village guards are a frequent target for revenge attacks by the PKK.

Road control is the central objective of routine Turkish milit-ary operations; the economic campaign aims to boost the richer peasants and to promote their loyalty to the central government. It is reminiscent of Ottoman rule in countries like Bulgaria, where there is a class known as the *chorbadzhii*, literally 'soup drinkers', the richer peasants who were loyal and responsible local leaders, or collaborators with the occupying power, depending on which way you look at it.

Even in oil-rich Batman, a wild and dissolute boom town in the remote far east with a Klondike atmosphere, peace is not expected to last for long. Businessmen are quietly taking their money out of the till in cash, and reinvesting in western Turkey. A store selling groceries to British and German tourists in Bodrum provides an easier way to make money than survival among the protection rackets and competing paramilitary groups in Batman. The eastern crisis spreads. In the middle of it all, traditional Turkey grinds on, as always. If there were an alliance, however loose and contradictory, between the radical elements in the Islamic movement and the PKK, the present situation in the east would be doomed. One of the few comforts for the National Security Council and the Ankara government is that the PKK and Hizbollah and similar groups are at each other's throats, to the point of open war.

An odd aspect of the life of cities like Van, Kars and Batman is that it is relatively difficult for businessmen to form their own mafia groups – the state is simply too strong. To run a business in such an environment is a lonely and difficult task, whereas the new mafias of the post-Communist world do at least provide a support mechanism for business in a hostile and confused environment. In Turkey, even in such anarchic and backwoods places, the state machine with its traditional bureaucracy has its long tentacles intact: forms have to be filled in and taxes paid, in theory at least. The key element in most East European mafia groups – the mixture of ex-nomenclatura interests and control of large amounts of cash generating business outside the state framework – simply does not exist in Turkey. The state bureaucracy is very much alive, and closely linked to the coercive power of the military and security apparatus. State functionaries usually regard the rich or even moderately successful Kurds as a source of bribe money and largesse for themselves, just as the Ottoman tax collectors in an outlying region would have done.

For many Turks living in the east, education is a particular problem. There is a university in Diyarbakir, but the teaching is not of a high standard, and students from other parts of Turkey who do not make it into higher education in Istanbul are allocated places there, often very unwillingly. It is not a satisfactory environment, and even ordinary secondary school education is in terminal crisis.

It is unfortunate for the Kurds that the resurgence in the national movement has coincided with the end of the Cold War. According to the British writer Philip Robbins, Turkey has become

one of the winners of the Cold War period. It is no longer a marginal player on the southern fringe of NATO. Rather, it is regarded as being 'in the eye of the storm'. It has replaced the Federal Republic of Germany as the member state located in the region of greatest uncertainty. In recognition of this new importance, Britain and the United States have set about bolstering the country's position. Britain used its presidency of the Council of Ministers to usher in an enhanced political status for Turkey. The United States led a massive transfer of military resources, both bilaterally and through the process of 'cascading'.

As has been argued elsewhere in this book, this process seems unlikely to increase regional stability in the long term – just as the vast flow of Western military equipment to the Middle East over the years has failed to prevent numerous local and regional wars, and the arming of the Shah of Iran in the 1970s did not assist the survival of his regime. If generals receive weapons, the lesson of history is that sooner or later they are used, and a rise in regional political tension is apparent, whether a war eventually takes place or not. The weapons build-up has perhaps contributed to tension in the Dodecanese area in early 1996 and the military manoeuvres over the disputed and goat-inhabited Greek island of Imia in February 1996. And, as we have seen, weapons are not only used externally in Turkey; they are a central part of the repressive internal security machine. Without the indirect support of NATO and the international arms industry, Turkey would find the war in the east very difficult.

The human-rights violations that the war involves are at the heart of the wider crisis. It is a dirty war, and some of the most savage repression takes place in Diyarbakir and the surrounding countryside. The police and security *apparat* operate special anti-terrorist squads from Diyarbakir central police station. The consequences of falling foul of them can be severe. For example in February 1995 Nevzat Ersonmez's body was found in a sack outside the offices of the minibus company for which he worked as a driver. He had been abducted by members of a police commando. When the sack was opened, his family found burn marks in the shape of TC (Republic of Turkey) on several parts of his body, and rope marks around his neck. He had been deprived of food and water and tortured for a long time before he died. He had worked as a minibus driver on the Diyarbakir–Lice route for five months. The owner of the minibus, a man called Salih Genc, who had been detained by the anti-terror squad three weeks earlier, was found dead on the road between Diyarbakir and Silvan, along with three other unidentified bodies. It is very unlikely that any action would ever be taken against the perpetrators of these crimes, and if they were ever arrested, they would be tried by the state security court in the city, dominated by officials from their own organization.

Turkish government officials like to claim that these abuses are sometimes inevitable in anti-terrorist campaigns and that the rule of law is still in operation in these provinces. There is no evidence to suggest this is the case, and a great deal to contradict it. In February 1995, the trial of seven leading members of the Turkish Human Rights Association began in the town. It did not receive much publicity, as few foreigners go to the far east, Western journalists may suddenly find it difficult to buy a seat on a Kurdistan-bound plane, and most ordinary Turks who live there have become as used to sickening violence as local people have in Northern Ireland. Whereas Istanbul tends to be classified as part of the 'West' by foreign news desks, the Kurdish areas are seen as part of the 'Middle East'. As most Western correspondents are based in Beirut or Cyprus or Jerusalem, and busy with the usual Middle East conflicts, Kurdish matters are not well reported unless there is a major crisis like the gassing of villages by Saddam Hussein in northern Iraq, or large-scale refugee movements after the Gulf War.

The death squads in Istanbul are a new and frightening aspect of the security crisis, and there are disturbing signs that they have begun to operate with impunity in the city. In 1993 and 1994, activists began to disappear in Istanbul in circumstances which made Amnesty International and other human-rights organizations claim that a pattern of extrajudicial executions had been established that was in essence the same as that in Diyarbakir and other far-east cities. For instance, on the morning of 7 August 1993 the 22-year-old journalist Aysel Malkac went missing after she left her office for a business meeting. She was working as a reporter on the Kurdish-owned newspaper *Ozgur Gundem*. Eyewitnesses reported that she was detained in the street by plain-clothes police. She has never been seen again. All efforts to establish her whereabouts have been unsuccessful, although an Istanbul petty criminal who was in custody at the time of her 'disappearance' made a public declaration that he had seen her in police custody on about 8 August. During the week before her disappearance, *Ozgur Gundem*'s offices had been under heavy surveillance by the police, who were patrolling streets in the neighbourhood, and monitoring telephone calls. Since this newspaper was launched in May 1992, it has consistently reported human-rights violations in the south-east. The authorities have repeatedly tried to close the paper on the grounds that it promotes 'separatism' and 'praises' the PKK.

Internationally, Turkey has never been seen as having a good human-rights record. Gladstone's condemnation of the Ottoman regime as an imperial state standing above any civil society that might exist has echoed down the years. It is an image the Ankara government can live with as long as not too much reality creeps in. That is increasingly difficult when the repressive process is applied to major literary figures, such as 71-year-old Yasar Kemal, who was put on trial in 1995 for what he termed 'crimes of thought'. Kemal has been the most prominent Turkish writer for some years, and is the author of wonderful, evocative novels of popular Turkish life such as *The Sea-Crossed Fisherman*, and *Memed, My Hawk*, for which he won the Varlik prize. He has often been mentioned as a possible Nobel prize-winner for his sustained and high quality output. With the prosecution of Kemal, the Kurdish struggle merges with the wider issue of freedom in Turkish intellectual life, and the right of the state to control critical intellectual activity. Kemal was charged with publishing 'separatist propaganda'. The grounds for this was his reference to the PKK as 'guerrillas', rather than the officially sanctioned term of 'separatist terrorists'. By condemning the military authorities in the south-east for atrocities, he was said to be 'insulting the moral personality of the Turkish republic'. This charge was brought under the notorious Article 8 of the anti-terror law, which Ankara has been promising to repeal for years but has never done. By targeting the most distinguished writer in Turkey under this law, it is almost as if the prosecutors *intended* to bring the law into disrepute, not least because, although Kemal is a Kurd, in his literary works he spends much of his time celebrating traditional Turkish values, and the diversity and vast energy of Istanbul life.

The military have opposed repeal of the law. In 1995 *Time* magazine reported the view of General Ahmet Corekci, the armed-forces deputy chief of staff: 'A change in Article 8 will affect our struggle against terrorism. We would prefer to see it untouched.' Prime Minister Ciller, anxious to help Turkey's passage into Europe and to stop the persecution of writers like Kemal, tried to change the law, but the outcome of her efforts was minimal. Great weight was put upon her reforming zeal by Western governments, although similar statements about human-rights reforms have been made by every Turkish leader for the last twenty years when it seemed necessary to do so, and with little tangible result.

In Kemal's *The Sea-Crossed Fisherman* a violent encounter in a Turkish fishing village on the Sea of Marmara results in murder.

A cycle of bloody revenge begins; a local criminal becomes a popular hero and a fisherman called Selim, the central character of the book, is unfairly blamed. In some ways the real victims are not the humans, but the dolphins of the Sea of Marmara, who are being cruelly massacred in the name of commercial profit, as Selim witnesses:

After a while he found himself in a forest of fishing boats. Hundreds of guns were blasting away and the sea was red with blood. Smitten dolphins shot up into the air, screeching like children, splashed down into the water and surfaced again, white belly turned up, bleeding. Some, screaming, dived out of sight only to rise a little later, white belly up, bleeding.

Kemal celebrates the richness, traditions and decency of ordinary Turkish life, and the massacres in the sea are a metaphor for the violence that has been at the heart of Turkish society for so many of the years he has been alive and writing. There are many others who share his values and commitment. In 1995 an anthology called *Freedom of Thought in Turkey* was published. It bore the names not only of the twenty-five authors but also of 1,050 Turkish writers and academics who endorsed its contents. The book was banned by the security police within two hours of its publication, and 700 of the signatories were charged under Article 8. Kemal issued an appeal at the time, ending with the words, 'It is the honour of my country, Turkey, which is at stake. The war the Turkish army is fighting against the guerrillas has no end. There is only one solution: make peace.'

In the meantime many intellectuals continue to bear crushing burdens in the struggle. The sociologist Ismet Besikci is currently serving a total of sixty-five years in gaol for his writings, and there are many other kind, brave men and women like him. In one of the most insidious recent developments, it is not only those who are suspected of involvement in the Kurdish struggle who are imprisoned or abused, but their legal representatives, and human-rights activists. The trial of members of the Diyarbakir

Human Rights Association has given particular cause for concern, as their local lawyers are often the only protection for many activists from the full force of the Turkish military and security *apparat*. They have also been impartial in helping anti-PKK peasants who have been subject to human-rights abuses committed by PKK guerrillas in the south-east villages.

Underlying the fears of many Turks about the effect of the war in the south-east on the country as a whole is the terrible, often unspoken fear that the war could precipitate another period of military rule. People seem to consider that the war is being contained if terrorist acts are not carried out in major Turkish cities, Istanbul in particular. The PKK bombing campaign against the tourist industry in some western towns on the coast in 1994 is the nearest that this stasis has come to being breached. If there were a sustained and effective bombing campaign that brought chaos to Istanbul (which would not be difficult from a practical point of view as the city teeters on the brink of it every day due to the urban crisis), an increased military presence on the streets would become inevitable. Then the 'creeping coup' scenario would unfold; there would be PKK retaliation against the security forces and a breakdown in public order reminiscent of the street battles between left and right in the late 1970s that precipitated the 1980 military government. The army would be forced to call on the National Security Council and the Ankara government would have to extend the emergency legislation that covers the south-east Kurdish provinces to the whole country. Gradually, *de facto* military rule would be established in the cities, particularly Istanbul, any façade of democracy that might remain in Ankara would become increasingly irrelevant, and civilian politicians, of whatever political colour, would be marginalized to the point of extinction.

There are a number of reasons this disastrous scenario seems unlikely, at least at the moment. Firstly, although the Turkish army does not appear to be very competent in many of its military operations in the south-east, the internal security and intelligence services are much more effective, and have so far succeeded in preventing the PKK from forming a large and effective underground organization in Istanbul. Informers are well placed within the Kurdish subculture, and the degree and severity of violence meted out to PKK suspects means that some of them occasionally give way under the pain and humiliation and agree to turn Judas for the Turkish state. The state's panoply of electronic surveillance is also important. Turkey is known to have invested heavily in state-of-the-art equipment, in the Cold War period with the active help of the United States. No telephone calls can be made in Turkey that the authorities cannot easily tap if they wish to do so. It is also possible that foreign agencies, such as the CIA, may assist the Turkish security *apparat* with information and technical advice.

But a deeper reason may lie in the character of the PKK itself. If the new underground is to appear anywhere, it is most likely to be in the diaspora, in Germany, where extreme radicals flourish and thrive. Ideology is also an important factor. The PKK leader, Abdullah Ocalan, is an old-fashioned Marxist in many ways, and is one of the last active proponents of the theory of a people's war, based in the countryside. The PKK iconography is that of an armed and determined people, seeking to recover their occupied country from a foreign occupation. Although fought ruthlessly within the villages, the Kurdish war is also an open and dignified military struggle, deserving the name of guerrilla warfare. It wins the PKK kudos among some foreign sympathizers in Arab governments, especially in Syria, and to a much less active extent in Greece, the Lebanon and Armenia. If the strategy changed to something more similar to the war the provisional IRA has fought in London and elsewhere with, for instance, large car bombs that brought many Turkish civilian casualties, the identity of the PKK would change. It would then begin to conform to the image the Turkish military so assiduously propagates, of the PKK as an amoral separatist terrorist organization, unworthy of humanitarian or political consideration.

There are also operational reasons why the PKK is unlikely to plunge Istanbul into violent chaos. It is organized and led from bases in the Bek'aa valley in Syrian-controlled Lebanon, where Abdullah Ocalan has his headquarters, and from an underground organization in Damascus. The supply lines and chain of command already make effective operations in south-east Turkey difficult. Supply lines would become impossibly long if a main focus were established in Istanbul, and, what is more, might mean the delegation of power for day-to-day operations to a lieutenant. Given the fissiparous history of underground political groups and their operations in Turkey, and the nature of the PKK itself, which has had to endure various leadership purges in the past, there would be a real danger to the integrity and organizational and political unity of the PKK if a terrorist campaign in Istanbul or the major western cities were initiated. Such a campaign would only play into the hands of the military, and risk dividing the PKK itself.

In an odd sense, the Kurdish *intifada* has become a victim of its own success. It has been able to tie up huge military resources over the last decade or so; it has put the Kurdish issue at the heart of the wider Turkish political and economic crisis; it has probably contributed substantially to the exclusion of Turkey from many European institutions and from large amounts of EU aid money and credits. But in a military sense it is a war that cannot easily be won, as so many nationalist opponents of the Ottomans in the Balkans found in the nineteenth century, with their small *cetas*, groups of armed fighters, on the mountainsides. Turkey has massive reserves of men and military equipment, and a devoted fighting spirit when the real or alleged division of the country is at issue. The shambolic troops who fought in the First World War disasters under Enver Pasha were transformed within five years by Atatürk into tigers who successfully defended the territorial unity of the Turkish homeland against the forces of the Entente powers. Generations of young Turks have willingly died in the sacred cause of national unity, and there is little reason to suppose contemporary soldiers are any different.

In the bazaars and mosques of the Kurdish towns, all this seems rather irrelevant. The *intifada* is still in progress, the PKK military leadership survives, with Mr Ocalan said to alternate between a deep bunker somewhere in Syria and offices in Damascus. In the 1995 elections, conservative Kurds on the whole supported the Refah Party, while younger and more radical people supported the HADEP, the People's Democratic Party. Without the support of the former, the latter did not get the necessary 10 per cent of the vote to achieve parliamentary representation. Although the Kurdish people make up about 7 million out of a total electorate of 34 million, HADEP only received about 4 per cent of the vote. Kurds remain alienated from the state, which is becoming a vehicle for representing and enforcing exclusively Sunni-Turkish interests. The programme of the coalition government formed in the winter of 1996 between Mrs Ciller's True Path Party and Refah contains no mention of the Kurdish issue at all. It will be addressed with the same mixture of military repression and lack of political dialogue. Over ten years, this has cost an estimated 75 billion dollars; it represents a cancer eroding state activity and finances, as something like a third of total state revenue is spent on trying to contain the Kurdish problem. The key to the future lies in whether the Refah Party's concept of Islamic brotherhood seems to offer a convincing prospect to the majority of Kurds. The mosque may well not fulfil the same function in Turkish or Kurdish society as in Iran or Algeria, but it will play an indispensable role in the future of Turkey's far east. As yet there is no sign that it will act in alliance with the secular radicals against Ankara. The Refah Party has set its face against any concessions on the Kurdish national issue, both on principle and for fear of losing support in their Anatolian heartlands. Some of its more radical figures are prepared to talk about an autonomous Kurdish region within a future Islamic commonwealth, but it is a vague

and distant vision that is unlikely to satisfy many Kurdish nationalists. In practical terms the Refah leaders had more than enough
to worry about in their relations with the army to risk being
termed 'separatist' by adopting a pro-Kurdish policy. In many
ways Refah coalition government followed military and security
policies identical to those of its predecessors.

The east has not only been a region of war, pain and disorder.
Over the years state economic investment in this area of arid
and unrewarding mountains, empty plateau and huge skies has
taken many different forms. The old pattern of corporatist activity can be seen through the history of the tea industry at the far
eastern end of the Black Sea coast. In the 1940s the Turkish
parliament approved an ambitious plan to make indigenous tea
the national beverage; it has succeeded, and tea has supplanted
coffee throughout the country. The state's contemporary
ambitions for the east are embodied in the GAP hydroelectric
schemes – over twenty-five dams are being constructed on the
Tigris and Euphrates to irrigate a huge area that has hitherto
been confined to 'dry' farming. It will give Turkey control over
the flow of the water from the two great rivers, something that
the riparian countries downstream are uneasy about.

The tale of the tea industry is a strange one, and something that
could only happen in Turkey. According to the anthropologist
Christopher Hann, it is really about democracy, and is full
of symbolic resonances, rather than being a simple industrial
investment plan. If he is right, then GAP may be seen in a similar
way, as part of the culmination of the Turkish state's modernist
technocracy. The role of the state is central to both projects, not
only in economic terms, but in terms of cultural self-assertion:
it attempts to bring a democratic culture and to solve the political
problems of a large part of the south-east by state investment.

Coffee was a great drink of the Ottoman world. It was brought
to Europe by the armies of the early sultans, and the coffee house
supposedly originated in the aftermath of the siege of Vienna. It

was, though, a drink for the élite, as it had to be imported, and was extremely expensive. It was the pre-eminent drink of both the Ottoman and the Hapsburg empires, and was soon adopted by the rest of Europe. To subsidize the creation of the tea industry was an exercise in import substitution that was very useful in cash-strapped Turkey and it was a further symbolic eradication of the Ottoman cultural heritage. Tea was democratic, and the national drink, according to the official ideology, whereas coffee was cosmopolitan, and therefore politically incorrect.

The only area of Turkey suitable for growing tea bushes successfully stretches along the far east of the Black Sea coast to the border with Georgia, east of Trebizond. It is a remote region today, but conditions were near medieval in the inter-war period – local communications were quite appalling and roads were frequently swept away by landslides. There is considerable ethnic diversity in the region: a few Greeks remain, there are many Roma, and the people who live east of the town of Pazar are Laz speakers, whose heartland stretches to the border with Georgia. Until the 1920s there were substantial Armenian settlements in the interior. The Laz language is part of what linguists recognize as the Georgian-Mingrelian family, and is under considerable official pressure, although it is flourishing locally. A German linguist who has spent his academic career studying it has been banned from Turkey, on the grounds that he 'encourages Laz nationalism', even though there is no sign of any known Laz political party. The reality is that the authorities in Ankara wish to eliminate the language, and he has been struggling to preserve it, particularly its stories and folklore. In the past the Laz were great wanderers, anarchic egalitarian spirits, often seamen who worked for the Genoese or the Venetians, outside the mainstream of Turkish society. Ankara's repressive reaction to the Teutonic scholar and his activities is linked to geography, or Georgiarphy as a friend once put it in a Joycean pun. The Laz live next to the eastern border with Georgia, and the last thing the government wants is another dissident and culturally self-conscious minority with potentially separatist ambitions that might seek border revision and unity with their Georgian cousins.

The tea grown in the Laz region has been a great success in Turkey, but it has failed as an export crop because of quality problems. It has produced a more democratic farming culture in the Rize region, the centre of cultivation, where even the big landowners have gradually gone over to tea production. It has kept an effective rural culture alive in an area that was prone to depopulation, and integrated the inhabitants into the economic culture of the Turkish state. It has not, however, really produced any capital, and it required a large capital infusion to establish the industry. Profit is a chimera in this industry, which is a paradigm for many of the activities of the Turkish state as an investor: production proceeds well, but nothing that could be exported or privatized results. Characteristically, the factory for processing the tea is owned and operated by Lipton's, a subsidiary of the giant Anglo-Dutch multinational Unilever. As in Ottoman times, Turkey produces the raw material – green leaf tea – and consumes the final product, but a foreign company makes a great deal of money out of the intermediate processes.

The GAP hydroelectric schemes in the south-east have given Turkey control of the headwaters of the Tigris and the Euphrates rivers, which are of critical importance for the agriculture and prosperity of Syria and Iraq. In theory, the dams should lead to a revival of agriculture in the south-east, if peasants can be successfully converted from dry to wet farming techniques. As with most large-scale infrastructure development projects, the actual economic and political consequences may be very different from what the Ankara government planners envisaged, and probably much more mundane. Although 'water power' is supposed to replace 'oil power' in the Middle East at some indeterminate date in the future, there are no signs of it doing so at the moment. If Turkish relations with Syria continue to deteriorate, an Ankara government could, in theory, use the GAP system to cut off the vital water flow from the two rivers and destabilize

Syria. But nobody has attempted to use control of water to do this before in the Middle East, and the outcome would be quite unpredictable. To restrict the flow of water would be against international law and might well produce national unity around President Assad or his successors rather than political change in Damascus.

The GAP dams are, above all, symbols of the power of Turkish technology and the civil engineering industry, monuments to the tradition of statist and centralist industrial development that Atatürk established. Like many Atatürkist projects, or those in many developing countries, there are great political interests involved in their 'success'. The dams are certainly impressive and are very useful for foreign investors' brochures. Whether they will ever be more than that seems doubtful. However great the engineering achievement, the claim that they are likely to revolutionize the politics, economics or society of the south-east is belied by the Kurdish war. The war has developed into a cancer that is eating away the heart of Turkish society over the same period as the dams have been constructed. The technocratic and political realities have little relationship to one another.

8. The Islamic Renaissance

> About this time a great change came over Hassan's mind. He had often heard tell of the Dervishes, of their strange dancing services in the dim-lit *tekkes*, of the mystic doctrines they taught, and of the contempt with which the *ulema* regarded them. Hassan had no very deep veneration for the *mollahs* and *hojas*, and all the official hierarchy of Islam. It was not that he had thought about his religion in any critical way. He accepted it as he accepted the established order in everything. But there was a mystic turn to Hassan's mind. The cold precise dogmas of Islam had never touched his soul at all.
>
> Victoria de Bunsen, *The Soul of a Turk*, 1910

On the bus that rolls slowly across the Anatolian plateau, a small, well-dressed man is reading *Zaman*, a stout old newspaper that has now 'gone Islamic' and generally supports Refah, the Welfare Party, and the renewal of Islam in Turkey. I ask him why he supports Refah. He indicates in sign language that he is dumb. But he has understood the question. He points to a small cartoon in the middle of the paper, showing a boy entering a mosque and leaving with a copy of the Koran tucked under his arm, having discarded his Game Boy video machine outside on the steps like an empty sweet packet. Islam represents traditional knowledge, the rejection of consumerism and technological mindlessness, according to the cartoonist. It has nothing to do with fanaticism, xenophobia, violence or conquest; it is concerned with preserving Turkish religious tradition. My companion removes a pad from his pocket and carefully writes, 'I have three children. How many do you have?' We begin a dialogue on paper. It is warm, dignified, humane and very Turkish. Islam for him is communication – without a good traditional education, in a country where literacy is far from universal, he would not be able to communicate with anybody. He probably sees it being surrendered for a diminishing amount of foreign aid, often with political strings attached, and very little real investment. In 1995 foreign investment in Turkey was a quarter of the multinationals' investment in Hungary, a country with a sixth of the population. Few people understand what a devastating blow the collapse of Communism in 1989 has dealt to Turkey, with the diversion of millions of dollars of international money to the Christian ex-Communist countries to the north. Islam does not provide any economic answers, but at least it gives a cultural response for nationalist Turks.

Yet, for hundreds of years in Europe, the word 'Turk' had nothing to do with the modern concept of Turkish nationality, whereas in countries such as England or France national consciousness, however limited by class and education, was at least partially independent of religious identity. To be a Turk meant simply to be a Muslim, and resisting the expansion of Turkey meant resisting the expansion of Islam. Most other Muslim societies were backward and tribal. Even nations that are now very important, such as Saudi Arabia, Iran or Iraq, were until the 1950s too marginal and too far away to pose any threat to Western Christian society. The enormous impact on the West of President Nasser's revolution in Egypt is largely forgotten now, but at the time signalled the end of the political quiescence of the Islamic world under Western colonialism. Turkey had been the enemy, on Europe's doorstep, a tangible military threat for two centuries, and an ideological threat for much longer. It is arguable how much of this psychology permeates European reactions to Turkey today, in however distorted and unconscious a form. Although the West has recently waged war on a number of Islamic states, such as Iraq, none of them has common land borders with Europe (even if some of them are uncomfortably close, as Algeria is to France), and they are perceived as tyrannical regimes. The fact that Iraq is an Islamic state was unimportant in terms of Western public support for the Gulf War in 1990–91. Most educated Westerners realized that it was a war about oil and power as much as human rights, but they also realized that the Iraqi regime was one of the most venal in the world, and so military means to overthrow it appeared to be justified. Islam was irrelevant.

In Turkey under Atatürk, religion was to be considered a private matter, something confined to the mosque or the church, if it remained at all. The old Ottoman institutions that imposed religious law on the whole empire were some of the first bodies to be abolished after 1922, in the initial wave of Atatürk's revolutionary reforms. Today the mullah in his working clothes is a common sight in Turkish streets, so it is easy to forget how rigorously the outward power of Islam was repressed. The images that survive from the 1920s and 1930s are the positive ones – the great hospital building programmes, the new capital city on the Anatolian plateau, the draining of swamps, the building of dams – a kind of beneficent Stalinism, without the repression or the cruel labour camps; that is certainly how Ankara would like it to be seen. The propaganda has been very effective, and very few people know anything about the savage repression of Islam under Atatürk. There were great vested economic and political interests involved in discrediting the claims of Soviet Communism, but Turkey was too backward and marginal a country to attract comparable interest.

In the inter-war period, it was convenient to blame almost everything that was wrong with the old Turkey on the mullahs and the mosques, much as the United States today blames radical Islam for almost everything subversive in the Middle East. But there was serious repression, and it is not a subject which modern Turkey finds it easy or convenient to come to terms with. Open and radical criticism of the Atatürkist project is still difficult even in academic circles, and more or less impossible in state bodies. The ever-present members of the police and security service on university campuses, especially at the influential University of Istanbul, are the real indicators of the limits of intellectual freedom in these respects.

Western writers before the Second World War overlooked the problem of repression, or saw what they wanted to see, in the manner of many contemporary visitors to totalitarian states, such as Stalin's Russia or Hitler's Germany. The aesthetic school of Turkophiles was preoccupied with Ottoman traditions and buildings and sensual pleasures, and cared little for religious matters. The modernists saw nothing wrong with Atatürk's reforms. A typical book reflecting this was the popular *Allah Dethroned* by Lilo Linke, published in London in 1937. This enjoyable and well-written, but deeply misleading, work portrays a country where, before Atatürk, the mullahs had almost untrammelled power over every aspect of life and where their removal and the abolition of shariah law brought almost universal happiness. If 'capitalism' were substituted for 'Islam', and the place names changed, much of it could have been a sympathetic account of the contemporary Soviet Union. Many of the main social themes are identical, such as the literacy campaigns and the 'emancipation' of women. Lilo Linke knew a good deal about modern Turkish history, and her picture of the crisis in Armenian life, for instance, is very sympathetic, but the imams do not get a fair or objective press. It is wrong to suggest that they were the decisive force in the country, as they were before 1830. As a historical generalization, the mullahs and the ulema always tended to be strong when the sultan was weak; the religious institutions filled a political vacuum, if there was one, and that could apply at any time in the empire's history.

After the abolition of the caliphate in 1924, and Atatürk's dispatch of his opponents, there was little popular opposition to the regime, but the Islamic authorities were in a difficult position. At first they were prepared to bide their time, as it was far from clear what the future would hold. Some appeared to believe that the Atatürk regime was an artificial product of the revolutionary period during and after the First World War, which would not survive. The mosques and their administrative and legal apparatus had had a privileged and honoured position in Turkish society for hundreds of years, and were also central to the identity of the Turkish state. The grandeur and magnificence of buildings like the great Sinan mosques in Istanbul embody the glorious public life of the Ottoman Empire in a religious setting. It must have been very difficult for the imams to believe that all of this was to be swept away, even though their influence had been in decline for a long time. The ramshackle structure of the central religious authorities in Constantinople and their courts had failed to function properly since the reforms of the 1830s if not before. In many ways it was easier for the Christian and Jewish communities to adapt to the process of modernization, since they had a long history of relative independence from the Ottoman state under the *millet* system of self-governing religious communities.

Foreign writers visiting Turkey during the early Kemalist years tended to have few doubts about the modernization process, as titles such as *Allah Dethroned* and *Through the Garden of Allah* reveal. There were also various books with the word 'modern' in the title, such as E. G. Mears' authoritative general reference work *Modern Turkey*, published in 1924, intended to provide accurate information, particularly for business people, about what was happening in this 'new' society. (Mears is interesting for the student of economic history, as he shows a society that was open to foreign investment and trade in some respects. The reality of Atatürkist *dirigisme* has always been exaggerated in this sphere.) However, even in volumes of this kind, consideration of the position of religion is central. At this stage, in the 1920s, the attack on Islam was the central feature of Atatürk's revolution that attracted British and American attention.

The repression was very real, and even those who had fought

honourably to defend the country during and after the First World War were affected. A good example is a philosophical writer with Kurdish roots, Bediuzzaman Said Nursi, author of *The Words*, a famous Koranic commentary. He was born in 1877 in eastern Turkey, deep in the old world, both geographically and intellectually. He died as a very old man in 1960 in Urfa, also in the far east. He lived through the revolutionary period, the repression and the slight liberalization in the position of Islam after 1950. He had been a religious student whose great abilities gave him an audience with the sultan in 1907, and he tried to found an Islamic university. But the times were not propitious, and although the foundations were laid in 1913, nothing came of the project. In the war, he volunteered as an ordinary soldier, and won a war medal on the eastern front, fighting the Russians. He was taken prisoner in 1916, and held by the Russians for two years, before escaping and returning to Istanbul via Warsaw, Berlin and Vienna. His travels in the West increased his interest in science, and he spent most of the rest of his life writing philosophical texts reconciling traditional Islam with modern science. But despite his progressive outlook, and his exemplary national credentials as a soldier, he was gaoled after the 1925 Kurdish uprising in the far east, and sent to Barla, a tiny village in the Isparta mountains. As he was not allowed writing materials while he was there, he had to dictate his work in secret to a local scribe. Printing presses were banned for Islamic texts, so copies of his work had to be made by hand and circulated illegally throughout Turkey. It was not until the period of relative liberalization after the Second World War that duplicating machines were allowed, and only in 1956 that his works could be printed. The whole unhappy odyssey, for a man who could not be described as anything other than a patriot and a moderate, illustrates the parallels between state repression under Atatürk and his successors and the suppression of religion in the Soviet Union. Even the dates of liberalization coincide, with 1956 a key date in both countries.

In the 1930s many European writers took the view that Islam had been vanquished, whereas in fact it had been driven underground, but the greatest mistake many commentators have made is to see Turkish Islam as a monolithic block. This stems from the fact that they confuse nationality with religion, which does not do justice to the variety of faith in the country, still less to the social implications of religion, as recent riots involving members of the predominantly lower class Alevi minority in Istanbul have shown. The history of Islam in Turkey is complex. The Ottoman conquest took hundreds of years to take over the whole country, large parts of which were already subject to independent Islamic influence from a number of sources, such as Iran, while some of the most important cities and centres of government, notably Constantinople, were not Islamic in their original culture and retained very large non-Muslim minorities. The rich Greek and Armenian business communities were incorporated into the Ottoman system, while many strands of Islam, such as the Bektashis, who appealed principally to the poor, or at least to non-privileged groups, became almost underground movements. When Atatürk attempted to finally dethrone Islam, he could be seen to be completing a process that had begun with the nineteenth century reforms; he formally banned the dervish and Bektashi movements, but they had been persecuted intermittently by the religious authorities and the government for hundreds of years.

The picture of a uniform Islamic society embodied in some modernist and technocratic Western definitions of Turkey is wrong and misleading. Although the history of the early Islamic states in Turkey is very complex, shariah law was never fully institutionalized in Turkey's government, as in some countries. The Sunni majority have always been 'moderate' compared with the rest of the Islamic world, and this was remarked on by visitors from the West throughout the Ottoman period. Since the early nineteenth century a reform process had been in train that was progressively reducing the power of the mosques and the imams, against a constitutional background that made it clear that the sultan, seeing himself as successor to the caliph, had never really ceded much power to the clerical authorities. Although the Ottoman Empire was basically a theocratic state, the sultan was the real arbiter on many issues that in a 'fundamentalist' Islamic state are exclusively reserved for clerical jurisdiction. (In that sense the defenders of Atatürk's heritage who accuse the Refah Party of wanting to put the clock back to Ottoman times are tilting at windmills.) Only under the weakest and most feeble sultans did the ulema become the decisive political power in the land. Turkish Sunni Islam has always had to live with a strong state, and never had the opportunity to aspire to secular dominance. It also had to live with religious minorities for hundreds of years, under the Porte, with very large minorities of Jews and Christians, such as Greeks and Armenians, inhabiting important areas of the capital city. Great sultans such as Selim II (1566–74) encouraged the settlement of minorities such as the Jews from Catholic Spain.

The victory of the Refah Party in the December 1995 elections has meant that mosque–state relations are likely to be at the forefront of Turkish politics once again, whether Refah remains in the government or not. The nature of the Refah Party has been subject to much debate and frequent distortion in the West. Too many commentators have lumped it together with Iranian, Algerian and Egyptian radicalism as part of an international conspiracy that threatens the West. In Turkey this is a serious distortion of reality. The *New York Herald Tribune* reported the results in the 1995 poll thus: 'Welfare won the most seats at the December 24 elections in the first victory by an Islamist party at general polls in modern Turkey's 72-year history as a strictly secular republic.' This begs many questions, notably whether Turkey has been 'a strictly secular republic' for any length of time. Even after the military coup of 1980, when avowedly 'secular' generals were in total control of the government, Islamist influence within the state increased markedly.

The career of the leader of the Refah Party, Necmettin Erbakan, exemplifies the realities, rather than the myths, of Turkish Islamic politics. He is a short, genial, formally dressed man in late middle age, who has been in Turkish politics since the late 1960s. Like so many of his peers, including Turgut Ozal, he was an engineer, one of the typical technocrats bred by the Atatürkist programme, with a high position in the statist industrial *apparat*. He was elected an independent Islamist MP for the conservative town of Konya in 1969, after a quarrel with the then prime minister, Suleyman Demirel, whom he accused of sacking him as head of a prestigious industrial group because of his Islamic commitment. This alone punctures the first, all-pervasive Western myth about Refah – that it has sprung from nowhere to head an Islamic radical mass movement. There has always been a number of serious Islamists in the Turkish ruling coterie, even in Atatürk's time, and, provided people kept their views to themselves, promotion to the highest levels was possible, outside the military sphere, even in the secularist 1930s. In the now legendary quarrel with Demirel, which certainly took place, it is likely that matters other than God were involved, including Mr Erbakan's frustrated ambition, and his business arrangements.

Necmettin Erbakan's family background indicates the strength and cultural importance of the lingering Ottoman heritage. He was born in the northern town of Sinope in 1926, one of six children of a father who served as a *kadi*, a travelling Islamic judge, in the collapsing Ottoman system. This did not prevent Erbakan, a man of obvious ability if of dissident views, from serving in traditional Turkish governments. He was deputy prime minister in two coalition governments in the 1970s – chaotic, ineffective administrations that in many ways prepared the ground for the military coup in 1980. His opponents nowadays claim that the then prime minister, Bulent Ecevit, distrusted Erbakan so much that when he left the country on official business in 1974 he refused to leave his deputy the powers of prime minister. At a superficial level, Erbakan's links with the old political élite may detract from his image as a popular, radical Islamic politician, but in fact this phase of his career typifies a particular stage in the development of Turkish Islam as a political force: a period of uneasy collaboration, mutual distrust and little practical achievement.

If the 1950s and 1960s meant the re-establishment of traditional Islamic culture and education as a social force in Turkey, in the 1970s and 1980s those who had benefited from this restoration were starting to emerge from universities and enter the labour market. The climate was not yet ripe for open mass struggle against secularism to create a more Islamic society. Erbakan made his way right to the top, but there were many others in less prominent positions in Turkish institutions. (The social basis for this movement existed because 'conservative' towns like Konya and Sivas had never been incorporated into the Atatürkist project in any real sense; some foreign diplomats might have been less surprised about the Islamic revival in the 1990s if they had ventured more outside Ankara and Istanbul.) Educated Islamists in these years gained increasing prominence in many professions and occupations and were at last able to penetrate the Ministry of the Interior, with its monopoly of regulation-making powers and influence over aspects of policing. In the 1980s, the struggle against pornography as a symbol of Western corruption was important, and Islamic influence in the Interior Ministry secured one of its first victories: the much derided green plastic bags that cover up magazines like *Playboy* and *Penthouse*. Islam's growing influence was the culmination of a natural process, in which the cultural struggle against empty Western materialism and consumerism was critically important, especially among the Turkish masses, who did not benefit from it but saw it as the ideology of a corrupt, self-serving and rich élite.

Another quiet achievement of the Refah movement in these years was the establishment of a national party organization.

One of the guiding principles of the Islamists has been to avoid the political fate of the Turkish Marxist left, with its rigid cadre structure. On many occasions information from the secret police has enabled the government to destroy opposition by selective arrests, imprisonment and torture of activists. The Refah Party is decentralized. It has a large network of informal party sympathizers who are never pressed to join as formal members if they do not wish to do so; a strong, open organization of local party offices that would be difficult for a hostile government to destroy; and a cautious relationship with the army that avoids head-on conflict. The party itself now boasts over 300,000 members, a formidable number, by Turkish standards. Local government is an important aspect of Refah thinking, and some of its appeal lies in its promise to restore aspects of traditional Turkish local democracy that have been eroded by centralism since the 1970s. Almost three quarters of the Turkish population now come under Refah-governed mayoralities after its victories in the local elections of 1994 and 1996. Different currents of opinion exist within the party, as is to be expected in such a large organization, and it has a moderate and radical wing.

If the movement were not Islamic, the organization might be seen as a product of Turkish democracy, but 1994 coincided with the growth of aggressive and revolutionary Islamic radicalism in north Africa, and some commentators assumed the same process was happening in Turkey. More importantly, the advance of Refah is anathema to the army and the secular middle-class establishment, who see it as the party of the poor and dispossessed, with an economic programme that would destroy many traditional privileges. The central issues are those of international relations and defence. Refah had promised to loosen Turkish ties with NATO when the party came to power, close important NATO bases and renegotiate the EU–Turkish Customs Union. This is often linked to a grandiose project to build a new Muslim world economic order. The rhetoric is calculated to send a chill down the spine of NATO officials, with Mr Erbakan recently denouncing 'world imperialism and Zionism as well as Israel and the champagne-drinking Turkish collaborators in the holding companies that feed it'.

Mr Erbakan's thinking, if not that of Refah generally, with his emphasis on 'the Muslim Commonwealth', is reminiscent of the old ideology of the Pan-Turkish right. An Islamic United Nations has been promised, as well as an Islamic version of NATO, and even an Islamic version of the EU. It could all be seen as a modern version of the Ottoman world, with Mr Erbakan casting himself as a charming and intelligent but slightly ludicrous successor to the caliph. What would happen in practice if there were a majority Refah government remains to be seen, but there is no doubt about the strength of its anti-NATO commitment, and the anti-Americanism involved. In government the Refah Party found itself with little room for economic manoeuvre, due to a collapsing currency and major economic crisis. Some Western pessimists have forecast a return to the 1970s, with armed left- and right-wing groups bringing the country to its knees. It is likely that the World Bank and the IMF and other similar agencies would prevent much change in the economic orientation of the country, so a much more independent foreign policy may be all that Mr Erbakan can offer his followers. His statements after the outstanding performance of the party in the 1995 elections brought it to the brink of government seem to reflect this:

The RP will now establish the new government and it will solve Turkey's problems. No one should have the slightest doubt about this. Let me immediately add, especially for the benefit of our foreign press members, that these results will also serve the interests of foreign countries.

He went on to say that Refah felt that until now Western countries had tried to interfere in certain areas of Turkish life, that the country had been driven to poverty on the basis of IMF directives, and Turkey had failed to develop as a result of this meddling and exploitation. It was an illuminating statement, not least because almost every word could have been uttered by Atatürk himself back in the 1920s, in particular the emphasis on the need to secure national control of economic resources.

Refah policy is based on three principles that may determine the future of fully Islamic government in Turkey. The first is populist democracy – the need to involve the grass roots in social and economic development – and an end to the centralist and authoritarian model of Atatürk's Ankara, with its dead weight of authority and bureaucracy. In Mr Erbakan's words in January 1996, 'We will do what the people want. We will not quarrel with the people, their history or their beliefs.' The second principle is an integration of Islam and the state, and an end to the isolation of Turkey from the rest of the Muslim world. This has meant a major policy change and a radical reorientation of Turkey towards countries like Iran and Libya. The third principle is to restore the authority of parliament. Although on the surface this is the most innocuous and uncontroversial provision, in practice it involves the most dangerous potential confrontation for Refah, as considerable power is still held by the National Security Council and its closed circle of military advisers. It means that Refah will have to take on the power of the military and security *apparat* in government to achieve this central objective, and it is here that the party is most vulnerable, as the outlook and orientation of this leading group is heavily influenced by the United States and NATO.

However much it caters for nostalgia, and the sympathy the mass of Turks have for traditional values, Islam cannot solve the problems of the population explosion and the shortage of jobs quickly or easily. Young men still sit in the cafés reading the German newspapers.

Adapazar is a dull, middle-sized town on the old main road between Ankara and Istanbul, famous in the past only for the aqueduct built by Justinian I in 560, which stretches majestically across a small river outside the town. It is fairly near the new Toyota plant – some Adapazarians work there. There is a plastics factory, some engineering and garage jobs, and the usual mixture of small shops and cafés of any Turkish town. And there are several mosques, with dusty, worn minarets that no writers of tourist guides ever bother to visit. As such it is typical of any town between Sarajevo and Bangladesh. There are no Christian churches in or near the town. Islam is strong here, the Refah Party polls well, but it is difficult to see what a more Islamic state could give to the loyal Muslim people that they do not have already. In Ramadan Adapazar could be a town in Iran; it is so quiet that the mew of a stray cat breaks the silence in the middle of the day.

Here Refah is very clearly defined; a vote for Refah is a vote against the bosses, for the poor against the rich and corrupt. Yet the endless complexity of Turkish society means there is another story to Adapazar, one that has nothing to do with class or money, but everything to do with religion and the Ottoman heritage. One reason for the piety and conservatism of the town is that most of the inhabitants are descended from Chechens and Circassians who were settled on what was a malarial swamp in the nineteenth century. They were Muslims, refugees from the tsar's wars in the Caucasus, driven from their homes by the scimitars of the Don Cossacks. They had to work very hard to make Adapazar a habitable town, and no doubt they did not feel they were well governed in Ottoman times, just as their descendants have little time for what they see as the manipulative foreigners, lazy and corrupt bureaucrats and the idle rich of Ankara today.

In the capital, of course, things look a little different. It is difficult and often depressing to try to govern a country like Turkey, when the headlines in the American newspapers read TURKISH ECONOMY REELS FROM MULTIPLE ILLS, or TURKEY, HELD BACK BY INSTABILITY, STRUGGLES TO BOOST COMPETITIVENESS (*Wall Street Journal*, February

1996). The bureaucrats have to try to move society and the economy forward. The working classes can leave if it all gets too difficult, and from towns like Adapazar hundreds of thousands do. In a country where most families still have several children rather than the two or so of northern Europe, it is as normal for a family member to try to get a job in Germany as it was in nineteenth century Ireland to try to buy a passage to America.

9. *The Turkish Diaspora*

Turkey is a land without unemployment.

Ankara government handbook, 1938

In reality, every country has its unemployed, even if they have to leave their native land to find work. Before the Second World War, Turks simply returned to their villages if they could not find a job in the city. Now there are other cities to work and settle in, far from Turkey.

The Wedding district of Berlin, four miles north of the city centre, with its tall factory chimneys dating from the 1920s, recalls the proletarian plays of Brecht and the revolutionary tones of Schoenberg's pupil Hans Eisler. The atmosphere is old working-class Germany, with its little dark *kneipers*, small local pubs that survived the RAF bombing, serving cheap *korn* schnapps. But the corner shops are full of *dolmades* and *kefliku*. The German workers have long since gone; probably few of them returned after the war, as this part of Berlin provided some of the last regiments that perished on the Russian front. It is now a *gastarbeiter*, mostly Turkish, suburb.

Until very recently Turkey has not had a significant diaspora, unlike Britain or France, despite its large and influential empire. Few cities in the ex-Ottoman world now have a recognizable Turkish quarter. Turkish influence of course remains, but is often confused by modern visitors with Arab or Islamic cultural traditions.

The nature of the Ottoman Empire did not lend itself to large numbers of Turks voluntarily settling abroad. Diaspora communities, from the ancient Greek colonists onwards, have usually been based on trade and commerce, and in the Ottoman world much of that was in the hands of minorities such as Armenians, Greeks and Jews. The typical Turk was a soldier or administrator, living a garrison life and returning to Turkey after a term of service expired, rather than a trader who for business reasons had to put down roots in the local community. The ethos of conquering and enjoying the fruits of conquest continued as it had for hundreds of years. Landownership was a major obstacle to the development of an independent diaspora, as all land remained, at least in theory, the property of the Ottoman state. The imperial administrators were directly answerable to the Porte and their lives resembled those of Western diplomats in difficult East European missions during the Cold War: they had little or no contact with local communities. The army officers often had a difficult time ingratiating themselves with non-Turks, as Atatürk himself found when stationed in Sofia before the First World War. A biographer, H. C. Armstrong, describes his difficulties with the Bulgarian women:

He frequented the drawing rooms and tried to become the society gallant, making love to the ladies of Sofia, but they found him excessively gauche. . . . They had no liking for Turks at any time. He understood nothing of the play of light flirtation, he bluntly demanded that each lady should bed with him; if she refused he ceased to be interested but, as bluntly, asked another. . . . He began to hate the fashionable women with their soft ways and their chatter, who would not make love wholeheartedly but teased and tormented his desire. With men – and with the loose women of the capital – Mustafa Kemal was far more at ease. With these, in the cafés and the brothels, he drank and revelled night after night far into the dawn.

If a man of the standing, intellect and personal magnetism of Atatürk encountered these difficulties in a civilized if dull and clique-ridden city like Sofia, the isolation and emptiness of the lives of most Turks in remote and primitive places like the Yemen and Mesopotamia can only be imagined. Atatürk wrote in a letter to his intimate friend, Corinne Lutfu, in 1913 that 'it isn't possible to see even one beautiful woman in Sofia'.

At the end of Rakovski street in Sofia the Military Club is an imposing *fin de siècle* building painted yellow ochre. Rakovski nowadays is *mafioski* mile, with gun shops and cheap hotels and quiet conspiracies taking place in the gloomy old Budapest restaurant. And it is dangerous: a contract killing costs only 2,000 dollars. Sofia has always had this dimension; in Atatürk's time it cost as little as five gold coins to pay for an Internal Macedonian Revolutionary Organization gunman to assassinate somebody. Half-way down the street on the left is the Slavanska Bessada Hotel, which was a front for the secret police under Communism. Now it is the home of Piotr from Leningrad, who deals in cheap caviare and handguns. There has always been violence and intrigue here; even the shadowy doorways by the Suzuki garage selling modern diesel generators embody the spirit of Ottoman intrigue, the plotter, the bomber, the double cross, secret assignations and flashing eyes in the darkness.

In Atatürk's time, Rakovski street was the most fashionable in town. When he arrived in Sofia in 1913, it was as the Porte's military attaché to all the Balkan countries. After the Balkan wars even these relationships had quickly returned to normal. The Turkish officers who frequented the bars and soirées at the Military Club were welcomed in the Balkan way, where an enemy can become a friend overnight, and vice versa. Suddenly they were honoured guests of the Bulgarians rather than oppressors. For Atatürk it represented political exile, a punishment for association with the failed Young Turk revolt in 1908. In retrospect, the boredom and humiliations of Sofia may have saved him from the Balkan terrorist *komitajis*, who were still part of the anti-Ottoman movement. But Turks of his class were not the only Turks in Bulgaria.

Many foreign travellers of the time seem to have hardly noticed the existence of an ethnic Turkish minority in Bulgaria, except for passing tobacco traders bringing their heavily laden wagons into towns, or Friday gatherings around the central Sofia mosque by the municipal baths. But not so Atatürk. He seems to have been impressed by the decent position of the ethnic Turkish peasants, their emancipation from the old ways – most women were unveiled and, like their fellow Bulgarian peasants, possessed a degree of self-respect and independence that were rare in Turkey itself. Some Turks were rich and had become businessmen, trading in food and *raki* with Thessaloniki and Constantinople. They helped Atatürk form an image of what Turkish peasants might be like if they were freed from the trammels of Islam and repressive patterns of landownership.

The poor who made up the Bulgarian diaspora in Ottoman times were often ignored, like the peasants who were moved into Macedonia in the late empire to try to boost Muslim and Turkish numbers, or stranded Turkish soldiers left in Albania in 1913. As a political factor in the Communist period it seemed completely irrelevant, and even today the interests of the Turkish minority in the Former Yugoslav Republic of Macedonia are often overlooked by outside powers when considering its future. The Turks who go abroad now are mostly economic migrants, except for large numbers of Kurdish political refugees. The Turkish Communists exiled abroad during the Cold War have mostly returned home. The vast majority of Turks abroad have always occupied lowly social and economic positions, and, unlike Greeks or Jews who may have started poor but prospered, Turks often stay that way. In the conflicts in Germany over the Kurdish issue, local Turkish spokesmen often appear inarticulate, incompetent in dealings with the media, and poor spokesmen for Ankara's cause.

The Bulgarian Turks, and those who were settled elsewhere in the Balkans, Central Asia and the Arab world, are part of the old diaspora. The new diaspora is very different. Like many poor nations on the periphery of the EU, Turkey provides a supply of cheap labour from rural areas to do the menial and badly paid jobs which Western Europeans do not want to take.

Germany is at the heart of this diaspora; 1.6 million Turkish people live there today, and as many as 5 million have lived or worked in Germany since the end of the 1950s, when the labour shortages of the booming German factories led to mass migration. In terms of class, they are as near the bottom of the heap as the poor peasants of the Ottoman diaspora. West Berlin was an early centre, with districts near the Berlin Wall like Kreuzberg becoming crowded with thousands of Turkish migrants. Mostly poor and uneducated peasants from Anatolia, unaccustomed to urban life, they were a pliable and docile labour force and accepted without question their lowly place in German society. As trade unions were either banned in Turkey or docile creatures of the government, they were ideal material for German employers. Although open racism was uncommon in the early days, social discrimination was normal and educational facilities for the immigrants in their own language were non-existent.

Gradually community facilities were developed, more enlightened employers provided industrial training, and a network of Turkish-owned small businesses has grown up around the *gastarbeiter* communities, such as travel agents, restaurants, specialist grocers and so on, which the more open-minded Germans accept has enriched German urban life. The mosque has followed – there are over fifty Turkish mosques in Germany, with more under construction. Some parts of cities such as Solingen and Munich are now completely Turkified.

But integration of so many immigrants is hard for any nation, especially a country struggling with difficult post-war conditions and the need to form a new national identity after the horrors of Nazism. A Turkish ambassador to Bonn once described the Turks in the old Federal Republic as a people of 1.6 million hopes, not 1.6 million problems, but the latter have often predominated. Alienation, alcoholism, family problems such as domestic violence and divorce, and vicious political infighting have become the norm in many diaspora communities. A minor industry of specialist social workers has grown up in Germany dealing with the problems of the Turkish community. Neo-Nazis and extreme right-wingers have benefited from these tensions. With no hope of becoming German under the present nationality laws, except by rare inter-marriages, and a climate of increasing anti-immigrant feeling that makes changes in the law politically impossible for any German government, however well intentioned, the long-term Turkish communities have been turning in on themselves and rediscovering their cultural traditions. In practice, that means the rediscovery of Islam. Home for workers such as Ovul Ozgur, a fat, quiet man from Bursa, has become the mosque as much as his small flat in Berlin. Ramadan is increasingly strictly observed, even by secular Turks. It is unfashionable in the more devout communities, such as Berlin's inner city, to be seen drinking alcohol during these weeks of the year, although the Islamic rules are often broken at private gatherings. Traditional festivals are being celebrated in public; many Germans are offended by the slaughter of sheep during the feast of Bajram the Great. Community relations worsen a little further, and racialist feelings become increasingly prevalent in large sections of German society.

The long days of grinding work at BMW have changed Ovul from the cheerful secular optimist he was five years ago into a gloomy and prejudiced Welfare Party stalwart – someone who works in the West because it is economically necessary but who is no more part of it than the Iranian militants who assembled in the same meeting halls in the 1970s. They sat there then and listened to traditional Iranian music before planning the overthrow of the Shah of Persia. They, too, worked on the track in the BMW factory and received excellent training and welfare benefits from the same employers and generous state social workers. Iranian Islamic passion and commitment were hidden under the same *gut ordnung* of German industry and under super-clean overalls.

The Koran offers hope of a just Islamic society where the traditional guidelines would be observed, and where the Turk would have self-respect and not be reduced to a mere hewer of wood and drawer of water for the often arrogant and indifferent Teutonic industrial Moloch. Unlike Greeks, Turks are often not good at living abroad; in cultural terms they suffer an inferiority complex and are easily offended. The Greek diaspora has a long and distinguished history and for many generations it has been normal for some members of Greek families to seek their fortune overseas. Something of Greek culture is known and respected, if not always well understood, in most host communities, in particular in the United States and Australia. This is not the case for Turks, whose history, language or culture is almost unknown outside the ranks of academic specialists. Most Turks, from all classes and viewpoints, feel their culture is completely misunderstood and distorted in the West, and the behaviour of the less sensitive German lower middle class on package holidays in Turkey or uttering racist sentiments in the bar does nothing to dispel this prejudice. Turkish education stresses the long and distinguished history of the country, the beauties of the Turkish land and sea, the glories of the early Ottomans, and the dignity and values of Turkish life. Turks see themselves as the heirs to Byzantium, ancient Rome and even to some aspects of ancient Greece, usually referred to as a 'classical society' in the Turkish school textbooks.

Germans see themselves as hard-working and progressive 'Europeans' and often equate cultural development and progress with economic materialism and the progress of industry. There are few points of contact between the communities, other than in the world of work, where most Germans give orders and most Turks carry them out. The relationship mirrors, in reverse, the world of the Ottoman *beys* and *rayahs*. Reduced to an underclass without effective political rights, it does not take conscious racism, only general insensitivity, to raise Turkish hackles, and most Turks in Germany are highly critical of their host country. It remains, though, the only country in the West prepared to take large numbers of Turkish immigrant workers, even though the palmy days of the late 1970s and early 1980s are over, when almost anybody, regardless of qualifications, could get a Federal German visa and work permit.

Turks are chained to the German industrial machine, like Prometheus to his rock, whether they like it or not. For many years, the Bonn view has been that the Turks are fortunate to receive training in an industrial society and to be able to accumulate a little capital that enables them to start businesses when they return home. The latter may be true, but most Turks do unskilled jobs in Germany, even now, and when they return home with their savings the height of their aspirations is to be a taxi driver or corner shopkeeper. While no doubt worthwhile occupations, this does not lead to the revitalization or structural modernization of the Turkish economy. There is little transfer of real skills, even if many people do manage some form of self-employment on their return. The small minority of young Turks educated in Germany who gain technical or professional qualifications tend to stay in Germany and become doctors, dentists or lawyers ministering to the diaspora communities, rather than returning to assist Turkish development. If they do return, it is usually to professional life in Istanbul or other large cities, rather than to their grandfathers' villages.

It is difficult for most Turkish women to gain acceptance in the German labour market, and the diaspora has done little to improve the chances of women in the national labour market if they return home. The stresses and strains of life in German society, and the absence of the extended family, tend to lead to women staying at home in the new ghettos in German cities, and the chances of employment after motherhood are virtually nil. This is also the case when a family returns, with the exception of part-time jobs such as helping out at the village shop.

Ankara's view of the diaspora used to closely mirror that of Bonn, except that undue emphasis was put on the likelihood of people returning home with substantial savings to invest. If the comparison is between the financial status of peasants in rural

Anatolia in the 1960s and 1970s and that of contemporary Mercedes assembly workers in Stuttgart, then Germany promises riches indeed, but what is not made clear is that this is not capital accumulation, merely high wages, much of which have to be spent immediately to sustain life in Germany. Ankara governments were grateful that Bonn provided *gastarbeiter* visa and residence opportunities, but were less keen on the politicization of many workers in Germany exposed to potentially subversive concepts like free trade unions.

Nowadays things have moved on from these simplistic economic relationships, partly as a result of the Kurdish crisis. With the war in the east dragging on, thousands of Kurds have moved abroad to seek safety, and a prime destination has been Germany, because of its liberal political asylum laws and the fact that Kurdish communities have existed in most German cities for many years. Residence and work in Germany has been a politicizing experience for most Kurds. The PKK, the Kurdish Workers Party, has established itself deep in these communities, and has developed an underground support network for the campaign in the east as well as ways of helping people on the run from the Turkish security services. Self-help educational provision has improved many Kurds' level of education, and literacy rates are much higher among diaspora Kurds than those who have remained in Turkey. In eastern Anatolia, illiteracy is still about 40 per cent, with even higher rates in the Kurdish communities as a result of the nationalist-led boycott of the monoglot Turkish education system.

In Germany, especially in cities with a radical political tradition like Berlin and Munich, many young Germans have 'adopted' the Kurdish cause. Education classes in the Kurdish language are often interspersed with political education and have produced an intellectual radicalization of the Kurdish communities. Large amounts of money have been raised by German supporters of the Kurdish cause, which is being used to produce a new generation of educated, radical leaders of the nationalist movement. The government in Ankara, especially the hardline National Security Council with experience of the war in the east, has expressed alarm at the implications for the country. They see it as developing into something similar to the support and weapons procurement networks that Irish radicals have always had in the United States, from the time of the nineteenth-century Fenians to the contemporary IRA. As a result, all Kurdish political activity in the diaspora is seen as support for the PKK and for 'terrorism', and there is at least some truth in the notion. A good deal of the responsibility for this must be attributed to the Turkish government. In a political climate that makes any assertion of non-Turkish identity potentially subversive, it is hardly surprising if the diaspora leads to a flowering of Kurdish cultural and political activity. The Turkish communities act as both a safety-valve for the crisis and an exacerbation of it. Although little is known about the organization of the underground PKK in Germany, unlike the more open military command in Syria and northern Iraq, it seems certain that the revolutionaries are steadily broadening their base of support in the diaspora. This is not a situation any Turkish government could neglect.

In response to intense pressure from Ankara, the German government banned the PKK in Germany in 1994, claiming it was a terrorist organization. According to independent press reports appearing since in Germany and Britain, this appears to have been counter-productive, and has not led to a significant decrease in PKK activity. If anything, the ban has heightened the alienation of many ordinary Kurds from German society, and, according to a survey published in Germany in mid-1995, has increased both the membership and the active sympathizers of the PKK by several thousand recruits. The democratically oriented German intelligence service does not appear to have either the will or the capacity to infiltrate the Kurdish movement in German cities, and as long as Kurds restrict their activities to Turkish rather than German targets, it seems unlikely that the

PKK and its front organizations will be seriously threatened by the German government.

An effective operation against the PKK in Germany would produce uproar in the Kurdish diaspora and the possibility of serious human-rights violations. Without infiltration of the PKK, the police would not have accurate information to act on, and many of the wrong people would be arrested. It would be almost impossible to obtain convictions in the courts if evidence were required from Kurdish witnesses, and, in the event of convictions upon false evidence, violent action against German government targets would be very likely. An immediate response from the German media and public to such a PKK campaign would be to call for the expulsion of entire Kurdish communities. As many of the members of these communities have been granted political asylum, this would be against most federal laws and wholly impractical, as well as being virtually genocidal if ever carried out. During Turkey's military campaign in Iraq against PKK bases in spring 1995, large demonstrations for and against the war were held in German cities by the opposed diaspora communities, and, while on the whole public order was maintained, the potential for widespread disorder and intercommunal conflict in Germany certainly exists. The government ban on the PKK did not affect the capacity of the Kurds to organize their protests. The noisy and militant gatherings will not have increased the popularity of the immigrant communities among respectable Germans who are already highly prejudiced against the Turkish *gastarbeiters*.

In Bulgaria this world of bitter and often dangerous political and military struggle seems remote, at first sight. The sleepy world of the Turkish peasants is that of tobacco growing, the café and the mosque, life lived in poverty and slow motion, far from the political turmoil of the German communities. But there is a link. In the aftermath of Communism many Bulgarian Turks have also sought political asylum in Germany, having suffered intense repression of their Bulgarian Turkish identity under the

Zhivkov regime. Relations between the ethnic Turkish minority and most Bulgarians had been poor for many years, long before Communism, and emigration from these communities to Turkey has been a consistent feature of Bulgarian life. The high birthrate of the Turks, compared to the very low Bulgarian birthrate, has meant that the proportion of ethnic Turks in the population has remained roughly the same over the years. In the 1980s Turks were threatened with long prison sentences if they refused to change their names to Bulgarian forms, and tanks and armed soldiers with savage dogs surrounded rebellious Turkish villages. Germany seemed to represent freedom and security, an alternative to the streets and car parks of Istanbul, where so many people who had spent quiet and productive lives in southern Bulgaria were forced to camp.

The situation of both groups is a metaphor for the inextricable role of Turkey's problems in Western Europe. Germany is the heart of the diaspora and it is possible that the fate of Kurdistan may eventually be decided there. However, conflict is not confined to German soil. In tranquil Berne, in Switzerland, Turkish diplomats opened fire on Kurdish demonstrators in 1994 from their embassy building, causing local outrage. In Greece there are many Kurdish exiles and some of the assassinations of Turkish diplomats and other officials over the years are probably linked to Kurdish nationalism.

Britain has avoided serious problems of this nature, largely because of the limited number of Kurds granted political asylum. In the late 1980s there were many applicants, but the Home Office claimed speciously that they were 'economic migrants', an example of the strong support the Thatcher government gave to the Ozal government in Ankara. There has been little real change since, with every effort being made to prevent the build-up of Kurdish *émigré* communities in British cities, the quiet exclusion of known PKK sympathizers, and even academics. No doubt intelligence information is exchanged with Ankara about *émigré* political activities, although given the limited expertise of Special Branch and MI5 in this field, its value may be small. British Kurdistan occupies a small square of territory in Hackney, although there are Kurds scattered all over north and east London and there are small communities in some provincial centres like Manchester and Sheffield. The traditional Marxist left is still quite influential in the Turkish diaspora in Britain, and relations between the Kurds and Turkish immigrants are not as bad as in Germany – the main Turkish bookshop in north London even sells some Kurdish material and Kurdish newspapers. The left has always claimed that the Kurdish issue is a product of the racist nature of the Turkish state and capitalist patterns of land ownership, coupled with the manipulation of Turkish internal policy by the United States and NATO.

A complicating factor in Britain is the existence of a large, well organized and politically influential Turkish Cypriot community, much larger than the mainstream Turkish diaspora. Most of these people have been in Britain since the turmoil in Cyprus in the 1960s and 1970s, and some for much longer than that. The leader of the Turkish Cypriots, Rauf Denktash, was a barrister in London in the 1950s before he returned to Cyprus. In the main the Turkish Cypriots are strongly anti-Kurdish, and support the most radical nationalist positions of their *de facto* government in Ankara, but they have their own separate quarrels which have prevented the Kurdish issue from dominating the communities, although there have been some bitter individual conflicts, with assassinations of leading figures on both sides. But the London quarrels seem more like family feuds compared to massive inter-community struggles in cities like Dortmund, Essen and Solingen.

The Cyprus issue dominates the British diaspora to the exclusion of all others. Even the relatively few mainland Turks in London and Birmingham often work for Turkish Cypriot employers and so are drawn into the periphery of the conflict with Greece and the Greek Cypriots. Most Turkish Cypriots in Britain live close to Greek Cypriots, and sometimes have common business interests, as was the case with Turkish Cypriot entrepreneur Asil Nadir. Greek Cypriots helped set up his company, Polly Peck, and some of the east London rag trade companies that formed the original core of Polly Peck were owned by Greek Cypriots.

These social conditions have meant that a separate, well defined Turkish identity has been slower to evolve in Britain than elsewhere in Europe. There is a scattering of middle-class Turks – exiled bankers, diplomats and representatives of the big Turkish companies – but little sense of an exiled community, as in Germany, Switzerland or even in Melbourne in Australia.

The British business associations tend to be right-wing; many companies are involved in defence-related industries which have close links with the military and industrial establishment in Ankara. Although these links are no doubt very favourable to the companies involved, they often do not present an appetizing picture of Turkey to the wider British public. The sight of, say, Rover riot-control vehicles on the streets of south-east Turkey intimidating unarmed Kurdish civilians is the kind of publicity the company prefers to avoid. The defence sales establishment has close links with the upper echelons of the Conservative Party in Britain, which has a long history of supporting the status quo in Turkey, ever since Disraeli found ways to apologize for the sultan in the nineteenth century. Moreover British diplomats who have specialized in Turkey often see the Kurdish problem as exclusively one of 'terrorism'; many become almost more Turkish than the Turks themselves.

To one strand of opinion in Ankara, these negative images hardly matter: what is important is the number of British tourists on Turkish beaches, which is increasing, and the revenue brought in from other commercial contracts. But this is a short-sighted, economistic view. If Turkey wishes to accomplish its foreign-policy objectives in Europe, it can only do so with the support of the educated European public. Turkey has had very limited influence among British politicians, for many reasons: the lack of Turkish commitment to the Allied cause in the Second World

War; the pervasive influence of Hellenism; the economic strength of the Greek Cypriot diaspora in London; distrust among liberals and the left of Turkey's pretensions of democracy during periods of military rule; and anti-Muslim feeling among some sections of the Christian church and Tory right. These are formidable barriers for Turkey to overcome, and many Turks do not really seem to understand them.

The diaspora could play a key role in overcoming prejudice in Europe, as the Jewish diaspora has been able to do over the years, working in support of Israel. But in order to do so, a sea change in Ankara's attitudes will be needed, and an end to what are often neurotic reactions to criticism. The great strength of the Jewish lobby in a country like the United States has been that it reflects a variety of political opinion and, although strongly defensive of Israeli interests, it has often vigorously criticized aspects of Israeli government policy. It is difficult to imagine Turks abroad feeling confident enough to do that, especially in Germany, where many feel their national identity and culture are being consistently undermined. The question also goes to the heart of Turkish political development. Without a fully functioning democracy in Turkey, it will be difficult to engage the energies of Turks abroad in defence of the interests of the country. The great majority of Turks in the coffee shops of Berlin and Munich were part of a largely non-political underclass at home, so it is not surprising that a significant proportion of them become adherents of extremist political or religious ideologies when they settle abroad.

Part Three

THE NEW EASTERN QUESTION

10. Turkey and the European Union

'*Haide, Chabuk*' – the usual expression used to hasten anyone, your *Suruji* (postilion), for instance, signifying 'Quick, make haste!'

Murray's Handbook to Constantinople, 1900

Two hundred miles west of Istanbul, across the plain of Thrace, the autumn wind blows dust over the barren fields towards the train. Puffs of black smoke drift across the earth from burning stubble in the far distance. The plain is desolate, the antithesis of the fertile, rich breadbasket for Istanbul that it actually is for the rest of the year. There are no villages in sight, only an empty arable landscape as forbidding as the Asiatic steppe – Asia on the doorstep of Europe. As the border with Greece comes closer, there are empty car parks, old First and Second World War gun emplacements, railway sidings long abandoned that were once used as marshalling yards for great armies, then endless high fences and towers with electronic listening devices. Freezing Turkish conscripts smoke furtively while still on guard. A honey buzzard from the Evros delta hovers between the lines of fences – the 10-metre mined corridor makes a lethal avenue for human refugees but an ideal hunting ground for birds of prey.

The train slows to walking pace and finally stops in a siding beside the Evros river, the border. Long and careful formalities are observed by the blue-uniformed Turkish border officials. The train transports refugees and the poor these days; the customers of the old Orient Express travel by air. The passengers include hard-up Bulgarian Turks with relatives in Turkey, students from northern European universities with huge rucksacks, a Romanian academic, a few Yugoslav black-market traders with carriages stuffed full of black plastic sacks of children's clothes. The Turkish officials are not interested in these people. It is the heroin smugglers and the Kurdish revolutionaries on the run who are their targets, young men known to cling to the underside of the train like flies to find safety in Greece, a clean bed and PKK comrades in the Lavrion refugee camp in Attica. The officials with their identikit black moustaches and clean pale blue shirts are aware of this. A little man in overalls moves along the train with a small mirror on the end of a long pole, a policeman bends beside him. A Kurd would have to be very small and very skilful indeed to escape detection. In the duty free shop, a pair of north German tourists watch uncomprehendingly.

The engine stands blowing diesel smoke into the air on the Evros bridge, a long narrow steel structure like a glorified bailey bridge that joins Greece and Turkey, Europe and Asia. It has a temporary air, as if the soldiers who built it for civilian use might suddenly take it away one day, and the route to Greece would be cut off. Below is the Evros, with a wet mass of dark green vegetation, reed beds stretching into the distance, overhanging poplar trees, a black stream swirling and rushing towards the Aegean and marking the boundary of Europe. In Greek eyes this is the edge of civilization, one of the finest haunts of birds of prey left in Europe, home of the Egyptian vulture and the golden eagle, a wild and primitive border for a wild and primitive country.

Eventually the train begins to move after an Asian with a pink shirt and yellow trousers and a pile of cheap luggage has been detained and is left sitting sadly by the customs shed. It crawls across the bridge, from Turkey-in-Europe into the Europe constituted by the Treaty of Rome. The landscape is still open, windswept. Scrubby hedges punctuate the fields, a small herd of sheep graze in the distance. Rural Thrace is one of the poorest parts of Greece, even compared to some of the more barren and remote islands, and there is virtually no tourism or industry to improve local incomes. The large Muslim minority who were stranded here by the Treaty of Lausanne in 1923 have remained, poor tobacco and cotton growers like their cousins north of the Rhodope mountains in Bulgaria, a fragment of the old Ottoman world hanging on within the new Europe. It is difficult to imagine that the new Europe exists here at all – the world of mobile capital markets, portable telephones and the ECU, the end of borders. The wind blows off the Rhodopes as it did in antiquity and stirs the shepherd's thick coat as he watches his sheep and a single goat gnaw and ferret at the bottom of a row of alders. A little way inland the train winds northwards towards Didymotichon, a strange direction to follow if trying to get to Thessaloniki as quickly as possible, but the line is a relic of the Ottoman Empire. It was laid out by the last sultan to link his main military bases of Didymotichon, Drama, Xanthi and Serres so that they could be reinforced by rail from Anatolia with fresh troops to hold back the bloodthirsty Bulgarians and the expansionist Greeks with their eyes on old Constantinople. The Greek army is the biggest employer in the region nowadays, just as the other side of the border is dominated by the Turkish military.

The train lumbers and rolls across northern Greece, following its slow and illogical route between two great Byzantine cities. It almost reaches Bulgaria before it finally turns south down the Vardar valley to Thessaloniki, home of Atatürk's family and the place where he grew to be a soldier.

Turkey-in-Europe means something a little different in Brussels, 1,800 miles north. The Turkish application to join the European Union has become something of a joke among the Brussels bureaucracy – 'Who has the deepest in-basket in Brussels?' 'The official who is dealing with the Turkish membership application' is one example. Hardly any other subject has been surrounded by more official double talk and cynicism. Negotiations have been in progress, in some form or other, for over thirty-five years: it was August 1959 when Turkey first presented its application to the European Community for 'associate status'. The long and tortuous history of the formal interchanges is illuminating, because the same themes recur despite the many changes in Turkey and the Community over the years.

Turkey is the oldest 'associate' of the European Union – an unenviable achievement, a little like that of a spinster who has seen her younger sisters sweep by her on their way to the altar. It took four years for the original application to bear fruit: an Association Agreement was signed in Ankara in September 1963. This was an important step forward, and in many ways could be seen as the only tangible achievement of the whole negotiating process. It took effect in December 1964, and had two main strands. The first was to set up a customs union, and the second was to plan for the convergence of Turkish and EC economic policies. The former meant that, provided Turkey and the Community moved closer together in economic terms, 'the possibility of Turkey's accession to the Community would be examined'. It provided Turkey with an open door to the Community, but there was no obligation on the Community's part to move any further. It has, though, given the modernizing elements in Turkey an ideal to aspire to over the years: the projection of 'Europe' into the Turkish body politic. The agreement laid down a time-scale and three stages to fulfil its objectives: a preparatory phase of five years (1964–69), a transition period of twelve years for the Customs Union, and a final stage, without a time-scale, to coordinate economic policies. Turkey was given a low-interest loan of 175 million ECU for economic modernization, and a number of import restrictions on Turkish goods were lifted.

Although these were useful advances for Turkey, of considerably greater importance was the framework for exporting labour from Turkey to the European countries, above all to the Federal Republic of Germany. Although some Turkish workers had begun to arrive in German cities before the agreement was in existence, numbers dramatically increased in the late 1960s and early 1970s. These movements were controlled by bilateral agreements between the two governments but would never have taken place on the scale they did without the EC agreement. It is interesting to compare them with the limited numbers of people allowed entry from non-EC countries such as Yugoslavia. All Ankara governments have cherished the ambition that Turkish workers would be allowed to move freely within the EC as a result of the agreement, but this has never really taken place. This would establish a Turkish identity within the EC countries, and avoid what seems to many of those involved to be a ghetto existence in Germany. The prospect of Turkish guest workers was unattractive to countries like France and Britain, with immigration sources of their own from ex-colonial countries, whereas Germany had few colonies.

But some slow progress was being made between the mid-1960s and mid-1970s, years of growth in the world economy and in Europe, which had low unemployment. A generous arrangement for Turkey seemed both possible and desirable as part of a worldwide movement towards tariff reductions and free trade. Many industries were short of labour, especially in booming Federal Germany, and local workers were becoming more and more unwilling to take unskilled, low-paid jobs. In January 1973 a transitional phase of the Customs Union came into force, with the removal of a wide range of EU duties on Turkish manufactured goods, a reduction on Turkish tariffs on EC manufactured goods, and specific deals on certain industries such as synthetic fibres and chemicals. Trade in textiles and agricultural products, both Turkish strengths, were encouraged. The sensitive question of the free movement of Turkish workers within the EC was dealt with by a promise to achieve it by the end of the twenty-second year after the agreement came into force – the end of 1986.

Until the military coup of 1980, Turkey was seen as a welcome and growing partner, able to offer the Community cheap and politically docile labour, if in larger quantities than the Community actually required. The internal troubles in Turkey in the late 1970s and the coup changed the situation. Discussions to revitalize the trade accords that were being held in the late 1970s collapsed, and relations were not normalized until 1986, with the return of civilian government. Most important of all, injections of Community finance into Turkey ceased, and negotiations for new loans were suspended. At the time these did not seem important problems. The Turkish economy grew quickly in the 1980s, and American capital and assistance from international institutions such as the World Bank and the International Monetary Fund continued, and effectively bankrolled the military government. Although closer association with Europe would have been useful to Ankara, it was not indispensable, and the movements of *gastarbeiters* continued as normal. By now, their earnings were of central importance not only to economic stability but also as a political safety valve. Opponents of the regime could be 'encouraged' by thuggish local police to seek a work permit abroad, with the strong implication that if they did not, their safety and that of their families would be compromised.

In some ways the Ozal years in the early 1980s marked a second industrial revolution for Turkey, at least on the surface. The cities expanded and hundreds of thousands of peasants abandoned the land for jobs in the urban centres. Places like Izmir experienced explosive population and economic growth. Some of the 'modernization' that EC countries like France and Italy experienced in the 1950s was taking place in Turkey, but without a Common Agricultural Policy to protect the interests of the farmers, nor a social security safety net for the poor in the new suburbs. It was a traumatic process, and the business class found the military government useful in repressing any dissent at the social consequences. This period did bring real economic growth and a substantial increase in GDP and establish many new industries and factories throughout the country. These were not only the traditional low-technology, low-wage industries, like shoe manufacturing and textiles, but in the world growth sectors such as electronics and high-technology consumer goods. For the first time since the Ottoman period, large foreign investments were being made in Turkish industry, often by countries such as Japan, which had no previous interest in Turkey at all. The Ozal government claimed a model of industrial development for Turkey resembling some of the 'tiger' economies in the Far East, where a combination of low wages, a cowed and highly disciplined workforce and an injection of high technology was bringing about economic regeneration. The reality was rather different, and inevitably contradictory. Alongside genuine high-tech and innovative operations, like the television manufacturing industry, using the skills of a somewhat better educated labour force, were factories that were merely 'screwdriver operations', where imported components from the Far East were assembled. His electronics factories were one of the more successful elements in the business empire of ill-fated Cypriot businessman Asil Nadir. It was ironic that in the 1980s Turkey seemed to be able to succeed in a process of modernization without the European Community that proponents of membership claimed was impossible.

Although industrial modernization seemed to be proceeding apace during these years, agriculture remained a vital industry and an obstacle to EC membership. Exports to the populous and rich countries of the Middle East, which all had difficulty in feeding their burgeoning urban populations, were capitalized upon by many of the most influential Turkish business dynasties, like the Koc empire. Sometimes international politics intruded. Iraq was an important and profitable market and the imposition of trade sanctions by the United Nations under American leadership was widely resented during the Gulf War, as was the closure of the oil pipeline that carried Iraqi oil to the outside world. During the 1980s the prospect of the integration of Turkish agriculture into the Common Agricultural Policy became more and more remote. If it was conceivable, at least at a technical level, in the 1960s, before the accession of Spain, Greece and Portugal, it ceased to be later. The entrenched problems of the CAP – overproduction of food and huge subsidies for farmers – would be magnified if Turkey became a full member of the Community. It is perhaps symbolic that the great GAP hydro-electric and irrigation scheme in south-east Turkey is in part designed to grow more food for export to the Middle East, and has no visible connection with Turkey's European aspirations. Turkey does trade with the Community in a few minor commod-ities, such as figs, where there is only limited production within Europe at the moment, but that is all. There appears to be little export potential for Turkish wine and spirits, and the traditional Mediterranean products such as tomatoes, grapes and fruit are in vast over-supply in the EU already. Although in theory pro-duction of some early spring vegetables could fill a gap in northern European markets, there are already trade agreements with pro-spective members like Cyprus for products such as potatoes, and it would be expensive to transport products to, say, Denmark, from south-east Turkey.

Proponents of Turkish membership have claimed that agricul-ture is less important to the Community than it used to be, and that now that Turkey has industrialized, there is a much healthier basis for collaboration and eventual membership than there was in the past. It is true that European social programmes would not have to absorb so many peasants, or ex-peasants, but a close look at the mechanics of the Customs Union agreed in 1995 does not bear out this claim. The areas where it proved most difficult to reach agreement between Ankara and Brussels were food products and the traditional Turkish export-oriented industries dependent on cheap labour, principally textiles. Turkish business is in direct competition with similar producers in northern Greece, Spain and Portugal, of leather, cotton and denim clothes. Turkish labour costs are much lower than those in Greece, even allowing for the fact that most of the Thessaloniki textile producers use low-paid home-workers in small towns like Serres and Drama. Some manufacturers have even moved production facilities to Bulgaria to reduce costs. The Customs Union would open up EU markets to cheap Turkish textiles on a large scale and Greek and Spanish producers have felt threatened.

Another central difficulty for Turkish agriculture is the effect EU membership would have on the traditional 'cheap food' policies that all Ottoman and Turkish governments of whatever political complexion have followed for hundreds of years. (It is worth noting a similar controversy in Britain over Commonwealth food in the 1950s and 1960s.) The social effect of raising Turkish food prices dramatically can only be guessed at, but there is every reason to think it would be profoundly destabilizing. No Ankara government would embark on it with anything other than trepidation.

Yet the European ideal is central to the aspirations of Turkish politicians, even if it seems increasingly improbable and remote. It contains many intellectual inconsistencies. A key problem, as in so many other areas of Turkish life, is the heritage of Atatürk. Although many of the statist planning mechanisms that his governments established have been removed over the years, some have not. Perhaps even more important, the strong informal networks and family links between members of the small Turkish business élite remain, with roots in the Atatürk period. If EU membership ever became a reality, the Treaty of Rome would require the abolition of the government planning bodies, and many decisions that are made in Ankara would be handed over to Brussels. In the view of many Turkish voters, foreigners have more than enough influence over the Turkish economy already through the international banks, financial institutions and multi-national companies, without giving away the few economic control levers that remain.

Despite these difficulties, Turkish integration is still seen as a priority by some politicians in the key EU countries. Pressure on the European Parliament to ratify the Customs Union proposals in 1995 was intense, and was applied by almost every significant EU leader, the argument being that Mrs Ciller's secular government would become a victim of Islamic radicalism if the agreement were not ratified. However, this special pleading came too late to save her government, and the results of the December 1995 election showed that the prospect of Customs Union meant little to the Turkish electorate. EU critics of Turkey and its human-rights record also found the efforts of government leaders achieved little, as a number of genuine improvements in legislation were lost in the legislative backlog that accompanied the fall of the Ciller government. There is an overwhelming sense that the more pressure is applied to change EU–Turkish relations, the more things stay the same.

Another fundamental change that has complicated relations between Ankara and Brussels, and hindered Turkish progress towards a closer relationship with Europe, has been the collapse of Communism and the consequent pressures for EU membership in countries such as Poland and Hungary. The strategic imperative to shore up anti-Communist forces in these states has made the Turkish lobby in Brussels seem feeble and ineffective. The fact that nearly all the ex-Soviet satellite states are coming closer to full EU membership than Turkey is deeply resented by the Turkish bureaucracy. The drive to push through the Customs Union proposal was all that the EU could offer in 1995–6. The demand for Turkish labour in Germany has been further reduced by the influx of ethnic Germans returning from ex-Communist states like Romania and Russia, and by the arrival of skilled and well-educated illegal workers from the ex-Soviet satellite states, quite apart from the new indigenous labour supply from the old GDR. The Yugoslav war has also added to the labour pool, with over 300,000 ex-Yugoslav refugees in Germany, many well educated and some with a good knowledge of the German language. They are not supposed to work while they have refugee status, but many of them do so. To many Turks, their legitimate interests with Europe seem to have been quite forgotten in a world of bewildering change and political realignment.

Religion is still seen as the hidden obstacle to EU membership by many Ankara commentators. There are frequent references in the Turkish press to the controversial speech made by Jacques Delors, then EC president, in Strasbourg in December 1989, in which he stated that 'Europe was a product of Christianity, of Roman law and of Greek humanism'. He was seen as excluding a Muslim country like Turkey, however ostensibly secular, from the European Community on an indefinite basis. He was speaking only hours after the then Turkish prime minister Turgut Ozal had made an appeal to the Council of Europe for a fundamental change of attitude to Turkish membership, claiming that as Turkey had shared for forty years the burden of the defence of Europe against Communism, it should share in the benefits of European economic growth. It was a logical and sensible argument, from the Turkish point of view, but the timing was unfortunate – with the end of the Cold War Turkey was becoming less important to Western defence and security strategy. At the cynical level of *realpolitik*, Turkey's capacity to pressurize its friends to produce changes in policy is very limited. The threats of military action that have been effective over the Cyprus issue, and over many small quarrels with Greece, as the row over the tiny Greek Aegean island of Imia in February 1996 showed, do not work with major forces like the EU and the United States. To them, Turkey is a dependent state. One of the reasons for the growth of anti-Western feeling and Islamic radicalism in Turkey has been the public's realization that this is the case, and that the struggle and sacrifice of the post-war period have not resulted in Turkish leaders being able to articulate the national interest very successfully within the traditional Western framework.

During 1995 and 1996, the question of the Customs Union was seen as central to the future of the EU–Turkish relationship, and, irrespective of the merits of the arguments involved, has become the focus of bilateral relations. The great difficulty both parties face is that it is largely a symbolic issue now. There will be winners and losers as it goes through, with some benefits to the more modern and competitive sections of Turkish industry, and job losses in the backward areas. It is unlikely to be a panacea for the many problems of the Turkish economy. The real question remains what will come after it. Negotiations between the EU and Cyprus for full membership are likely to open after 1997, and ex-Communist countries such as Hungary are moving closer and closer to the EU. Questions associated with the Maastricht Treaty and monetary union dominated the inter-governmental conference on the future of the EU that opened in April 1996, at the expense of the question of Turkish membership. In that sense, the debate has not moved forward much since 1959. The EC was always willing to talk to Ankara about specific economic agreements that might bring benefits to both parties, but it has never really been prepared to seriously consider full membership, or even a form of associate status that would allow Turkish politicians to claim to their electorates that they have indirect political influence in the inner councils of Europe. The membership application being put forward by Cyprus is unlikely to make the relationship easier. It will bring the most difficult issue in the south-east Mediterranean into the heart of the EU.

The period since the Customs Union was ratified in 1995 has once again demonstrated that the more relations between the European Union and Turkey seem to progress and change, the more they stay the same. The Customs Union agreement failed in its first, critical objective, which was to bolster up the centre-right Ciller government, and prevent growth of support for the Refah Party. The general election results showed that the Turkish people found Europe wanting and increasingly irrelevant, after so many years of delays and broken promises. In practical terms the same intractable problems remain: credits and financial agreements are still held up by Greek vetoes, and there is a general sense in Ankara, across the political spectrum, that Greece will always ultimately control policy in Brussels, and Turkey will never move closer to the Holy Grail of full membership.

It is difficult to see what else Europe can offer at the moment, except, perhaps, the increasing number of tourists who sit on Turkish beaches every summer. However welcome, they are a poor substitute for integrated institutional relationships. European Union countries with close historic connections with Turkey, principally Germany, will no doubt try to develop further links, and Germany has already shown in its initiatives with Iran, so strongly disapproved of in Washington, that it can deal with Islamic regimes. Some EU countries such as Britain still seem to assume that an Islamic government in Turkey will be a temporary phenomenon, an aberration which will disappear and somehow business will return to normal. There are many reasons to doubt whether this will be the case, but in the meantime, the European policy vacuum plays strongly into Refah's hands, irrespective of the immediate future of Mr Erbakan's government. To many on the centre-right, it seems as though the option of EU membership, which has been put forward for two generations as a solution to the nation's problems, has been withdrawn, and the nostrums of the Islamists often seem the only valid alternative. In these matters, as in many others, Refah has what President Bush used to call 'the vision thing'. The vision of a fully European political future for Turkey now seems dead to a large proportion of the Turkish people.

On the beach at Ciplakada, Europe is clearly visible. In the obvious sense, there are the low cliffs and pine-forested hills of Lesbos a few kilometres across the straits, the romantic tower fort of Molivos, the rough tracks through the woods used only by the collectors of pine resin for Greek retsina. Greece and Turkey here are so close as to be almost part of one country. On the waterfront there are echoing, empty Ottoman warehouses, a relic of the days when there was a prosperous trade across the water. It is now routinely patrolled by the Greek navy. Politics on Lesbos has a strongly Turkish flavour; all the traditional prejudices of the frontier town are there. The territory is on the fringe of civilized Europe, and of Christendom, in the view of the inhabitants, who believe the citizens of Ciplakada live under near-despotism and a tyrannous religion, without the generous financial assurance which has improved material life out of all recognition on Lesbos since the 1950s.

But Turkey here is becoming Europeanized. There is a German holiday village up the coast, and British accents on the beach that come from Manchester and Milton Keynes, not Ankara. Despite the bomb threats, the doubts about water supplies and the dangers on the roads, Europeanization is in full flood here and in thousands of similar places up and down the Mediterranean coast of the country. It is perhaps significant that the Mediterranean coast is virtually the only area in the country where the old secular right did well in the 1995 general election.

11. Turkey and the Balkan Imbroglio

> Allah, Allah, oh Turkey,
> What befell you on that night?
> In the darkness of that night
> Was wasted such a horde,
> When they entered the horde in the first rank,
> They slew all the Albanians.
>
> Northern Albanian folksong, *c.* 1840

My friends in suburban Istanbul refer to the cheese and pastry shop opposite, which also sells milk, as *shqiptare*, meaning the Albanians' place. Albanian-descended Turks dominate much of the dairy trade in Istanbul, as well as having a strong presence in many other small retail businesses. It is difficult to buy a pastry in some parts of the city without buying it from an 'Albanian'. About a million people in Turkey claim some Albanian descent, making them one of the larger ethnic groups in the country. According to a study conducted in the 1980s by independent experts from the University of Tübingen in Germany, there are no fewer than thirty-seven sizeable ethnic groups in Turkey. As well as the large Muslim communities and well-assimilated groups such as the Albanians, there are people whose ancestors came with the Byzantine trade routes – Poles and Estonians, bearers of amber and furs in the middle ages, who ventured south down the great Russian rivers. They mingle with indigenous groups, such as the Laz people on the Black Sea coast.

Many ethnic groups in Turkey have recent as well as ancient origins. Today Russians are colonizing parts of Istanbul, but

Russians were also there in the ninth century. Albanians, too, have lived in Turkey since Ottoman times, as Muslims, and played an important role in the administration, providing several grand viziers, the Ottoman equivalent of prime minister, as well as many leading soldiers and other imperial functionaries. The Albanian national hero, Skanderbeg, who fought the Ottomans in the fifteenth century, was trained as a soldier in the sultan's army. He changed faith and became a deadly enemy of the Porte. Turkey has been a refuge for Albanians in more recent times, as when tens of thousands of Kosovars fled to Turkey in the aftermath of the Communist victories in Albania and Yugoslavia at the end of the Second World War. The defeated Kosovo uprising against Tito's partisans led to a mass exodus of Albanians from southern Yugoslavia, so much so that some towns in south Serbia which had a significant Albanian presence before 1939 do not have a single Albanian today. Most of the refugees and their descendants are running small shops throughout the country. As with so many other Turkish minorities, outward conformity is everything, and nothing on the surface would reveal their non-Turkish descent, apart from the Gheg Albanian still spoken by the old granny who sits crocheting at the back of the shop in a dark grey Paisley pattern overall, and she is only speaking it to the shop cat.

Separate political organization for such groups has not been encouraged, even for those deeply entwined with Turkey by religion and tradition such as the Albanians. They are on the whole conservative, old-fashioned Muslims, usually hard workers running small businesses – exactly the kind of group conservative governments admire, particularly in Turkey, where they have been long respected and share the dominant Sunni ideology. But ethnic diversity is not encouraged, particularly in the political sphere. In the days before the Yugoslav war, silversmiths from Kosovo used to make an annual trek to Istanbul to buy a year's supply of silver for their filigree work. Now the buses carry desperate Kosovar Albanians looking for work and safety in Istanbul or in Bursa, the other great centre of Albanian settlement in Turkey. They are attracted to Turkey and its culture by tradition, belief and political necessity, yet the 'system' treats them as outsiders as much as any Kurdish Marxist. Here the legacy of nationalism and the racial assumptions derived from the Young Turk movement and embodied in Atatürk's republic are a profound handicap to modern Turkey. In all the verbiage about Turkey's 'European' destiny spoken by eurocrats, ethnic diversity is usually passed over in polite silence. This is perhaps another example of the Western foreign-policy establishment only having eyes in Turkey for what it wants to see. In the Ottoman world careers were open to talented Albanians and many other minorities that are now largely closed if they wish to maintain their cultural identity. According to an Ottoman proverb, 'To the Armenian the pen, to the Albanian the sword'. (Even establishment figures can have difficulty with the continual emphasis on 'Turkish' identity and descent – the late prime minister Turgut Ozal suffered continual taunts from the ultra-nationalist right that he was soft on the Kurds because he had a very small amount of Kurdish blood in his family.)

Turkey has other strong links with the Balkans. There are some 100,000 Turks in former Yugoslav Macedonia and Thrace, and minorities in almost every Balkan country, even Serbia. The largest is in Bulgaria, making up about 10 per cent of the population, the smallest in Montenegro, which the Porte never succeeded in integrating into the empire – the mountainous country prevented the development of towns, which was where Muslims tended to settle as part of the imperial administrative and military system.

The role of Turkey in the painful and intractable Balkan crisis did not receive much attention or publicity during the years of turmoil since 1990, except for a short time at the end of 1993 when it was clear that Turkish troops were to join the United Nations peace-keeping force in Bosnia. This produced protests from predictable quarters, particularly Belgrade, and a feeling that the deployment was likely to bring many problems in its wake. In fact it did not: the contingent was small and largely symbolic, it was not used to protect Muslim 'safe havens' such as Srebrenica or Tuzla, and so the chance of a clash with Serbian or Croatian forces was removed. Whatever else might be said against the United Nations, they were well aware of the risks that Turkish troops faced in Serbia and Bosnia. Turkish food and medical aid were important in some stages of the war for the Bosnian Muslims, but they fell far short of early expectations raised by the late prime minister Turgut Ozal. When the war in Bosnia began, some Bosnian leaders made it clear that they expected considerable material assistance from Turkey, but very little arrived.

The only sense in which Turkey has played a central role is in the equations the outside powers have pored over concerning Kosovo and the Former Yugoslav Republic of Macedonia (FYROM). It has been assumed from the beginning of the crisis that conflict in Macedonia would involve Turkey on the side of its ethnic minority and as an ally of the Albanians, as fellow Muslims. The logic of this argument illustrates clearly that Turkish participation in Balkan politics was seen as a potential threat by Europe, rather than as a possible contribution to a balance of power within the Balkans, as Washington has seen the situation. International fears have in essence been based on a rerun of aspects of the Second Balkan War, when Turkey sought to re-establish influence over its lost territories of Turkey-in-Europe. Did these fears have any foundation? The peace-keeping force in FYROM was supposed to prevent military invasion from Serbia, yet there is very little evidence of aggressive intentions by either the Serbs or the Turks in Macedonia. The Yugoslav Federal Army withdrew quite peacefully from FYROM in 1991, and Turkey has not threatened military interference in the future of the state.

The prevailing view of aggressive Turkish intentions seems to rest on an odd concoction of demography and irredentism. It is assumed, for instance, that as Turkey is settling peasants from

Anatolia in Cyprus, it may wish to do so in the Balkans. This view seems to be out of touch with both history and political reality. Turkey did make attempts under the Ottoman Empire to settle people in the Balkans, but it was never very successful in the later stages of the sultan's rule.

These speculations about conflicts that may never happen seem a long way from the blood and turmoil of the Bosnian war, with the horrors of ethnic cleansing, enforced movements of people, and a quarter of a million dead. At the Royal Institute of International Affairs in London, during an official visit in 1991, Prime Minister Turgut Ozal promised that Turkey would 'not allow the human rights of the Bosnian Muslims to be violated'. The terrible reality has been all too obvious: neither Turkey, nor any other country, has been able to do much to prevent the attacks on the Bosnian state, despite the deployment of peace-keeping forces.

During the first crucial months of the war in Bosnia, Turkish aid to the Muslims and the Bosnian government consisted of little more than the dispatch of old army boots and out-of-date military first aid units. Mr Ozal's London speech expressed the central dilemma for Turkish Balkan policy very neatly. It is a region that was governed from Turkey for hundreds of years, there are millions of people in the Balkans who are Muslims and are in some senses 'Turkish' in culture and outlook, as well as some hundreds of thousands, mostly in FYROM, who are wholly Turkish in their culture and identity. Yet their relations with Ankara have been problematic, and often they seem to have been almost forgotten by the Ankara and Istanbul establishments, much as the interests and human rights of the Greeks in Istanbul and on islands like Imbros have been neglected by Athens governments.

The reasons for this are complex. Firstly, the Balkans were the setting for some of the most dramatic and humiliating defeats the Turkish army suffered in the last stages of the empire. The endless pitched battles between the forces of Greece, Serbia,

Bulgaria and the Porte spelled the end of empire. They were waged with such ferocity that the savage massacres of Turkish soldiers by the Bulgarians are remembered in Turkey even today. The popular memory of Turkish activity in the Balkans is not of wealth, opportunity or political influence, but of military defeat and suffering, when unarmed and surrendered soldiers, poverty-stricken and despised civilians were massacred and helpless women and children were incinerated in their homes. The problems involved in controlling the Balkan mountains were never fully solved by the sultan's generals, any more than they were by the Byzantines or the Romans before them, or by the United Nations at the present time. Turks see the West's obsession with Armenian and Greek historical grievances as unbalanced and ill-informed; the Armenians do not have a monopoly of suffering in this region.

Not only were the Balkans a terrain of bloody defeat, but Turkey suffered heavy economic losses there at the end of the empire, a factor that is often forgotten. Some of the most progressive and developed 'Turkish' industrial and economic enterprises were in Thrace and parts of Macedonia, the territories that were lost after the Balkan Wars and the Treaty of Lausanne. Cities that were eventually returned to Turkey, such as Edirne (Adrianopolis) suffered dreadful damage and destruction at the hands of Christian occupiers, and took a generation to recover, if they have ever fully done so. Although other cities such as Smyrna, modern Izmir, were gained in the war, in the sense that they became fully 'Turkish' after the genocide of the Greeks and Armenians, other valuable land in what we now think of as the Balkans was lost. It was yet another hangover of empire.

The modernist ideology of the Turkish regime after 1923 ignored this, and more recently links with Western Europe have appeared to jump the Balkans and have been formed directly with Germany. But the geography of the ex-Yugoslav war has defeated the modernists and aided those who wish to link Turkish foreign policy inextricably with Islam. As the war has gone on,

Turkey has become more and more involved, first as a provider of humanitarian aid, then as a lobbyist for the Bosnian Muslim cause, a source of peace-keeping troops, a source of arms for the Bosnian government, and now as a surrogate for the United States in strengthening the Bosnian Muslims' military *apparat*. Washington has Islamized Turkish Balkan policy.

The Balkan crisis has complicated Turkish relations with Europe and especially with the countries of the European Union in a number of ways. The importance of Turkey has increased as a function of the participation of the United States as a separate power in the peace process, in particular after the Dayton agreements were signed in the autumn of 1995. In the early stages of the war, it was a priority for the Europeans to keep Turkey out of the conflict except as a provider of humanitarian aid. Although this policy succeeded, the continual television coverage of Muslim suffering and apparent Western indifference had a radicalizing effect in Turkey itself. It enabled the Islamic radicals in the Refah Party to stigmatize Europe as a conservative, almost imperialist force, and its leader, Mr Necmettin Erbakan, to claim that the Customs Union with the European Union was part of a 'Christian-Zionist plot to undermine Turkish leadership of a future Islamic Union'. There seems little doubt that the media reporting of the plight of the Bosnian Muslims has had a significant effect on radicalizing Turkish public opinion towards the conflict, and strengthening Islamic influences in Turkish life.

Lord Owen, the chief EU negotiator for three years, embodies the conventional European view of Turkey's role in the Balkans in his important memoir *Balkan Odyssey*:

Another essential before fixing the map [of Bosnia] was to try to carry Turkey with our policy and we felt it important, therefore, to visit Prime Minister Demirel. [Cyrus] Vance and I met him in Ankara . . . and found him persuasive when he told us of the real frustration throughout the Islamic world about Western 'idleness' and 'inactivity' over Bosnia-Hercegovina. He put the case for lifting the arms embargo and also criticized the ineffectiveness of sanctions; his call for a tightening up was instantly passed on by Vance, who advised Boutros Ghali that this was something the Security Council should be 'prodded on'. But there was also a strand of practical realism from a man we both knew as a practitioner of the art of the possible. We did not convince him, but we felt we had not alienated him.

The same cannot be said for public opinion in Turkey and many other Islamic nations. It may be that the conflict will have significant long-term effects not only in the Balkans but also in surrounding countries. It has fuelled the arguments of Islamic radicals and religious conservatives in Ankara and Istanbul who maintain that Turkey has little to gain from a closer association with Europe. It was frequently pointed out in the Turkish press that one effect of the UN 'safe areas' policy was to prevent any active intervention by Islamic powers on behalf of the Bosnian Muslims, at least until covert assistance began to arrive in 1994–5. As well as failing to protect the Muslims from their enemies, the UN soldiers cut them off from potential friends.

But the geographic imperatives remain. The Balkans have always been the route to Europe for the Turks, whether it was the Ottoman armies marching northwards towards Vienna or the *gastarbeiters* travelling by train through Yugoslavia towards jobs in the car factories in Munich and the Ruhr. In the Cold War years the Balkans were mostly subsumed under Communism and the only democratic state, Greece, was a hostile and unfriendly neighbour to Turkey. Many conflicts associated with Greek and Turkish interests in the nineteenth century have spilt over into the larger canvas of the eastern Mediterranean in the twentieth. Turkey's relations with Yugoslavia improved somewhat in the later Tito years, but remained bad with Bulgaria as a consequence of the Zhivkov government's policies of forced assimilation and name-changing inflicted on the ethnic Turkish minority in Bulgaria. The Turkish and Muslim minorities in ex-Yugoslavia generally remained at the bottom of the economic heap, except in a few cities like Sarajevo. Some Western liberals have put forward a partial and one-sided view of conditions in the old Yugoslavia, based only on the prosperity of the urban Muslim élite in Bosnia. Far more typical were the ethnic Turkish peasants of western Macedonia, who scratched a living in the mountains by gathering wild herbs and mushrooms in the forests, or the obscure and poverty-stricken peasant people of Sandjak, in south Serbia. Ankara paid them little attention, except for the odd visit of an important Turkish politician or dignitary when a docile group in national costume would perform folk-dancing displays. Access to higher education was more or less barred, on language criteria, and illiteracy rates remain high. Families are very large and the position of women is very backward. The Sandjak Muslims living on high land are some of the poorest people in the entire Balkans.

With the end of Communism in 1989, before the collapse of Yugoslavia, it seemed for a short while that the old Balkan trade route might be open again. Turkish traders flocked to places like Skopje in former Yugoslav Macedonia, and street markets were suddenly full of sacks of Turkish rice and denims and shoes. Turgut Ozal and the Motherland Party were in pro-European mood, and prospects for a closer relationship with the European Community were improving. The Balkans did not seem to present an obstacle, certainly not compared to the intractable Cyprus problem, which has always led Greek governments to say that they would veto Turkish membership. It might be said that the same is true now, in that Turkey's difficulties in negotiating the 1995 EU Customs Union were mostly associated with the Kurdish war, Cyprus, human-rights abuses, and the undemocratic and repressive nature of the post-1980 military coup constitution.

Whatever the long-term effects of the Balkan turmoil on Turkey and its international relations, the practical reality is that Turkey's military *apparat* is too well integrated into NATO and Western command structures to play an independent role in the defence of Muslim interests. The military has made it clear to the Islamists that a change to an anti-NATO, anti-European position will not be permitted. This has been a good guarantee against active Turkish military participation in the Balkan conflict. The NATO framework in which the peace-keeping force operates will also limit a possible independent Turkish role.

One danger of the military's stance is that it will encourage Islamists within the Turkish army to pursue their support for Muslim causes in underground organizations, or even in military conspiracies. There have been some signs of this happening already, at various levels. For example Turkish army officers played a part in the Sarajevo government's attempt to break the international arms embargo in the latter stages of the Bosnian war. There was a new and potentially very important 'garrison vote' for the Refah Party in the 1995 election, particularly in the Kurdish south-east. If these trends within the military continue, they could have a seismic effect on the orientation of the army and the Turkish state, as one of the foundation stones of the whole social order is the secularism and unity of the army. There are some uncomfortable parallels here with the development of armies in certain Middle East and north African states, where the army, which began as a secular, conservative force, became the nursery for Islamic and social radicals like Colonel Gadaffi in Libya, or the leaders of the Sudan. The situation has not yet developed to this point in Turkey and immense international pressure will be applied to prevent it, but, in the absence of a general Balkan settlement, it would be foolish not to see it as a possibility.

The Turkish government tends to deny or overlook these developments, in the interests of a harmonious relationship with the military. Discreet Refah Party activity among army personnel in the 1995 campaign was ignored. It remains to be seen, though, whether events are fully under Ankara's control. The Bosnian government moved much of its arms purchasing to Turkey in 1993–4, and other Islamic states are passing their aid to Bosnia through Ankara. Many militant meetings have been held in support of Bosnian interests, which placed the Ciller government of 1994–5 in a dilemma. Apart from the problems with NATO allies in taking a more active role in events, the government in Ankara could not afford to be seen to act under pressure from the Islamic lobby and the Refah Party. In practice, underground Bosnian Muslim military or terrorist organizations would be able to establish themselves in Turkey quite easily if they wished to do so.

A more active military role for Turkey in Bosnia has evolved under American tutelage, particularly after the conference on re-arming the Bosnian army that was held in Turkey in March 1996. The re-armament programme proposed by the United States at this conference appears to envisage a special role for Turkey, an institutionalization of Turkish Balkan involvement that may have dramatic long-term implications for the region. The obvious danger foreseen by the Europeans is that the United States will at some stage withdraw from its current engagement in the Balkans, perhaps as a result of domestic pressures, and that it will then bestow on Turkey an independent political role as protector of the Balkan Muslims. Some elements in the US administration seem to believe that this is necessary, as Turkey is a 'moderate' and 'secular' country, and will keep the Sarajevo government on the right path, unlike some of the other Islamic forces at work in the area, such as Iranian and Afghan radicals. In other respects, though, it would take Balkan power relationships back to the pre-First World War period. It is an example of how far US policy is conceived internationally, with little regard for specific Balkan conditions, and how far resisting Iran and its influence still seems to lie at the heart of US policy-making. It also rests on specious political logic, in that Turkey may not remain as secular as it is now, and, whatever happens, Ankara will find it difficult to influence developments in Bosnia directly. In the nineteenth century Bismarck could declare that the Balkans were not worth the bones of a single Pomeranian grenadier, but nowadays it is impossible not to feel that the new Eastern

Question that is evolving is at least partly focused on a renewal of Turkish influence in the Balkans.

For many people in Belgrade it is ironic that at the beginning of the crisis there was a good deal of scaremongering, even among respectable Serbian intellectuals, about what role Turkey would play in the conflict. A pamphlet published by Miroljub Jevtic, a leading Serbian ideologist, in 1994, 'Pan-Turkism and its role in the Yugoslav crisis', is typical. It sets out a Pan-Turkish and Muslim conspiracy theory for the Balkans, where the various Muslim minorities are subjected to external manipulation as part of a plan to reassert Turkish control over the region in what the author sees as a neo-Osmali confederation. It is not a convincing argument, and the author is unable to produce much evidence for his theory, except, perhaps, for the Muslim political leadership of the Sandjak in south Serbia, who do seem, in the early stages of the war, to have asked Ankara to assist their struggle towards independence. The author's claims of deliveries of Turkish small arms to the Muslim forces in Bosnia seem far-fetched. Even if they took place on the scale alleged, they would still be a drop in the ocean compared to the overall flow of small arms during the war. The pamphlet is full of melodramatic and confused allegations that mix up political conditions of a century ago with the present. It received consider-able attention in the Serbian media, just at the point when conditions were beginning to be created by the United States to bring about the 'Pan-Turkish' influence in the future that the author had wrongly attributed to the past.

The official Turkish view of the Balkan future is very different, of course, and envisages peaceful trade and business exchanges in which the Ankara-sponsored Black Sea Trade Co-operation Area will play an important part. This is supposed to bring both Turkey and the Balkans closer to the EU. High-level repres-entations by the Turkish government, such as the visit of Prime Minister Demirel to Bulgaria in 1995, have sought to promote these laudable aims, but in essence, they are little more than glorified trade delegations. The results so far have been disappointing, with representation dominated by Ankara officials. Turkey has not yet begun to compete effectively with the freewheeling Greek businessmen who have monopolized parts of the economies of Bulgaria, Romania and Albania. Although many Turkish goods are traded in Balkan street markets, they are often smuggled in by Serbs experienced in sanctions busting and the evasion of customs duties. As with many Turkish economic dealings with central Asia, there is not enough free capital to invest outside Turkey, and, besides, Balkan conditions do not encourage much investment. The size of many of the Balkan markets is small – the total population of former Yugoslav Macedonia is only about a sixth of that of Istanbul. The entire population of Montenegro is much less than that of Ankara or Izmir. Many other producers are competing to sell goods in the Balkans, often with unorthodox black-market trade arrangements, such as the cross-border meat and cheese trade between Greece and Albania. There is entrenched anti-Turkish political prejudice throughout most of the Balkans, except Albania and Kosovo, which will discourage many economic relationships for the foreseeable future. This has been accentuated by the advance of Islamic politics in the 1995 elections, which has fuelled the propaganda of the orthodox nationalist right in all Balkan countries. It is impossible to imagine, for instance, a Turkish bank being allowed to open in post-sanctions Serbia or Montenegro in the immediate future. The deeper question is the real nature of the Turkish border with Europe, both in terms of minorities and cultural influence. Elements of Turkish life continue far beyond the border of the current Turkish state.

The road from Bulgaria to Istanbul is grim: a pitiless, dusty motorway across the plains of Thrace, with scarcely a sign of habitation in sight. Then Edirne, old Adrianopolis, appears on the horizon, with the minarets of Selimiye mosque, designed by Sinan, the greatest Ottoman architect, dominating the town from a small hill. It was an Epirote town originally, named Adrianopolis to honour the Emperor Hadrian. It fell into sharp decline in late Ottoman times, was occupied by the Russians in 1829 and 1867, and was captured by Bulgarian troops in the Second Balkan War in 1913 and by Greece between 1919 and 1923. Only the deliberations of the Great Powers embodied in the Treaty of Lausanne stopped it being part of Greece, which in turn may have saved Sinan's magnificent structure for posterity. Important Ottoman mosques and market buildings have not been well looked after in Greece since the Second World War, as some of the Turkish buildings in Ioannina and Trikala show. Le Corbusier was fascinated by the Edirne mosque. Today, lonely on its magnificent terrace, the Kavak Meydani, it stands above a wealthy but uninspiring frontier town, full of off-duty soldiers.

The train journey to Constantinople, once glamorous and attractive, is now no better: a slow rattling 'express' winds past endless new suburbs that ruin this part of the coast of the Sea of Marmara.

In the small Kosova town of Prizren, a Serb refugee family from Croatia is carrying bundles of clothes and cardboard boxes tied with string into an old Turkish building. It is a fine, square white house, with overhanging black wooden balconies. A makeshift sign on the door reads FEDERAL REPUBLIC OF YUGOSLAVIA REFUGEE CENTRE. Hundreds of miles from the fighting, they arrived here in autumn 1995, after being removed from their homes in the Krajina area of what is now southern Croatia, as part of the largest piece of ethnic cleansing in the war. The leadership of Franjo Tudjman in Croatia, in alliance with the Bosnian Muslims, has produced the first ethnically homogenous state in the Balkans. Serbs had lived in the region for hundreds of years, planted like trees by the Hapsburgs to protect Europe from the Ottoman armies, 'the guardians of the gate'. Now these hapless refugees are pawns in the United States' ambitions to build up Croatia. The old woman looks dazed at the government sign, the young man has a small bullet wound on his forearm. The building they are entering was probably built by a local Ottoman *bey* in the nineteenth century. It would have been used by mostly Muslim Albanians to campaign against the Turkish yoke; now the Albanian majority within this part of Serbia have to watch it being taken over as a refugee centre. All the people from Krajina would know the Serbian proverb 'Where the Turkish foot trod, no grass grows'. Yet they are grateful for a Turkish building to shelter them. For the Albanians, seen as proto-Turks by the Serbs, Belgrade's decision to put refugees in their historic buildings is an insult. Saki, who was Balkans correspondent for the *Morning Post* from 1902, wrote that the Balkans produced more history than could be consumed locally. That is certainly the case in Prizren, as it is almost everywhere in the ex-Ottoman world.

The most obvious legacy of the past is often empty property – half ruined and burnt-out buildings, a few barely recognizable possessions left behind in a pool of muddy water – both in the Balkans and in so many parts of Turkey, from the ruined churches in the Fener quarter of Istanbul to the damp mansions with collapsed roofs on Princes Island. Sometimes Greece is criticized by its European Union partners for what appears to be intractable and irrational hostility to Turkey, but the houses on Princes Island do have owners: dispossessed living owners, Greeks who happened to be born outside Turkey and as a result, under the Turkish government inheritance laws, cannot pass on their property to their legitimate heirs, even if they live in Istanbul, work hard, speak Turkish and pay their Turkish taxes. Greeks in Turkey have been subjected to a form of slow ethnic cleansing over many years. According to conventional wisdom, the Balkans stop at the Evros river, and the decisions embodied in the Treaty of Lausanne have ended one aspect of the Eastern Question. Yet in the centre of Istanbul, and on these islands on the doorstep of the city, the Balkan heritage is alive every day and the treaty might as well never have existed.

Greece is given a heavy responsibility by its Western partners in dealing with Turkey in these circumstances. At one level the illusion of normality must be maintained, and Turkey be seen as a reasonable, modern and Westernized state, while in practice the recent history of practical relationships between Greece and Turkey often does little to justify such a view. Greece has a central responsibility in relations between the two countries in the Balkan region, yet has to face incessant criticism for dealing with the local consequences of policies that originated in Brussels or Washington. An example was the often acrimonious debate over economic issues that accompanied the EU Customs Union negotiations in 1994–5, where intense pressure was put on Greece to conform to general European Union policies. In some important industries, such as textiles, the agreement will bring serious negative consequences to the Greek economy while the agreement has no practical consequences whatsoever for the vast majority of EU member states. As a result of the development of the new eastern question, Greece will have to bear a heavy defence burden for many years, while in many European capitals, particularly Bonn, it will be denied that such a problem with Turkey exists at all. The Balkan crisis and the social and economic deterioration of the states in the Balkans on the northern border have produced a fundamentally new situation of conflict and regional rivalry for Greece and Turkey which neither country seems well equipped to resolve.

12. Cyprus: Apple of Discord

> The Conquest of 1571 introduced into Cyprus, the bulk of whose inhabitants had hitherto been, as we have seen, Greek in religion and language, a large element of Ottoman Turks.
>
> Sir Harry Luke, *Cyprus under the Turks*, 1921

> The Turkish government undertakes to take, as regards non-Muslim minorities, in so far as concerns their family law or personal status, measures permitting the settlement of these questions in accordance with the customs of those minorities.
>
> Treaty of Lausanne, Article 42, 1923

The United Nations' Green Line in Cyprus is a survivor of the inter-communal disturbances of the 1950s and 1960s, and of the United Nations peace-keeping efforts after the 1974 Turkish military occupation of half of the island. The Cyprus conflict seems to be one of the most intractable international problems, with some of the longest-serving politicians on the world stage, such as Doctor Rauf Denktash, who has been the Turkish Cypriot leader for over forty years. The political crisis seems to have acquired a timeless quality for many diplomats, politicians and journalists, with many articles and telegrams being recycled over the years, with only the date and a few names changing. A Dutch MP, Erik Jurgens, summed up the general atmosphere in spring 1996, when he wrote in a human-rights report to the Dutch parliament, 'It is important for the international community to be reminded of Cyprus. I think the

Cyprus problem has become a forgotten thing in the international community.'

Meanwhile the Green Line has become a nature reserve: there are butterflies on wonderful March-flowering mimosa trees along the fence, wild flowers in profusion in the middle of the divided city of Nicosia, frogs flourishing in little ponds made by the United Nations vehicle tracks. It is also reminiscent of the more distant past – a rambling, ramshackle structure of barbed wire and old oil drums, piles of bricks and little soldiers' foxholes that would not have been out of place in the local conflicts in the nineteenth century Balkans. The haphazard observation posts built on top of Venetian walls could have been built at any time in the Ottoman Empire over five hundred years. Cyprus is a small island, and its wretched and apparently interminable conflict is fought and watched on a small and human scale. The burnt-out Armenian shops by the Leda Palace hotel in Nicosia used to be full of bustling people; now their absence is close, personal, tangible – individuals who have disappeared, voices arguing in throaty vowels about the price of cotton and velvet. Birds nest on shelves that would have held rolls of cloth.

But this conflict is only the most recent in a long series of wider disputes between Greece and Turkey. In Greek minds it represents both the last stage of Ottoman decolonization and the urgent need to restrict current Turkish expansionism. The twentieth century has never been free of the Greek–Turkish conflict. As it opened, the Cretans and peoples of northern Greece were seeking to liberate themselves from the last restraints of the old empire. They succeeded between 1908 and 1913, when the garrison at Ioannina was finally abandoned. At the end of the First World War Greek troops occupied large areas of what is now mainland Turkey, and, under the Treaty of Sèvres, it seemed that Greece, as one of the Entente powers, with France and Britain, might be able to carve out an empire in Asia under the protection of the greatest imperial powers of the day. It was the culmination of the 'Great Idea' that had dominated nineteenth-century Greek politics, an irredentist vision fired by the Orthodox church. But the Greek forces were over-extended and were unable to contain the armies of Atatürk and his generals. The British and French were unreliable allies and had their attention distracted elsewhere.

In 1922 Smyrna, modern Izmir, fell to the Turkish troops, who engaged in an orgy of destruction that has been known in colloquial Greek ever since as the *catastrophe*. Although relations improved a little in the inter-war years, Greece was subject to intense internal strains as it accommodated the hundreds of thousands of refugees who had to move country as a result of the war and the exchange of populations agreed in the peace treaties. After this, there was a period of calm for a generation, assisted by the relatively neutral position of Turkey in the Second World War. The Cyprus problem ended this optimism, and has plagued many governments since then. It may appear to be a relic of the decolonizing era, but many aspects of it recall the political and military realities of the Ottoman world. Cyprus has a fiercely nationalistic Greek majority of over 80 per cent of the population, and the Church plays a central role in the political and economic as well as religious leadership of the community. Turkey controls an area of land in northern Cyprus through the deployment of infantry troops. There is Great Power involvement, in the shape of British and American security interests in the region – the British bases of Akrotiri and in other parts of the island are still important. The island as a whole is a focus for several regional problems: it aspires to be a centre for regional business and economic co-operation, but in reality is the most important single obstacle to *rapprochement* between Greece and Turkey, and to a settlement of the outstanding security problems in the eastern Mediterranean.

The conflict has also recently acquired a wider contemporary significance. In the disorder that has developed in the ex-Communist world since 1989, the invasion of Cyprus by Turkish troops in 1974 seems symbolic. A large population made up of one ethnic group was forced from their homes by a foreign military force, thousands of people were killed, many more lost their homes, and the international community – that increasingly vague entity when any difficult or principled action is required – did nothing to stop it. The event could have taken place in the Balkans, the Caucasus, or the Horn of Africa in the mid-1990s, and mirrors the pattern of ethnic, religious and national conflicts spawned by the end of the Communist era. Yet at the time, in 1974, Operation Attila, the Turkish intervention in Cyprus, was seen as something unresolved from the decolonization process of the past, and the product of out-of-date religious and political extremism in Greece and Turkey. National feelings and ethnicity were not taken seriously in some respects by the Superpowers. The logic of international relations watered down the case for effective humanitarian action to redress the consequences of the Turkish action. Decolonization had many problems, but they would all come out in the wash, it seemed. With Cyprus, they never did.

In 1974 the battle with Communism was still being fought, with the last stages of the American involvement in Indo-China. Turkey's invasion of Cyprus was the first successful attempt to change borders in Europe by force since the Second World War, but it was regarded as an aberration at the time. The Turks were vital clients of the United States, and Greek society had been rent by years of dictatorship. Greece was not yet a full EC member. There had been inter-communal problems in Cyprus for many years, which were seen as inevitable but temporary hangovers from colonialism. It was possible to isolate the whole episode from the mainstream of social and political developments in a way that would be much more difficult now. It was also possible for Turkey to avoid the worst international consequences of the invasion, thanks to the priorities of the United States. For example, despite international neglect of many aspects of the Balkan crisis, there has been an attempt to bring to justice those responsible for the worst crimes of ethnic violence in

Bosnia. There was no effort to do the same in Cyprus, and the invasion and its aftermath still finds its apologists among the staff of some Western foreign ministries.

At a popular level in Western countries, the Cyprus problem is often now overlooked as a major factor in Greek–Turkish enmity and difficulties in bilateral relations. The great figures of the struggle for independence, particularly Archbishop Makarios, seem remote, although he died as recently as 1977. Equally distant seem the main British participants, such as Sir Hugh Foot. Today the island is somewhere to go for a cheap holiday. It offers many reminders of British colonial rule, from the post boxes to the street signs, the near universal use of English, and, in Christopher Hitchens' telling phrase, 'the wide availability of the Church of England'.

It is fashionable for the middle classes to prefer the occupied zone in the north for holidays, on the grounds that it is much less 'spoilt' than the Greek side, which is true in terms of the landscape. Cyprus has suffered some of the worst environmental vandalism in the Mediterranean, with random and ugly ribbon developments of concrete blocks, forests of signs and nonexistent public facilities. Many criminals and people having trouble with the legal authorities in their own countries also prefer the 'north', as it has come to be known in England, but not on environmental grounds. Substantial quantities of heroin pass through the Turkish zone. It is a strange place, whereas Greek Cyprus is lively, economically successful, and appears to be on the brink of European Union membership. The Greek Cypriots have built a thriving modern economy since 1974, but there has been a high environmental price. There would also be a price to pay for EU membership. It would probably mean the collapse of most of the remaining traditional manufacturing on Cyprus, in textiles and leather, and problems for the tourist industry as drinks prices rise to European levels.

Some foreign visitors find the entrenched anti-Greek attitudes they come across on the Turkish side of the Green Line hard to understand. But Turkish Cypriots feel they did not get a fair deal under independence, and in the classic pattern of a national minority getting support from an adjoining neighbour, the northern half of the island has been populated by many Anatolian settlers over the last generation. There may well now be a majority of Turks from the mainland living in the occupied areas. This holds great dangers for peace in the long run, especially once Dr Rauf Denktash, the elderly leader of the Turkish Cypriots, dies. The continued political tension has affected relations between Cyprus and Greece, notably in the area of defence. A pact has been signed between the two countries, committing Greece to go to the defence of Cyprus if any further Turkish military expansion takes place. Greece has helped Cyprus to acquire sophisticated defence equipment, and to resist Turkish attempts to get the occupied part of the island admitted into international organizations.

None of this has hindered Cyprus's economic achievement since the mid-1980s. In May 1996 Richard Boucher, the US Ambassador to Cyprus, announced that US exports to Cyprus had doubled virtually every year in the last ten years, and that most of the goods were re-exported elsewhere in the region. This underlines the importance of the island as part of the Middle East trade bloc. Although divided and damaged by its own war, Cyprus has since done very well out of its neighbours' conflicts. Huge amounts of money are held in the offshore accounts of Cyprus-based banks for nationals of every Middle East country. This has been augmented, in recent years, by money from Russia and ex-Yugoslavia. The Cyprus banking system was important for the very survival of Serbia in the early stages of the Yugoslav war, and the Bank of Belgrade has one of the larger and more impressive tower blocks in downtown Nicosia today.

At a human level, little changes in the conflict. In London, where many Cypriots live, the two communities are divided by mutual mistrust and a sense of political impotence. Some of this may stem from the limitations of exile, but there is an almost universal feeling that the future of the island will be decided by outside powers, and that there is little the Cypriots themselves can do about it. This sentiment is particularly strong among Turkish Cypriots, who know privately that democracy in the occupied part of the island is limited and that the degree of political independence enjoyed by the Denktash government is minimal. The growth of Islam in Turkey is generally unwelcome to Turkish Cypriots, who tend to be secular, and who see the Turkish army as a protective force whose operations have effectively been sanctified by NATO. A potential conflict between the army and a future Islamic government would be anathema in Cyprus, where the dominant ideology of the state and its civil service is imbued with secular, nationalist values. If Turkey ever became a partly or wholly Islamic state, it would confirm the deepest prejudices about Ankara held by Greek Cypriots. Nationalists would feel vindicated in their view that Cyprus is at the forefront of Western defence against Islamic expansionism.

As with mainland Turkey, relations with the European Union are central to the future of Cyprus. The thriving economy of the Greek side of the island already meets most of the Maastricht Treaty criteria for monetary union and Cyprus has a rate of growth in excess of the EU average. There are over 9,000 foreign offshore companies now registered on the island, and the number is rising by about 100 a year. They are mostly involved in service industries such as insurance, banking and shipping. In 1995 the International Monetary Fund praised the 'government's excellent record of prudent fiscal management', and welcomed plans to keep government debt under stringent control. These undoubted achievements were a main factor behind the re-election of the government coalition parties in the spring 1996 general election, under President Clerides.

There is the possibility, though, that despite this effort and virtuous hard work, Cyprus will not receive the expected reward of EU membership. Turkey has firmly opposed European Union membership without a settlement of the basic political and inter-communal problems on the island, and has been lobbying hard in the United States and in European capitals to make membership conditional on a political settlement. Turkey wishes to engineer a position where it effectively has a veto on Cypriot membership of the Union. Although this is in theory unacceptable to most foreign leaders, as British Foreign Secretary Malcolm Rifkind stated in April 1996, Turkish involvement by proxy in the projected final negotiations may have much the same effect. Turkish diplomats in the United States have claimed that their government has been backed by the US State Department over the issue, although recent observations by US representatives do not bear this out. The Turkish Cypriots have threatened to withdraw from the United Nations peace process if the EU proceeds with membership accession for the Greek part of the island. So far this threat has been firmly rejected by the EU, but it remains to be seen whether the line would be held in the event of major tension in the region or on the island itself which would involve the UN as peace-broker. Earlier in 1996, the EU Commission Vice President for External Relations, Mr Hans van den Broek, confirmed that a political settlement was not a condition for accession, even though it would undoubtedly help the negotiating process.

A good deal may also depend on the new United Nations peace initiative. The situation is confusing for Greek and Turkish Cypriots alike, with peace plans being suggested by the European Union, the United States and the United Nations. The United States' effort resembles in many ways its leadership on the Balkan settlement: the formidable personality of Mr Richard Holbrooke was to be used to bang heads together within a specific time framework. The whole process rests on the self-appointed leadership of the United States, and the fact that attractive settlements on these foreign-policy issues were important to the re-election prospects of President Clinton. US concern over the failure to make progress on Cyprus has been linked to concern over rising political tensions in the eastern Aegean in general. Speaking at a conference in April 1996 in Washington, the State Department's coordinator on Cyprus, James Williams, spoke of the 'anachronism' of the Cyprus problem, which had done more to damage peace and stability in the region than any other issue. The latter is undoubtedly true, but the problem is far from being an anachronism, given that so many aspects of the Cyprus situation mirror the typical conflicts of the post-Communist era, with its emphasis on ethnicity, land, nationalism, revenge, territorial and population exchange, and, above all, religion.

The demands of the Clerides government in Nicosia will make the task of the international negotiators difficult, as they call upon the Turks to abandon any attempt to create a state in the occupied areas, and to accept United Nations Security Council resolution 939, which calls for a federal settlement based on the undivided sovereignty of the island. This is anathema to Ankara and could lead to a collapse of the peace process.

During the summer of 1996, the Cyprus problem began to take on a new dimension. The military build-up by Greece and Turkey continued, in the context of the dispute over the island of Imia and other points of conflict in the eastern Mediterranean. Greece and Cyprus held regular joint military exercises, sometimes involving brushes with Turkey over the use of air space. Diplomatic initiatives were accelerated; Britain appointed Sir David Hannay as London's special negotiator, and there was increased European Union activity. American efforts to bring the parties together were delayed by the Greek Cypriot elections in June, but were resumed soon afterwards. It seemed as though a Dayton-type negotiation might be in the offing, whereby America would draft an outline peace plan with its allies and impose it in an overall settlement on both Greek and Turkish Cypriots.

But these plans came to nothing when new factors appeared on the scene: independent political action by the Greek Cypriots themselves, and military reaction to their struggle by the Turkish occupation forces. For many years some Greek Cypriot groups have demonstrated peacefully against the 1974 invasion and the resulting division of the island and loss of Greek property. The women's movement staged regular protests, demanding information about relatives who had disappeared in the aftermath of the 1974 invasion. In August 1996 groups of motorcyclists from the Cypriot diaspora assembled all over Europe and rode to Cyprus to protest against the division of the island. At first their plan did not attract much attention either in Cyprus or in the international media. Turkish Cypriots dismissed it as a publicity stunt, while extremists in Turkey, and on the island itself, were conscious of the opportunity to use the protest for their own purposes. Members of the Fascist Grey Wolf organization began stirring up anti-Greek feeling in the occupied zone, and when the demonstrators arrived in Cyprus and rallied at the Green Line, there was serious, if localized, violence; a Greek Cypriot was beaten to death by the Turkish military in full view of the cameras of the local and international media. From apparent obscurity, the Cyprus problem had reached the front pages again. A factor in what happened was the very small and ineffective presence of the United Nations peace-keeping force of 'Blue Helmets'. The UN had only about 1,100 men and women in uniform on Cyprus in April 1996, to patrol a boundary hundreds of miles long, and the troops had not been reinforced by August. Cyprus has been a victim of the appalling pressure on UN resources in the 1990s. Further violence has followed, and the cease-fire line between the occupied and the free parts of Cyprus has become as tense and difficult as it was thirty years ago.

Although the events of August gave rise to deep concern in many countries, progress to resolve the issue has been minimal. Speaking to the United Nations General Assembly in late September, Cyprus' president Glafkos Clerides said that he had been encouraged by the 'rekindled interest and more active engagement of the international community'. It is hard to see what this consists of, to date. The United States promised to renew its peace initiative after the November presidential elections, but all that has been mentioned so far is a 'preparatory stage', for a 'federal solution' of the problem, before the 1998 Greek Cypriot presidential elections. As with so many other foreign-policy initiatives of the Clinton administration, it is high on idealism but short on specifics. The British Foreign Secretary has said that there is a 'window of opportunity' emerging in 1997. Most other European Union governments seem to consider that some progress can be made over the division of the island in the negotiations over Cyprus' membership of the EU.

Here the issue interconnects with EU–Turkish relations in general. Given that closer links with Turkey appear unlikely, the EU will have very little leverage in Ankara over Cyprus policy. A disturbing sign of this, from the Turkish point of view, is the freezing of EU budget funds for Turkey under the programme of assistance for Mediterranean countries: in 1996–7 95 million ECU will be blocked until 'the Turkish government adopts measures to help resolve the Cyprus problem'. This move is similar to the 'outer wall' of UN sanctions still in place against Yugoslavia, and will add to the anti-European feelings among the Turkish and Turkish Cypriot public. The Ankara government does not accept that it has any official role or involvement in the August or September killings.

As in many of its relationships with the outside world, the Cyprus problem puts Ankara in the position of an imperial power dealing with a colonial problem which makes the use of force seem indispensable to defend Turkish national interests. This is also the case with Kurdistan. Regardless of the political debate, certain military realities remain and from the Turkish point of view seem to rule out many political options. Of course the situation does not look the same to the rest of the world, although traditional allies in the Middle East like Israel face many of the same problems and have been quietly supportive of Turkey over the years.

One of the conundrums affecting policy in the region is whether a Refah government is likely to be a permanent feature in Ankara;

if so, any meaningful concessions to the Greek side are very unlikely indeed, and the European Union will find it difficult to bring effective pressure on the government to secure a peace settlement and the end of the division of the island.

Another important factor in Greek and Greek Cypriot minds that may make any progress on Cyprus difficult under the present Turkish government is the background of Mr Erbakan himself. The prime minister was a member of the Ankara government in 1974 when the invasion took place, and has since expressed the view that it was a mistake for Turkey not to take over the whole island. This is a rare occasion where his views on a major issue coincide with those of much of the Turkish army leadership. The fierce Ankara reaction to the purchase of advanced Russian anti-aircraft weapons by the Greek Cypriots in early 1997 indicates a further deterioration in the long-running crisis in the region.

13. The Challenge of Central Asia

Oh race of the Turks!
Oh, children of iron and fire!
Oh, the founders of a thousand homelands,
Oh, the wearers of a thousand crowns!

'Turana Dogru', Mehmet Emin Yurdakul (1869–1944)

If Cyprus is a small island with too much difficult history, well known in Britain due to long and close military association and millions of package holidays, Turan is very different. Turan is invisible. It cannot be visited, whether by car, plane or train; it belongs, in Koranic terms, to the 'world of the unseen'. It has never existed outside the imagination. The writer Mehmet Yurdakal was a Pan-Turkist: he believed in a greater Turkey, to be called 'Turan' – a new nation state, a vast sprawling territory encompassing most of the central Asian steppes. To create a new state there, which was to include all of modern Turkey and many of the new central Asian republics, was the object of the nineteenth-century Pan-Turkists. In scale, it would have been an enterprise only equalled in modern history by the creation of the United States of America or the USSR. It appears to be a strange political fantasy.

As an ideology, Pan-Turkism seems even more remote today than its fellow nineteenth-century phenomenon, Pan-Slavism. The latter still has some intellectual resonance in the West – it affected the thinking of great writers like Dostoevsky, and it is occasionally mentioned in analyses of Russia's reasons for supporting Serbian security in the Balkans. Pan-Turkism seems a weird and recondite vision; to understand it requires a knowledge of the peoples and politics of central Asia and the intellectual currents in vogue in Turkey during the late Ottoman Empire. Most Pan-Turkists posited the union of all the Turkic peoples of the world in a future super-state, based on the contemporary view of an 'ancestral home of Turks' in the Asiatic steppes. In modern guides, official publications and popular histories, this is usually referred to as the 'Motherland of all Turks', a slight but important ideological and semantic shift, implying that, as children leave their mothers, so the modern Turkic states have 'left' the original 'Turan' family home, are sovereign and without territorial or other claims on the 'Turan' lands. It is an anti-irredentist, modernist definition.

Most nations possess a primordial myth of origins, but Turan remains a current in contemporary ideology. And, like stories such as that of Moses being found in the reed bed, it has its poetic and its practical dimension. Sometimes it veers towards the absurd. It is possible to read some official schoolbooks and documents, particularly those of the last generation, and to come away with the impression that most people living between Dulwich and Outer Mongolia are really 'Turks', if they did but know it – although what action they should take if they did is unclear. Government maps published as late as 1991 show almost the whole of the Eurasian world as having been inhabited by 'Turks' at one time or another. A government hand-out of the late 1980s claims that 'the Turkish tribes were scattered over an area of 18 million square metres between the twentieth century B C and the twentieth century A D, and founded sixteen empires'. More rational projections of identity and origins see Turan as a minor part of the modern Turkish background, which is officially dual-istic, with an equal cultural heritage derived from the amazing achievements of the Seljuk Turks and from their descendants in Anatolia. In the most liberal version of all, that espoused by Turgut Ozal in the last years of his life, the classical and Byzantine inheritance is openly acknowledged, although in a way where the Greek heritage is appropriated to boost Turkish tourism.

In the late nineteenth century some intellectuals, writers like Yurdakal especially, looked towards the restoration of what now seems a largely mythical Greater Turkey. This important political current appeared to die a political death with the national renaissance under Atatürk. Until very recently, Pan-Turkish ideas were largely confined to the lunatic fringe in Turkey, although a few prominent intellectuals have always articulated them. Critics of Turkey, in Greece particularly, have always claimed that they had a marked ideological influence on the army and in nationalist circles, contributing to permanently antagonistic Turkish relations with Russia and justifying expansionist ideas elsewhere. How far this was or is the case seems extremely doubtful. In the past Turkey and Russia have had many competing interests that long pre-date Pan-Turkism, going back to Byzantine times. Greek–Turkish and Byzantine–Ottoman affairs have not been harmonious at any period in history, despite many statesmen in both countries, including Atatürk himself, who wanted mutually good relations.

In Turkey itself, Pan-Turkism did not survive the Kemalist revolution even as a minority current in mainstream politics and Turkish life. After the military catastrophes of the late Ottoman sultans, and the struggle to resist Russian incursions in the east in the aftermath of the Bolshevik Revolution, there was little popular appetite for vague and misty visions of a vast new Turan super-state with unspecified and wholly indefensible borders. Securing stable national boundaries for the post-Ottoman state was an absolute national priority when Turkey itself was suffering economic and political collapse, and was partially occupied by outside powers under the Treaty of Sèvres. The genuine affection Atatürk evokes in ordinary Turks' minds rests, above all, on his achievement in stabilizing the national borders of the country, rather as Churchill is admired in Britain as a national saviour in the Second World War even by those who do not share his political outlook.

Even when Russia was most weak militarily, during the Civil War that followed the Bolshevik Revolution in 1917, there was no Pan-Turkist attempt to seize Russian territory. In the view of its proponents, Turan was, emphatically, a Muslim state that would absorb huge areas of territory belonging to the old enemy, Orthodox Russia. This was anathema to the secular Kemalists, the apostles of Turkish modernism, who saw it as an imperialist vision belonging to the past. But as in so many other spheres of life, the collapse of the Soviet Union has resulted in a resurgence of the past, and of apparently defunct ideologies. A chain of new states with Turkic or partly Turkic populations of about 42 million people, has been created, from the eastern border of Turkey through the Caucasus – independent Azerbaijan, Dagestan and Tajikistan – and beyond, towards China. This has had profound regional repercussions, even in China. Many sinologists consider that a relaxation of repressive Chinese policy in Tibet is unlikely, partly because of looming Turkic minority problems elsewhere in China. Nearer home, Turkey has become involved by proxy in the long and bitter struggle between Armenia and Azerbaijan over the disputed enclave of Nagorno-Karabakh. Turkish officers have 'advised' the Azerbaijanis in their military operations against Armenia, and Turkish military aid has played an important part in the Azerbaijani campaigns.

In this region, as elsewhere, the vistas of free-market development and international harmony of 1989 have turned into civil strife and bloody ethnic and nationalist conflict. In the most important war of all in the Caucasus, between Russia and the Chechen separatists, Turkey has played only a passive role, but further involvement is possible, given that thousands of people of Chechen descent live in south-west Turkey. As always, religion plays a central role in conflict in this part of the world. Chechens are not Turks, ethnically, but they are Muslims, and have a long history of links with Turkey during the nineteenth century in their fierce resistance to Russian domination.

In April 1995 the heads of the Russian and Turkish intelligence services met in Moscow to discuss matters of mutual interest. According to *Jane's Intelligence Review*, Moscow's concern was the use of Turkish territory as a refuge for Chechen guerrillas, while Ankara wanted the Kurdish representative office in Moscow closed down, and an end to other PKK-related activities on Russian soil. John le Carré's view that spies often carry with them the real preoccupations and subconscious fears of a nation was vindicated by these two men, representing solid middle-sized world powers with disturbing nationalist movements on both their frontiers. The retired Turkish Chief of Staff, General Dogan Gures, who is of Circassian origin, is said to have lobbied heavily for support for the Chechen rebels. In total there are estimated to be about 8 million people of Caucasus origin living in Turkey.

After what the leaders of the new Turkic republics see as hundreds of years of exploitation by the Tsarist and Soviet empires, they have naturally looked for new partnerships and allies in the post-Soviet era. This should not, on the face of it, unduly disturb Turkey's neighbours, except perhaps Armenia, with its endemic war with Azerbaijan. In the late-Communist era the political leadership of virtually all these republics was notoriously corrupt and nepotistic, and this has given the emerging states a degree of stability in the complex interaction between traditionalists and modernizers among their élites. They would have remained sleepy, marginal small states, were it not for a dramatic new factor which now dominates all regional political calculations: the discovery of vast new oil and gas reserves in Azerbaijan, on a scale that is likely to mean the Baku region will have an equivalent importance in the next century to the Middle East in our time. The republic of Turkmenistan, to the east of the Caspian Sea, also has enormous gas reserves. The population there is also of mainly Turkic origin. And, just as the lethal rivalries engendered by the oil politics of the Middle East have from time to time dominated world events, there is no reason to suppose the situation will be any different in the Caucasus in the medium term.

Turkish relations with the new republics to the east are not only concerned with international oil politics. These countries offer great opportunities for Turkish business, in that they are starved of consumer goods and, in some cases, food, and they all have natural resources to sell, often minerals. Theoretically it should be a natural partnership, with Turkey setting up joint ventures with local companies and building up businesses which should be extremely profitable and bring Turkey great political influence in the region. In the early 1990s it looked as if much of this promise might be fulfilled: Turkey was involved in strategic infrastructure schemes in central Asia, such as the modernization of the telephone networks and their integration with the Turkish system, and the placing of a Turkish television satellite above western central Asia, so that Turkish programmes can be watched as far away as the borders of China. Turkish businessmen were frequent visitors to central Asia, and new air and bus routes were opened up – the international bus station in Istanbul is full of dusty vehicles with glamorous names on the front, and it is easy to buy a ticket as far as Iran. Great lorries make up convoys to cross the empty expanses of steppe and desert, like the road trains of the Australian outback. They often have *Allah Korusun* – 'God Protects' – painted above or across the windscreen, as if the drivers do not have full faith in Mercedes Benz or Volvo engineering.

The establishment of Turkish cultural, media and transport links was cheap and easy, whereas the problems of politics, international relations and economic development are more difficult. All the emerging ex-Communist states of Eastern Europe are capital hungry, with antiquated and backward economies, and little hard currency to pay for what is required. Turkey is itself a highly indebted country, with many serious structural economic problems, and few large companies with the necessary resources and management structure to operate in an international sphere. The great industrial dynasties such as the Koc empire are very much Turkish businesses, having evolved in a specifically Turkish context over the last fifty years, and until recently they have had little or no tradition of overseas investment. They have often depended on joint ventures with more technologically advanced and financially stronger international partners in order to achieve significant growth within Turkey in some spheres of the economy. A typical example of a successful joint venture in the agribusiness field is the huge growth in the production of tomato paste, making Turkey the third largest producer in the world, after the USA and Italy, and the largest supplier to the Japanese. However, the foreign multinational is the dominant partner and provides the capital for Turkish operations; it is not a source of money for Turks to invest abroad in speculative ventures in the new Turkic republics.

The markets in some of the Turkic republics are quite small, national income levels are often very low, and substantial sections of the population do not play a role in an urban consumerist economy, or hardly in a monetary economy in the case of the smallest pastoral tribes in the Caucasus. This means a very small return on capital is available for investors. It is also unclear what kind of political environment a company would be operating in. All of the new central Asian republics have strong links with Russia, and some have sizeable Russian minorities, who often occupy leading posts in the political and economic system. These people are not instinctively friends of Turkey; they are more likely to be supportive of fellow-Orthodox Greek businessmen. The Turkish companies that do have a tradition of operating abroad, principally the advanced and internationally respected civil engineering companies, have developed in the Middle East market, and depend on a flow of petro-dollars to fund their contracts. In contrast the virtually bankrupt ex-Communist countries of central Asia have no access to large sums of international capital to pay for projects in this field.

At a deeper level, many of the problems are political. The last years of the Communist Soviet Union were not disadvantageous for Turkish business interests. The Western investment community has tended to assume that Turkey was suddenly given access to new markets after 1989 in the ex-Soviet Turkic republics that had been largely closed hitherto. This was not the case. Turkey had been trading with them for many years, on a very large scale. Between 1987 and 1991 Turkish–Soviet trade more than trebled, to 1.8 billion dollars. The star performer was the civil engineering industry, which had an order book in the Soviet Union worth 1.5 billion dollars. Much of this work was in central Asia. The Soviet Union was then bound by trade agreements to spend at least 70 per cent of the hard currency it received from sales of Siberian natural gas on Turkish goods, which was a boon to the Turkish leather, food and mining industries. The two centrally directed economies fitted together rather well: cynics maintained that the two groups of privileged and undemocratically controlled technocrats understood each other, despite deep ideological differences. Turkey was even seen by some nations to be akin to Finland, a country with so much knowledge and experience of the Soviet Union that it could serve as a trade bridge. The Turkish banks continued to make large loans to the Soviet Union during the decline of the Gorbachev regime, when some other lines of credit to the USSR had been cut off. For this short period, Turkey seemed to be the ideal partner, with the right geographical position and experience to balance interests between the centre in Moscow and the emerging, often Turkic, southern republics.

With the end of Communism, some of these hopes foundered. The Turkic republics had to be evaluated for trade purposes by foreign companies on their own investment merits. Their governments had to deal independently with Moscow, often in the absence of stable policy or administration under President Yeltsin. Some trade finance loans had to be written off, denting some Turkish banks' balance sheets. Many important construction projects have ground to a halt because there is no money in the new Russia to meet local commitments or to buy raw materials. Although trade in Turkish food and consumer goods has developed well, much of it is in the hands of mafia-linked groups, and revenue gained does not find its way to either central government.

In the absence of the increases in trade envisaged in the early 1990s, attention has increasingly refocused on to the oil issue, or, rather, on the transport of oil from the new Caspian fields. The position is portrayed by some nationalists as a struggle between civilized, Muslim Turkey and Orthodox, chaotic, gang-ster-ridden Russia. In so far as the issue is essentially tied up with political and military control of this part of central Asia, this is not true. Between the two great powers lies the Caucasus, little known and as marginal in the Communist era as the Balkans. Over twenty nationalities live there, speaking over fifty languages and dialects. They vary from large nationalities like the Armenians and Chechens, with many native speakers, to tiny Dagestan mountain groups like the Rutuls, with 15,000 native speakers, and the Tsez, with only half that number. Virtually all the countries still have Russian bases, even if they are nominally independent, except for Azerbaijan itself. Local and regional wars have flourished since the end of Communism. Control of these conflicts by the international community has proved to be difficult and is likely to become more so as the financial stakes in the oil increase.

Azerbaijan could be the Kuwait of the next century, but there are some important differences. Small oil-rich states often have problems with large aggressive neighbours, and need powerful friends within easy reach. Baku and the country surrounding it is not easily defensible, as the White Russians found after the Bolshevik Revolution, whereas Kuwait has been rescued from the aggression of its powerful neighbours on more than one occasion since it was set up as part of the British post-imperial reorganization of the Middle East. Military commitment by the strongest Western powers has been central to its survival. Before the Gulf War in 1991–2, British troops had defended the territory from the Iraqis. Kuwait is adjacent to Saudi Arabia, a friendly power deeply embedded in the Western ambience, which can be used as a base for military operations. The long tradition of Western military intervention in the region is linked closely to the preservation of conservative local power structures. In the Gulf there is an advanced technological infrastructure capable of supporting a modern war, which is certainly not the case in the central Asian republics.

Azerbaijan has few advantages should it have to resist external security threats. Instead of pliable Saudi Arabia and the docile Emirates, the local Superpower is Russia, which is generally hostile and has recently engaged in a war against neighbouring Muslim Chechenia. While Turkey is able to be a useful protector in the local war with Armenia over Nagorno-Karabakh, it is not able to provide the wide-ranging security guarantees that Azerbaijan needs to cope with its new-found wealth and relative geographical isolation. (Even in such a localized war, Turkey was not in the end able to prevent great Armenian strategic advances.)

The Azerbaijan economy is being reshaped by foreign invest-ment, in contrast to the extreme backwardness of most of its neighbours. The investment is still fairly small, but it is having a dramatic effect, and most of it is from US and European companies. But unlike in the Middle East, the Western powers are not the dominant military and political influence, and Russia is not able to provide a security framework for the region that functions properly. In 1996 there were at least five separate wars in progress in the Caucasus, involving no fewer than twelve ethnic groups. Even a relatively minor conflict such as that between the north Ossetian and Ingush peoples in the central Caucasus has caused over 50,000 people to become refugees. In many respects the chaos and violence in the mountains present Turkey with far more problems than co-existence with Commu-nist Russia ever did.

This is not simply a matter for Ankara of securing oil and oil transport business, although that is very valuable in itself. Turkey's eastern frontier has historically always been an area of worry. Although the Armenian issue has had its day within Turkey itself, Turkey is rent with dissent over the Kurdish war, and there is no shortage of other internal tensions between different social groups. The eastern border has reverted to being a cordon sanitaire against the contagion of ethnic and religious conflict to the east. The advantages of increased economic participation in the region have to be set against the increased risks of involvement in the lethal feuds of the new Turkic nations. There is also the question of cultural affinity. In the eyes of the sophisticated, secular, Western-oriented middle classes of Istanbul or Izmir, there are already far too many 'primitive' people coming from the east, who are often seen as upsetting the nation's social, religious and political stability. The modernist middle classes feel that they have little in common with illiterate tribesmen from the Anatolian or Kurdish mountains, who are often seriously Islamic, and whose claims to be 'Turkish', in any meaningful sense, seem remote.

Fears about the future have crystallized around the question of oil transport. The pipeline routes from Azerbaijan have been subject to much political and financial controversy and international intrigue. In 1995 the Azerbaijan government opted for the so-called 'two pipeline solution', at least for the first flow from the new fields. This provides for a flow of oil through Russia, and also through the Caucasus to a terminal in south-east Turkey. The preferred Russian route also involves a terminal in northern Greece, at the small backwoods port of Alexandropolis, and runs through Bulgaria. The project is very close to fruition and a little oil began to be pumped in late 1996, but the overall project has been disrupted by quarrels between the pipeline company, dominated by Greeks and Russians, and the Bulgarians, who want a greater share of the construction work for allowing the pipeline to cross their territory. The Bulgarians claim that far too much of the construction work will be dominated by Greek contractors, and they wish to have a substantial minority shareholding in the pipeline company. The Russians and Greeks do not wish to give, in effect, a veto over the operation of the pipeline to the Bulgarians, who will contribute almost nothing towards the costs of construction. The issue is complicated by the wider uncertainties of Bulgarian–Russian relations, and by Bulgarian-Greek tensions – the fact that Greek businessmen are acquiring ever greater economic influence in Bulgaria is not always welcomed in Sofia government circles.

There is also a deeper problem. At the moment the Azerbaijani oilfields are perceived by Turkey as a source of enormous wealth and accompanying political power, once the question of oil transport is resolved. Yet with oil prices often under pressure the multinational oil companies who control the refining and marketing of most of the world's petroleum products have shown no sign of wishing to bring Azerbaijani oil quickly to the market, nor have the existing oil producers who make up the Organization of Petroleum Exporting Countries (OPEC). Leading members of OPEC, Saudi Arabia in particular, have been lobbying against the reopening of world markets to Iraq, which would increase the world supply and could cause oil prices to drop radically. The Saudis are still paying for the vast expenses of the Gulf War and show no sign of wanting Iraqi crude in world markets until those debts are paid, especially since the kingdom is not as economically secure as it used to be. The solution proposed by the Azerbaijani International Oil Consortium, the Western oil giants who will ship the oil in the future, is to lift a limited quantity of 5 million tons a year, the so-called 'early oil', to bring some revenue to Azerbaijan and to begin to introduce the product to the world market. Even this apparently positive proposal is seen as a possible stalling device by some Turkish oil experts, as it would be completely uneconomic to build a pipeline to transport so little oil.

It is possible that the wealth the Azerbaijanis and many Turks dream of will never be realized, and that they will have to be content with a much smaller quantity of oil shipped across Turkey. Without it, there will never be a rich Turkic bloc dominating the region between Istanbul and the Caspian Sea. As many other countries have found, oil guarantees a place in the highest councils of world politics, and offers the greatest potential wealth, but it also brings small and often militarily vulnerable countries into conflict with some of the most powerful and ruthless global vested interests – those of the major oil companies and the existing producers in OPEC. The oil companies claim that the Azerbaijani boom will only be delayed, not aborted; but in the twenty or thirty years that oil men say it may be necessary to wait before the real wealth comes through, many other oilfields may be found in less politically difficult surroundings.

In 1995 Prime Minister Tansu Ciller stated that her two main goals before the Turkish general election were to see that Turkey entered the EU Customs Union, and that the pipelines carrying Azerbaijani oil to the West should pass through Turkey. Her strategic reasoning was clear in both cases, although neither ambition was fully realized before the election. The second is much the more difficult, as rapid development of Azerbaijani oil would benefit Turkey and the adjoining Turkic states alone. It is not currently in the interests of Russia, the major oil companies, or the existing oil producers. A showdown with Russia over the issue is politically impossible, as Russian gas for the time being has a near monopoly in Turkey and powers much of Turkish industry. Perhaps understandably, the excitement over the prospects for Azerbaijani oil that dominated Turkey in the early 1990s has largely evaporated, as the political and economic fog over the mega-project shows no sign of lifting. There are also increasingly widely felt environmental concerns about the prospect of hundreds of new tanker passages through the already crowded Bosphorus if the Azerbaijani fields are ever fully exploited.

In late 1996 major decisions over the pipelines appeared to be suspended, as the United States and other Western powers awaited the outcome of President Yeltsin's heart operation and of the power struggle in the Russian leadership. Turkey's best hope of securing international financial support and political commitment for the Azerbaijani pipeline proposals would be a strongly nationalist or Communist government in Russia, which would make a Turkish-controlled route seem desirable for Western security reasons.

The other factor that would act as a catalyst for the Azerbaijanis and their friends in Ankara is the possibility of increasing instability in the Middle East. In 1995 and 1996 the growth of anti-US sentiment was evident in Saudi Arabia, and if the renewed assertiveness of Iraq led to another Gulf War, the West would be under pressure to secure more diverse oil supplies.

The windswept hills beyond Batman are some of the most lonely in Turkey, severe, unforgiving, and very poor. Beyond them is the remote province of Hakkari and the Islamic Republic of Iran, considered by many the most threatening terrorist state in the world, the exporter of Islamic revolution, and the central threat to Turkish stability. Yet, as borders go, it is calm. It has none of the tension of the Balkan *granitsas*, with tough guards who really believe that they are the last line of defence against Vatican imperialism or Serbian expansionism, nor the prim efficiency of the old Iron Curtain countries. Some trade carries on: old lorries laden with fruit and vegetables cross the border; Kurds sell cartons of Marlboro cigarettes by the roadside. A group of Belgian doctors from Médecins Sans Frontières change a wheel on their Land Rover, a dusty lump of Birmingham metal lost among dry scrub. Debt-laden peasants are paying a village shop-keeper and money-lender his dues after returning with hard-earned money from cotton picking on the plains far away. There is much less of the front line atmosphere of the Syrian border, with its free-fire zones, ethnic cleansing of Kurdish villages nearby, and high-technology military equipment. The Iranian border is not a friendly place, not least because of the difficult climate, but it is not somewhere where death seems to be waiting in the acacia bushes with an AK, or laying a mine behind a carob tree. Although most of the population here is Kurdish, the Turkish security forces' main effort is to control the towns and often to enforce a night-time curfew; the countryside is too remote and under-populated to justify the systematic 'counter-insurgency' warfare that has destroyed so many villages nearer the border with Syria. The Iraqi border to the south is now quiet because of UN sanctions, but was once the focus of thriving trade that Ankara claims was worth 3 billion dollars a year. (The 612-mile-long pipeline between Kirkuk in northern Iraq and the Turkish Mediterranean port of Yumurtalik earned the country about 250 million dollars a year.)

In central Asia, Iran is now a rival even if the Erbakan government has signed a major gas deal with Tehran in 1996. This is symbolized by the opening, in May 1996, of a new railway linking the landlocked central Asian republics with Iran and the Indian ocean. Iran has always been strategically important. Under the British Empire it was a key point on the road to India, just as it was in the time of Alexander the Great. As well as offering an outlet to the sea for the countries of central Asia, it is a source of oil and trade. It will be surprising if religion and business do not accompany the railway, just as in the nineteenth century missionaries and traders accompanied the railways that opened up the American West or the interior of Africa. It remains to be seen how successful the Iranians will be, and whether they will become the major influence in the region, but Ankara's optimism that these new Turkic nations would easily fall into its sphere of influence seems misplaced. In the same way, in the far eastern states, like Kazakhstan, the Chinese are very active in trade and commerce, with very low priced goods to sell, and here it seems unlikely that Turkish economic penetration will be significant in the future. Since 1993 the dramatic vistas of expanding Turkish influence in central Asia have been obscured and a modern 'Turan' seems as far away as ever.

14. Turkey, the Middle East and the Future

Adet (custom) in Turkey is at the root of civilized life. But all over the world custom dies hard.

Victoria de Bunsen, *The Soul of a Turk*, 1910

All realized that at last their glorious city had been freed from the Turkish yoke. Howling dervishes ran in front of him, dancing and sticking knives into their flesh, while behind him came his column of picturesque Arabian Knights. For months they had heard of the exploits of Shereef Lawrence, but now for the first time they saw the mysterious Englishman who had united the desert tribes and driven the Turks from Arabia.

Lowell Thomas, *With Lawrence in Arabia*, 1928

Turkey means many things now to those who visit the country – the warm sea on a holiday at Bodrum, the minarets and monuments of Istanbul, hermits living in caves in Capadocia – but never the bleak and sandy wastes of the Yemen or the Syrian desert. Yet it is arguable that the foreigner who had most influence on the definition of Turkey among the educated British in the early years of this century scarcely set foot in Turkey itself. The Ottoman desert was his playground, where the sultan's Arab empire was in its death throes. Lawrence of Arabia is no longer a fashionable figure in Britain; his ascetic homosexual infatuation with the Arabs, and his committed and idealistic British imperialism are not politically correct these days. His main work, *The*

Seven Pillars of Wisdom, is little read, after being Sir Winston Churchill's favourite book and enjoying best-seller status between the wars.

The romance of the discovery of Arabia as *Arabia felix*, with its noble and dignified Bedouin inhabitants, has been replaced in the West by a popular image of Arabs as corrupt sheikhs, venal dictators, religious fanatics, or potential terrorists. It is difficult to recapture the excitement felt by Lawrence and his contemporaries at the alliance between Arab nationalism and British interests against the Ottoman sultan, and the affirmation of Arab culture this involved. As the Ottoman world has disappeared, so the Arab revolt became more difficult to understand. Lawrence had little interest in the future of Turkey itself, and was more than content for Atatürk to try to drag it into the modern world if he could. This is perhaps a pity, because, whatever the weaknesses and limitations of Lawrence, his perspective and his momentous life's work in the Middle East were a testimony to the fact that the Turks are not Arabs, and vice versa. He would have found the idea now prevalent in parts of the West that Turkey is a secular, Muslim country and an example of what the Arab world should become quite absurd.

The West has always tended to define Turkey as part of the Arab Middle East, and that remains the case today, especially in the United States. Yet it is a view that ignores much of twentieth-century history. For example the British Empire's influence in the Middle East after the First World War was based on the opposition between Ottoman Turks and Arab nationalists. One of the reasons for the German débâcle in the war in southeastern Europe was the fact that the Kaiser was fighting with Ottoman troops gained as a result of Germany's alliance with Turkey in 1914. But at least a quarter of the Ottoman army was of Arab stock, and most of them deserted if they could, rather than fight the Kaiser's surrogate battles. They were hungry, maltreated and never paid, and they disappeared like water in the desert sands from where so many of them had sprung. Another example of historical amnesia surfaced when correspondents covering the Gulf War in Iraq in 1992 recalled the Battle of Kut, which lies on the road to modern Baghdad. Whereas the Battle of the Somme is indelibly etched on British memory, the Battle of Kut in Mesopotamia has been completely forgotten, although it was the largest British–Turkish encounter in the war, and tens of thousands died in the burning sands. Troops on both sides suffered appalling hardships. It is a telling sign of how much history shared with Turkey has disappeared from our consciousness.

However hard various Turkish political leaders and publicists have tried to create a European identity, where it matters most – in the US State Department and the Pentagon – the country is seen principally as a piece on the Middle East chessboard and the second largest recipient of US military aid in the region after Israel. Of course the fortunes of Turkey are inextricably bound up with the Middle East, a fact that is perhaps less easy to appreciate in the middle of Istanbul than in the desert near the Syrian border, or in the bleak and windswept limestone border hills near Iraq. Within living memory, many of these neighbouring countries were part of the Ottoman Empire. Most of Syria was part of the *vilayet*, or Ottoman province, of Damascus and, while countries such as Egypt had gained some independence in the nineteenth century, many vestiges of the sultan's authority remained. In the days before oil wealth transformed the area, most of the Middle Eastern territories mattered little in world affairs. But this was to change with dramatic rapidity after 1920, as T. E. Lawrence and those close to him, like the young Winston Churchill, appreciated. It was Turkey's misfortune that the greater part of the Middle East oil reserves in the Ottoman *vilayets* was being discovered just as the empire was collapsing and Constantinople was losing control of the territories concerned. It is ironic that one of the central planks of Atatürk's policy – national control of resources – often meant little within Turkey itself, but was to become a central determinant of international politics in the twentieth century. If the Ottoman Empire had survived until 1935, it would have contained a large proportion of the known oil reserves of the world, apart from those of the southern United States, which would have given Turkey a position of real world economic influence in the 1930s. The loss of what is now Iraq and the oil-rich Gulf regions has never been forgotten in Turkey, and contributes to the sense of lost national greatness that many Turks feel about the immediate past. This in turn is linked with the unwillingness of many Turks to make concessions on the Kurdish issue: Kurdistan is seen as a last imperial possession that has to be defended and kept after so many have been lost. The fact that some of the Middle Eastern *vilayets* were found to contain untold riches is a particular source of regret. For example, the key *vilayet* of Mosul, in what is now northern Iraq, not only contains great petroleum reserves, but has a large indigenous population of entirely Turkic origin. It was an irony of the Gulf War that these people formed the core of Saddam Hussein's Republican Guard, as some of the finest soldiers in the country, just as they joined the Ottoman élite in earlier days. One of the many reasons why the United States did not overthrow Saddam at the end of the Gulf War concerns the various neighbouring claims on Iraqi territory, such as the Iranian claim on the Shiite areas in the south, and the Kurds in the north of the country. Although Turkish ambitions towards Mosul are less well known, it is unlikely but possible that they would be articulated in the event of a total collapse of central authority in Iraq.

The 'official' view of Turkey's role in the Middle East that prevails in the United States and elsewhere is that it is an exemplary but secular Muslim state. In addition, Turkey has been prepared to recognize Israel, which until the Camp David agreement in 1978 had been ostracized by all other neighbouring countries, and has been prepared to allow her territory to be used for key American military bases. Turkey is certainly seen as an intermediary between East and West by many in the

Middle East, and this applies to matters of religion as well as business.

The crumbling slums of the Balat district in Istanbul, on the west side of the Golden Horn, are the nearest the old Ottoman city ever came to having a Jewish ghetto. Balat nowadays is very sad, like Fener. The streets that once were a vibrant commercial district are derelict and smelly, and most of the synagogues, centres of piety and the study of the law for centuries, have been transformed into warehouses and storage sheds. Trees self-seed and grow out of holes in the walls. It is as if there have been pogroms. The Greeks left the adjoining port district over the years and so have most Jews, although the language of the Sephardic Jews, Ladino, based on medieval Spanish, can still be heard spoken by old men in the coffee shops in some of the narrow streets. Some Jews have prospered and moved to the outer suburbs, as in all European and American cities, but many more have left Turkey altogether.

It is a great and abiding myth that there is no anti-Semitism in Turkey, and that there is a special quality of tolerance in Jewish-Turkish relations that is absent elsewhere. This is based on the generous welcome the early sultans gave to Sephardic Jews leaving Spain under the Catholic persecutions. It is a view projected strongly in some accounts of Jewish history in Turkey, particularly that put forward by the American Turkophile authority on the Ottoman Jews, Stanford Shaw. Greek anti-Semitism is contrasted with Turkish tolerance. Yet as long ago as the Second World War there was substantial Jewish emigration from Turkey in protest against excessive, virtually confiscatory, taxation of the business community in Istanbul and other cities – a fact that is glossed over in Shaw's otherwise authoritative work. His critics have accused him of neglecting the Armenian massacres in his view of Turkish history, and trying to build a pro-Turkish lobby among the politically influential US Jewish community. The 1950s and 1960s also saw considerable Turkish

Jewish emigration to Israel as a result of economic difficulties. In recent years there have been some attacks on synagogues by Muslim militants, and there is a sense of a loss of self-confidence in some parts of the Istanbul Jewish community.

This change in attitude is important at the human level in any consideration of Turkish relations with the Middle East. At the height of the Cold War, Turkey fitted into a pattern of international relationships designed to reinforce Israeli security as the centre-piece of United States Middle East policy. One of the beneficial effects of the Cold War was to insulate Turkey from many aspects of the Middle East and its lethal quarrels. Turkey had a clear and well-defined role to play within Western security structures. Most of the time this meant Turkey kept out of active participation in the wars and conflicts of the Middle East. Some internal problems in Turkey, principally the Kurdish struggle, had external repercussions, but they were containable by the US and its allies.

This is not necessarily the case today, and has added to internal tensions within the Turkish body politic. The Gulf War in 1991–2 was a watershed, which made a major economic, political and cultural impact. As soon as the prospect of war with Iraq over the invasion of Kuwait loomed, the United Nations imposed economic sanctions on Iraq. This meant the important pipeline exporting Iraqi oil running through Turkey had to be closed, at an estimated cost of 250 million dollars a year. Iraq was also an important market for Turkish agricultural exports, particularly from the farms of the south-east benefiting from the new irrigation schemes. Although the international community promised to meet the cost of these measures, it never really did so, and many Turkish companies in industries like road haulage were badly hit, and some were bankrupted. The long-running crisis with Iraq since then has meant that pre-1991 trade levels have never been recaptured. Other changes in the region have also adversely affected trade prospects. The end of the war in Lebanon has reduced demand for Turkish food in Syria, as many products on the Syrian market are now supplied locally. The fertile acres of occupied Lebanon have taken over much of this important market. Iran has suffered growing economic problems since the early 1990s, and business prospects are no longer so optimistic. Central Asian states to the north of the Middle East have difficulty in paying for what they want to buy. Saudi Arabia has a small domestic market and is no longer the cornucopia for Turkish civil engineering contractors that it was in the 1980s.

The geography of the 1995 general election may provide a good indication of Turkey's likely future. Over the great mass of central and eastern Anatolia, Refah was the largest party, with Islamic victories stretching to the heart of Istanbul, not only in the poor working-class suburbs but also in fashionable districts. Islam has become chic among the critical middle classes. Along the Black Sea coast and in the Mediterranean towns the old secular parties, which represent Atatürk's heritage in however uncertain and contradictory a way, still have secure majorities, while Thrace, with its history of settlement by refugee families from Balkan countries, is still firmly secular and anti-Islamic, and the main power base of the centre-left. In the south-east, in the Kurdish provinces, the Kurdish parties dominated local voting but did not reach the 10 per cent of the national poll required to secure parliamentary representation. Many soldiers must also have voted for the Refah Party, given the importance of the garrison vote in these parts of the country.

The Refah Party has put religion firmly back into the centre of Turkish life, and that religion is Islam. The home of Islam is in Saudi Arabia, and the states which are most closely tied to theocratic concepts of government surround it. The opening of Turkey to the East, with the possibility of some kind of Islamic Commonwealth or Islamic Common Market or Comecon, is an awe-inspiring prospect. However unlikely it is to come to fruition in the form its Refah Party advocates envisage, it may be an idea whose time has come. The great strength of Refah is that it is more than a political party; it has some of the same characteristics, in the minds of its supporters and members, as Andreas Papandreou's Panhellenic Socialist Party (PASOK) in Greece in the 1970s and 1980s. Although both are highly effective orthodox political parties that grew from small beginnings to become governing parties over a short period of time, they are also movements for fundamental change in society. They encourage loyalties much deeper than mere party loyalty. Before old age and decrepitude overtook its leader, PASOK could draw on passion and commitment of an entirely new kind. The old right in Athens was discredited by the Colonels' dictatorship in the same way as the entrenched right in Ankara has been discredited by nepotism and corruption. Both new parties arose at a time when the public was tired and disillusioned with the old parties and when society seemed to have reached an impasse; both provide a vision of what a really independent Greece or Turkey might become. Both had a charismatic and effective leader from the older generation who was part of the traditional ruling class but also in rebellion against it. Many of the consequences for the friends and allies of Greece and Turkey may be similar, and there is confirmation of this in Refah's performance in government in 1996. An irritating unpredictability was the hallmark of PASOK in the 1980s, with Greece cast as the gadfly of the NATO alliance. Refah has so far behaved similarly, particularly over foreign policy, where conformity to some NATO and American policy keystones, such as the Turkey–Israel defence agreement, has been combined with independence on other issues, exemplified by the visit of the prime minister to Libya in October 1996, which led to a government crisis and a parliamentary vote of censure. It was a victory for Refah, and a sign of a new reorientation of foreign policy of a genuine kind, one that is not afraid of a degree of nationalist assertion.

It is arguable how far the Refah government began to affect the Islamization of Turkish life. It did not introduce a legislative programme jettisoning secularism, partly for the obvious reason that Refah is only a coalition partner in a government with a 'secular' party, but also because Islam continues to advance without legislative assistance. The massive mosque-building and Islamic education programmes long predated Refah in government and will ensure Islamic cultural dominance in thousands of communities throughout the country. The millions of Western tourists on Turkish beaches will exert a countervailing influence. Despite the election of Refah, tourist numbers grew strongly in 1996 on the back of the weak lira: some 9.5 million visitors brought in revenues of no less than 6 billion dollars. Tourism now accounts for 26 per cent of external revenues, and 3.3 per cent of gross national product. With an annual growth rate of 15 per cent, it is a source of income that the government cannot afford to see threatened by images of Islamic extremism.

The thinking in most European capitals has been that Refah government would be a passing phase, and it would collapse in acrimony between the two coalition partners. In fact the government had to be forced from power by action from the National Security Council in mid-1997, with a mere veneer of parliamentary sanction. The confidence vote after the Libya visit had showed Turkey could develop its own foreign policy in defiance of the United States and NATO. Economic independence will be much more difficult to achieve, as awesome problems remain. A large gas deal with Iran has been signed, which will considerably reduce Turkey's reliance on Russian energy, but it will take time before the benefits come through. The structural reorientation of Turkey's entire economy and trading patterns that the Islamists seek will take years, if not decades, and in 1996–7 Refah was not in government long enough to attempt them. It was much more hopeful of short-term gains in industries like civil engineering, where Turkish contractors are owed large sums of money by countries such as Iran, Iraq and Libya; in theory they could receive some of what is owed if good political relationships in the nascent new Islamic 'Commonwealth' come into existence. How much was achieved in this direction is an open question.

Perhaps Refah counted too much on the famous patience and endurance of the Turkish people in the economic sphere, the stoicism and fortitude of ordinary people who will be prepared to wait a long time for the benefits of Islamic government to come to them. But the government does need to be able to offer them something other than wage rises that are immediately eaten away by inflation, and it is difficult at the moment to see how popular measures can be financed. Nevertheless, the results of the local and regional elections in November 1996 were reassuring for Refah: the party topped the poll with almost 31 per cent of the votes and made significant gains in the Aegean and Black Sea regions, where hitherto it had been weak. Its coalition partner came second, with 27 per cent of the votes, whereas the Motherland Party, in government for so long during the 1980s, only polled 8 per cent.

Another critical issue for the government has been relations with the military. Some foreign observers predicted an immediate aggressive reaction to a government with a Refah prime minister – a coup to save the Atatürkist tradition, although all previous interventions have had the blessing of the United States, which was unlikely to be forthcoming in this case. Recent American policy over Turkey has run a wandering course. There has been overblown rhetoric which strengthened the old élite's sense of self-importance. For example in September 1995 Mr Warren Christopher, the Secretary of State, stated that Turkey was a 'front line state', while another State Department official said that its importance was the equivalent of West Germany's in the Cold War. Such statements have not been matched by the economic and military aid actually disbursed. In particular the US has failed to come to terms with the burgeoning cost for Turkey of sanctions against Iraq, estimated at 27 billion dollars since 1991. In military terms, the Clinton administration has been seen in Ankara to be controlled by the Greek lobby, with the result that Ankara's requests to buy ten Cobra helicopter gunships and three frigates have been halted in Congress. In 1991 US economic aid to Turkey ran at about 120 million dollars a year; now it is only a quarter of that figure. Real commitment to Turkey is seen to be increasingly limited, and the old school of senior generals and admirals may come to realize that some sort of accommodation with Refah and its successors is necessary in the absence of strong US support for military intervention against the Islamic movement. Washington's policy clearly relies on the hope that the Refah movement will self-destruct quickly. It is a high risk strategy, as the Clinton administration found when trying to obtain Turkish support for the US missile attacks on Iraq in the autumn of 1996. Both Erbakan and Foreign Minister Ciller refused to support the US, knowing that Washington has little real leverage over the Ankara government, and that there was little for them to gain by following the policy of the old Gulf War coalition.

The current state of Turkish politics is very confused, with the military having achieved the ejection of Refah and the Islamists from government, at least temporarily, and the law courts have banned the party and Mr Erbakan from politics. But the underlying realities of the deep crisis in Turkish society remain the same, and it may well be that in a future election Refah will benefit from public sympathy over the undemocratic pressures applied by the old Ankara establishment to try to stifle the Islamic movement. In the short term it is a political victory for the old political system and for the United States, but the long-term cost may be high, with the old secular political parties showing little sign of coming to terms with popular alienation from the elder generation of politicians.

Epilogue

Across the Golden Horn, the workmen are crawling like ants on the dome of Hagia Sophia, once a church, once a mosque, now a museum. God here was banished by decree, much to the chagrin of irredentist and romantic Greeks, on one hand, and Islamic fundamentalists on the other. Both would like to see the greatest surviving monument from the Byzantine world cease to be a museum, the mausoleum for Atatürk's ideals of secularism and tolerance. To all intents and purposes these workers are engaged in necessary repairs, but the repairs are not exempt from controversy. In Athens in 1995 anonymous leaflets were being distributed, in the style of the outpourings of the Greek junta, accusing the Turks of neglecting the greatest Byzantine monument of all.

By the restored Ottoman houses below the west walls, a tall amiable man in an immaculate uniform stares aimlessly into space; his official role is to shepherd visitors in the right direction, encouraging them to rent a room in one of the little hotels – superb period restorations, with thick rugs, neat bottles of mineral water, scented soap, latticed wooden window shades designed to prevent ladies of the Porte in the late nineteenth century from being spied on. When he takes off his uniform and returns home to his cramped flat in Karakoy, he has nothing much to look forward to except the fortunes of Galatasaray, the football cult. The blood spilt nearby to defend or attack the Cross or the Crescent mean nothing to him; he is part of Atatürk's heritage – obedient, formal, devoid of ambition, his motto, *basa gelen cekilir*, 'one must endure what comes'.

Santa Sophia is echoing, empty. It has endured earthquakes,

sackings, fires, civil upheaval, then the end of the Byzantine Empire, the end of Rum, the new Rome. An overwhelming amount of history has passed through it, including some of the central events that have determined all European life since. History has been absorbed by the building and the city, by time itself, the opposite of the Balkans, where the past surges back into the present, death into life. But it has a chilling, decimated emptiness. Guides report that visitors in conducted parties often disperse as if in a trance, unable to bear the company of others for long inside the great cathedral. The Byzantine world of which it is the monument is more remote to many of them than the ancient world that predated it.

A few minutes walk along the street is the Cistern of Justinian, dark and oblong, wet and echoing, with hundreds of lined columns and patterns of light and shade in the subterranean darkness. The architecture is mathematical, regular, a tribute to the last intellectual flowering of Byzantine optimism. Along a walkway is the entrance to the next world, carefully restored. Music from *Phantom of the Opera*. Drips of water fall from the ceiling into the dark shallow water beneath the wooden planks. Japanese shuffle along into the nether darkness. It recalls the world of Byzantine conspiracy, assassination, casual violence. Above ground half a mile away in the damp soil near Topkapi Serai are the strangled brothers of Murat I. There must have been many sudden deaths down here. The living move uncertainly towards the end of the walkway. They know they must move that way, but they do not know why. Then in the water at the far end of the cistern they see the great head of Medusa lying on its side, holding up a column, a pagan goddess brought low, betrayed. The great theme of Turkey is betrayal of hope and promises. It is perhaps the most thrilling sight in modern Istanbul inside an ancient monument. The sculptor must have remembered a sensual and beautiful woman who he imagined lying in this prison. Her face recalls the lies of the late imperial officials, barking inanities to the people:

the walls will hold, the barbarians will for ever be held at bay.

Five minutes walk away is the Column of Constantine, perhaps the ugliest and most disappointing of the old monuments of the *polis*, a blunt, broken stump sticking up into the air near the Covered Market, a diseased old phallus of dirty grey stone held together with rusty iron rings which embodies the corruption of the old city. But below it are the Cemberlitas baths, reached through an unprepossessing open door in a stone grey wall.

This is a cleansing *hamam*. Wet marble. Two strangers approach from opposite directions, a man from the train that has wound laboriously through Thrace, a woman from the east. They bring with them the emptiness of Anatolia. One is a Turk, small, squat, with a little grey woolly hat. The other is a Kurd, thin, tall, with the eagle nose of her mountains, an olive skin. The baths bring a kind of democracy, a shared facility provided by the state.

Twelve o'clock. Eight hundred miles to the east, in the heights near Boghazkoy, dust, vast skies that remind visitors this is the edge of the Eurasian steppe. You can walk to Peking from here. Boghazkoy was the citadel of the Hittite kings, who built walls as long as sections of the Great Wall of China. Away from the city, there is no illusion of security. The remains of Hittite walls rise barely a few inches above the ground, not enough to protect mice and voles from the birds of prey who patrol them. Once they were the only barrier against anarchy. Turkey is the land of walls, built to protect a modicum of interior freedom. Here they have been reduced to a human irrelevance. The landscape stretches into infinity over the piles of scree and close-cropped spring grass. This is the land of the lost god, the Hittite myth of the missing god who has fled from Anatolia, from the endless stony wilderness that makes Turkey more a continent than a country. If he could be found and enticed back to favour his people through ritual and sacrifice, he reinvigorates the land and all the crops will grow. There had been famine, the gods and men and women had begun to starve, but then he was found. In the twentieth-century myth, the Turkish people had been starving for hundreds of years; then the god returned. He was called Atatürk. In Turkey today his bust and presence are everywhere, but his capacity to make rain and gentle sun and turn the landscape green is waning. In Hittite times vines and olives, the plants of civilization, grew here. But then the god was lost. In this terrible, poetic land, no one could find him.

Chronology

1071	Defeat of the Byzantines at the Battle of Manzikert, by the Seljuk Turks. Beginning of the Turkification of Anatolia.
1389	Death of Sultan Murat I in Kosovo.
1453	Fall of Byzantine Constantinople to the Ottoman Turks.
1521	Fall of Belgrade to Sultan Süleyman I, the Magnificent.
1826	Sultan Mahmut II's suppression of the janissaries.
1831–76	The age of imperial reform.
1876	Abdül Hamit II becomes sultan.
1877	Russian invasion of Turkey.
1878	Congress of Berlin.
1881	Birth of Mustafa Kemal Atatürk.
1895	Atatürk enters the Military Academy at Monastir.
1902	Atatürk graduates from Staff College in Constantinople.
1908	Young Turk Revolution.
1909	Deposition of Sultan Abdül Hamit II.
1910	Atatürk serves as chief of staff in the suppression of the revolt in Albania.
1912	First Balkan War.
1913	Second Balkan War.
1914	Archduke Ferdinand assassinated in Sarajevo, 28 June.
1915	Allied landings at Anzac.
1916	Allied evacuation of Gallipoli peninsula. On 1 April Atatürk promoted to General and Pasha. On

	7 August he recaptures Mus from the Russians.
1918	Death of Sultan Mehmet V. Atatürk returns to Constantinople.
1919	Versailles Peace Conference. Greek forces land at Smyrna, 15 May. Atatürk establishes HQ at Angora, 27 December.
1920	Military occupation of Constantinople by the Entente powers. Atatürk condemned to death by the sultan's government, 11 May. Armenian Republic established 2 December.
1921	Battle of Sakarya. Turks check Greek advances. Atatürk given title of *Ghazi* by the Grand National Assembly, 19 September.
1922	Flight of Sultan Mehmet VI from Constantinople. Peace conference opens in Lausanne, 20 November.
1923	Treaty of Lausanne. Turkish Republic declared, with Angora as the capital.
1924	Abolition of the caliphate.
1925	Uprising in Kurdistan.
1928	Introduction of Latin alphabet.
1932	Turkey joins the League of Nations.
1938	Death of Atatürk. Ismet Inonu follows him as president.
1939	Start of the Second World War. Turkey follows a policy of neutrality.
1950	Victory of the Democratic Party in the general election over the Atatürkist People's Party, led by Adam Menderes.
1960	Military coup. Execution of Menderes.
1965	Victory of the Justice Party in the general election. Mr Demirel becomes prime minister.
1980	Military junta takes over the government, under General Evren.
1987	Victory of Turgut Ozal in the general election.

1993   Death of Turgut Ozal. Mrs Tansu Ciller becomes prime minister.
1995   Islamic Refah Party becomes the largest party in parliament after the general election.
1996   Refah Party forms government in coalition with the True Path Party.

Select Bibliography

There is a vast literature in many languages on the history of the ancient, Byzantine and Ottoman periods in Turkey, and a considerable number of books on the modern period. Readers needing an accessible general introduction in English to the main themes of Turkish history will benefit from reading the monumental works of Lord Kinross, *The Ottoman Centuries* and *Atatürk*. An invaluable picture of late Ottoman Turkey-in-Europe is to be found in *Grèce et Turquie d'Europe* by Émile Isambert (Hachette, Paris, 1881).

Turkish studies of Atatürk are numerous but often difficult to obtain in the UK or the USA. A useful volume is *Atatürk: Founder of a Modern State*, ed. Kazan, Cigil and Ozbudyn, London, 1981. G. A. Armstrong's biography of Atatürk, *Grey Wolf*, is a riveting short account of the life of a great man, although presenting a controversial view of his personality. For the post-Second World War period, Geoffrey Lewis Lewis's *Turkey* gives an unrivalled picture of the world of the 1950s and 1960s, and there is much to be learned from the work of Professors William Hale, C. H. Dodd, and Dr Philip Robbins on contemporary problems.

A guide book that contains scholarly and generally objective views of Turkish history and monuments is the *Blue Guide to Turkey* by Bernard McDonagh. The *Blue Guide to Istanbul* by John Freely is an authoritative and learned survey of the contemporary city. Much contemporary British travel writing about Turkey closely reflects the Ankara government's preferred views of history and society and should be read critically. An exception is the work of William Dalrymple. In previous generations this was not the case, and writers such as George E. Bean, Freya Stark, Rose Macaulay, A. Goodrich-Freer, and A. Locher are helpful to the student of Turkish politics, economics and society as well as to the traveller. Richard Stoneman's *A Traveller's History of Turkey* is a useful book which gives due space to Greek and other minority issues.

The Turkish government produces a large number of official publications. Although the statistics are more accurate than they used to be, and the viewpoints less dogmatic, an independent assessment of controversial issues is essential, notably concerning ethnic minorities, the war in Kurdistan, Greece, Aegean boundaries, the history of the Balkans, Armenia, the Orthodox Church in Turkey, the recent history of Cyprus.

The list that follows comprises works mentioned in the text and some useful background volumes.

AMNESTY INTERNATIONAL, *Reports on Turkey*, London, 1972–

H. C. ARMSTRONG, *Grey Wolf*, London, 1938

Neal ASCHERSON, *Black Sea*, London, 1995

David BARCHARD, *Asil Nadir and the Rise of Polly Peck*, London, 1992

David BRAUND, *Georgia in Antiquity*, Oxford, 1994

A. BRYER and D. WINFIELD, *The Byzantine Monuments and Topography of the Pontos*, Washington, 1985

Fredrick BURNABY, *On Horseback through Asia Minor*, London, 1898

Noel BUXTON, *Travels and Reflections*, London, 1929

G. CHALIAND and Yves TERNON, *The Armenians: From Genocide to Resistance*, London, 1983

Richard CRAMPTON, *A Short History of Bulgaria*, London, 1987

W. E. CURTIS, *The Turks' Lost Provinces*, London, 1921

Victoria DE BUNSEN, *The Soul of a Turk*, London, 1910

Roderick DAVIDSON, *Turkey: A Short History*, New Jersey, 1968.

M. H. DOBKIN, *Smyrna 1922*, London, 1972

C. H. DODD, *Politics and Government in Turkey*, Manchester, 1969

Edith DURHAM, *The Burden of the Balkans*, London, 1905

— *Twenty Years of Balkan Tangle*, London, 1921

Charles ELIOT, *Turkey in Europe*, London, 1900

Edward GIBBON, *The Decline and Fall of the Roman Empire*, London, 1776

Philip GLAZEBROOK, *Journey to Kars*, London, 1984

John GRANT, *Through the Garden of Allah*, London, 1938

The Greeks in the Black Sea, Panorama, Athens, 1991

E. A. GROSVENOR, *Constantinople*, Boston, 1895

Guide Bleu Turquie, Paris, 1958

O. R. GURNEY, *The Hittites*, London, 1952

William HALE, *The Political and Economic Development of Modern Turkey*, London, 1981

Christopher HANN, *Tea and the Domestication of the Turkish State*, London, 1990

Lord HARDINGE, *Old Diplomacy: Reminiscences*, London, 1947

F. W. HASLUCK, *Christianity and Islam under the Sultans*, Oxford, 1929

Metin HEPER, *The State Tradition in Turkey*, London, 1985

Aubrey HERBERT, *Ben Kendim*, New York, 1925

Z. Y. HERSHLAG, *The Contemporary Turkish Economy*, Tel Aviv, 1988

Tim HINDLE, *The Sultan of Berkeley Square*, London, 1991

Eva HIRSCH, *Poverty and Plenty on the Turkish Farm*, New York, 1970

Christopher HITCHENS, *Cyprus*, New York, 1984

HMSO, *Treaty of Lausanne*, 1923

Peter HOPKIRK, *On Secret Service East of Constantinople*, London, 1995

George HORTON, *Report on Turkey*, Athens, 1985

Tim KELSEY, *Dervish*, London, 1966

Yasar KEMAL, *The Sea-Crossed Fisherman*, London, 1993

Lord KINROSS, *Europa Minor*, London, 1956

— *Atatürk*, London, 1964

— *The Ottoman Centuries*, New York, 1979

Mesrob K. KRIKORIAN, *Armenians in the Service of the Ottoman Empire 1860–1908*, London, 1977

K. KRÜGER, *Kemalist Turkey and the Middle East*, London, 1932

Jacob M. LANDAU, *Panturkism in Turkey*, London, 1981

— *Panturkism: From Irredentism to Cooperation*, London, 1995

S. LANE-POOLE, *Turkey*, London, 1910

Bernard LEWIS, *The Emergence of Modern Turkey*, Oxford, 1961

Geoffrey L. LEWIS, *Turkey*, Oxford, 1955

Lilo LINKE, *Allah Dethroned*, London, 1937

Sir Harry LUKE, *Cyprus under the Turks*, London, 1921

— *The Making of Modern Turkey*, London, 1936

Rose MACAULAY, *The Towers of Trebizond*, London, 1956

Compton MACKENZIE, *Gallipoli Memories*, London, 1929

Mahmut MAKAL, *A Village in Anatolia*, London, 1954

Philip MANSEL, *Constantinople*, London, 1995

J. A. R. MARRIOTT, *The Eastern Question*, London, 1926

Karl MARX, *The Eastern Question 1853–1856*, London, 1858

David MATTHEWS, *The Cyprus Tapes*, London and Nicosia, 1987

David MCDOWALL, *The Kurds*, London, 1992

E. G. MEARS, *Modern Turkey*, New York, 1924

William MILLER, *The Ottoman Empire and its Successors 1801–1927*, Cambridge, 1927

W. S. MONROE, *Turkey and the Turks*, New York, 1908

Bernard NEWMAN, *Turkish Crossroads*, London, 1951

Philip NEWMAN, *A Short History of Cyprus*, London, 1940

H. E. NORRIS, *Islam and the Balkans*, London, 1993

Bediuzzaman Said NURSI, *The Words*, Istanbul, 1994

Dimitri OBOLENSKY, *The Byzantine Commonwealth*, London, 1989

OECD Economic Surveys, *Turkey*, Paris, 1976–

H. Collinson OWEN, *Salonica and After*, London, 1922

David OWEN, *Balkan Odyssey*, London, 1995

Alan PALMER, *The Decline and Fall of the Ottoman Empire*, London, 1992

N. M. PENZER, *The Harem*, London, 1984

Hugh POULTON, *Minorities in the Balkans*, London, 1992

G. Ward PRICE, *The Story of the Salonika Army*, London, 1922

Sir Reginald RANKIN, *Inner History of the Balkan Wars*, London, 1916

Philip ROBBINS, *Turkey and the Middle East*, London, 1991

W. Kinnaird ROSE, *With the Greeks in Thessaly*, London, 1897

Jonathan RUGMAN, *Ataturk's Children, Turkey and the Kurds*, London, 1996

Stanford SHAW, *The Jews of the Ottoman Empire and the Turkish Republic*, Stanford, 1989

S. R. SONYEL, *Armenian Terrorism*, London, 1985

Constantinos SPYRIDAKIS, *A Brief History of Cyprus*, Nicosia, 1974

Freya STARK, *Riding to the Tigris*, London, 1959

John STILL, *A Prisoner in Turkey*, London, 1920

Richard STONEMAN, *A Traveller's History of Turkey*, London, 1996

Lowell THOMAS, *With Lawrence in Arabia*, London, 1928

Leon TROTSKY, *The Balkan Wars*, New York, 1938

Miranda VICKERS, *The Albanians: A Modern History*, London, 1995

Miranda VICKERS and James PETTIFER, *Albania: From Anarchy to a Balkan Identity*, London and New York, 1997

K. WAGNER, *With the Victorious Bulgarians*, Boston, 1913

Christopher J. WALKER, *Armenia*, London, 1990

C. W. WILSON, ed., *Murray's Handbook to Constantinople*, London, 1900

Sir Reginald WYON, *The Balkans from Within*, London, 1904

Mehmet Emin YURDAKAL, *Collected Works*, Istanbul, 1931

Index

READ MORE IN PENGUIN

In every corner of the world, on every subject under the sun, Penguin represents quality and variety – the very best in publishing today.

For complete information about books available from Penguin – including Puffins, Penguin Classics and Arkana – and how to order them, write to us at the appropriate address below. Please note that for copyright reasons the selection of books varies from country to country.

In the United Kingdom: Please write to *Dept. EP, Penguin Books Ltd, Bath Road, Harmondsworth, West Drayton, Middlesex UB7 0DA*

In the United States: Please write to *Consumer Sales, Penguin Putnam Inc., P.O. Box 999, Dept. 17109, Bergenfield, New Jersey 07621-0120*. VISA and MasterCard holders call 1-800-253-6476 to order Penguin titles

In Canada: Please write to *Penguin Books Canada Ltd, 10 Alcorn Avenue, Suite 300, Toronto, Ontario M4V 3B2*

In Australia: Please write to *Penguin Books Australia Ltd, P.O. Box 257, Ringwood, Victoria 3134*

In New Zealand: Please write to *Penguin Books (NZ) Ltd, Private Bag 102902, North Shore Mail Centre, Auckland 10*

In India: Please write to *Penguin Books India Pvt Ltd, 210 Chiranjiv Tower, 43 Nehru Place, New Delhi 110 019*

In the Netherlands: Please write to *Penguin Books Netherlands bv, Postbus 3507, NL-1001 AH Amsterdam*

In Germany: Please write to *Penguin Books Deutschland GmbH, Metzlerstrasse 26, 60594 Frankfurt am Main*

In Spain: Please write to *Penguin Books S. A., Bravo Murillo 19, 1° B, 28015 Madrid*

In Italy: Please write to *Penguin Italia s.r.l., Via Benedetto Croce 2, 20094 Corsico, Milano*

In France: Please write to *Penguin France, Le Carré Wilson, 62 rue Benjamin Baillaud, 31500 Toulouse*

In Japan: Please write to *Penguin Books Japan Ltd, Kaneko Building, 2-3-25 Koraku, Bunkyo-Ku, Tokyo 112*

In South Africa: Please write to *Penguin Books South Africa (Pty) Ltd, Private Bag X14, Parkview, 2122 Johannesburg*

READ MORE IN PENGUIN

A CHOICE OF NON-FICTION

Citizens Simon Schama

'The most marvellous book I have read about the French Revolution in the last fifty years' – *The Times*. 'He has chronicled the vicissitudes of that world with matchless understanding, wisdom, pity and truth, in the pages of this huge and marvellous book' – *Sunday Times*

1945: The World We Fought For Robert Kee

Robert Kee brings to life the events of this historic year as they unfolded, using references to contemporary newspapers, reports and broadcasts, and presenting the reader with the most vivid, immediate account of the year that changed the world. 'Enthralling ... an entirely realistic revelation about the relationship between war and peace' – *Sunday Times*

Cleared for Take-Off Dirk Bogarde

'It begins with his experiences in the Second World War as an interpreter of reconnaissance photographs ... he witnessed the liberation of Belsen – though about this he says he cannot write. But his awareness of the horrors as well as the dottiness of war is essential to the tone of this affecting and strangely beautiful book' – *Daily Telegraph*

Nine Parts of Desire Geraldine Brooks
The Hidden World of Islamic Women

'She takes us behind the veils and into the homes of women in every corner of the Middle East ... It is in her description of her meetings – like that with Khomeini's widow Khadija, who paints him as a New Man (and one for whom she dyed her hair vamp-red) – that the book excels' – *Observer*. 'Frank, engaging and captivating' – *New Yorker*

Insanely Great Steven Levy

The Apple Macintosh revolutionized the world of personal computing – yet the machinations behind its conception were nothing short of insane. 'One of the great stories of the computing industry ... a cast of astonishing characters' – *Observer*. 'Fascinating edge-of-your-seat story' – *Sunday Times*

READ MORE IN PENGUIN

A CHOICE OF NON-FICTION

The Pillars of Hercules Paul Theroux

At the gateway to the Mediterranean lie the two Pillars of Hercules. Beginning his journey in Gibraltar, Paul Theroux travels the long way round – through the ravaged developments of the Costa del Sol, into Corsica and Sicily and beyond – to Morocco's southern pillar. 'A terrific book, full of fun as well as anxiety, of vivid characters and curious experiences' – *The Times*

Where the Girls Are Susan J. Douglas

In this brilliantly researched and hugely entertaining examination of women and popular culture, Susan J. Douglas demonstrates the ways in which music, TV, books, advertising, news and film have affected women of her generation. Essential reading for cultural critics, feminists and everyone else who has ever ironed their hair or worn a miniskirt.

Journals: 1954–1958 Allen Ginsberg

These pages open with Ginsberg at the age of twenty-eight, penniless, travelling alone and unknown in California. Yet, by July 1958 he was returning from Paris to New York as the poet who, with Jack Kerouac, led and inspired the Beats . . .

The New Spaniards John Hooper

Spain has become a land of extraordinary paradoxes in which traditional attitudes and contemporary preoccupations exist side by side. The country attracts millions of visitors – yet few see beyond the hotels and resorts of its coastline. John Hooper's fascinating study brings to life the many faces of Spain in the 1990s.

A Tuscan Childhood Kinta Beevor

Kinta Beevor was five when she fell in love with her parents' castle facing the Carrara mountains. 'The descriptions of the harvesting and preparation of food and wine by the locals could not be bettered . . . alive with vivid characters' – *Observer*

READ MORE IN PENGUIN

A CHOICE OF NON-FICTION

Time Out Film Guide   Edited by John Pym

The definitive, up-to-the-minute directory of every aspect of world cinema from classics and silent epics to reissues and the latest releases.

Flames in the Field   Rita Kramer

During July 1944, four women agents met their deaths at Struthof-Natzweiler concentration camp at the hands of the SS. They were members of the Special Operations Executive, sent to Nazi-occupied France in 1943. *Flames in the Field* reveals that the odds against their survival were weighted even more heavily than they could possibly have contemplated, for their network was penetrated by double agents and security was dangerously lax.

Colored People   Henry Louis Gates Jr.

'A wittily drawn portrait of a semi-rural American community, in the years when racial segregation was first coming under legal challenge ... In the most beautiful English ... he recreates a past to which, in every imaginable sense, there is no going back' – *Mail on Sunday*

Naturalist   Edward O. Wilson

'His extraordinary drive, encyclopaedic knowledge and insatiable curiosity shine through on virtually every page' – *Sunday Telegraph*. 'There are wonderful accounts of his adventures with snakes, a gigantic ray, butterflies, flies and, of course, ants ... a fascinating insight into a great mind' – *Guardian*

Roots Schmoots   Howard Jacobson

'This is no exercise in sentimental journeys. Jacobson writes with a rare wit and the book sparkles with his gritty humour ... he displays a deliciously caustic edge in his analysis of what is wrong, and right, with modern Jewry' – *Mail on Sunday*

READ MORE IN PENGUIN

A CHOICE OF NON-FICTION

Mornings in the Dark   Edited by David Parkinson
The Graham Greene Film Reader

Prompted by 'a sense of fun' and 'that dangerous third Martini' at a party in June 1935, Graham Greene volunteered himself as the *Spectator* film critic. 'His film reviews are among the most trenchant, witty and memorable one is ever likely to read' – *Sunday Times*

Real Lives, Half Lives   Jeremy Hall

The world has been 'radioactive' for a hundred years – providing countless benefits to medicine and science – but there is a downside to the human mastery of nuclear physics. *Real Lives, Half Lives* uncovers the bizarre and secret stories of people who have been exposed, in one way or another, to radioactivity across the world.

Hidden Lives   Margaret Forster

'A memoir of Forster's grandmother and mother which reflects on the changes in women's lives – about sex, family, work – across three generations. It is a moving, evocative account, passionate in its belief in progress, punchy as a detective novel in its story of Forster's search for her grandmother's illegitimate daughter. It also shows how biography can challenge our basic assumptions about which lives have been significant and why' – *Financial Times*

Eating Children   Jill Tweedie

'Jill Tweedie re-creates in fascinating detail the scenes and conditions that shaped her, scarred her, broke her up or put her back together ... a remarkable story' – *Vogue*. 'A beautiful and courageous book' – Maya Angelou

The Lost Heart of Asia   Colin Thubron

'Thubron's journey takes him through a spectacular, talismanic geography of desert and mountain ... a whole glittering, terrible and romantic history lies abandoned along with thoughts of more prosperous times' – *The Times*

BY THE SAME AUTHOR

The Greeks
The Land and People since the War

Our perception of Greece conjures up many potent images: an ancient civilization brought alive by fable, hillsides dotted with sun-baked villages, lazy beaches lapped by crystal blue waters, the warmth and humour of its people.

Yet if we look behind the picture-postcard imagery, the painful contradictions of the country begin to emerge. In this century alone the birthplace of democracy has been riven by civil war and dictatorship. Shackled by deficit and weak currency, Greece struggles to compete with its EC partners. Even the traditional roles of the church and family are gradually shifting.

In *The Greeks* James Pettifer argues that it is vital to understand this country's present by looking at the far-reaching effects of its troubled past. As current events see the return of the Macedonian question and the wider Balkan crisis, he surveys the roots of Greek social, economic and political realities with intelligence and convincing clarity.

'A very good book' – Peter Calvocoressi in the *Oldie*

'He has the credentials necessary to air the most embarrassing of Greek secrets, without being deemed an enemy of the people ... accessible yet authoritative' – John Torode in the *Independent*